REVENGE

REVENGE
On the Dynamics
of a Frightening Urge
and its Taming

Tomas Böhm and Suzanne Kaplan

Translated by *Pamela Boston*

KARNAC

Revised English edition published in 2011 by
Karnac Books Ltd
118 Finchley Road
London NW3 5HT

This book is a revised version of the German book *Rache: Zur Psychodynamik einer unheimlichen Lust und ihrer Zähmung* and a revised version of the Swedish book *Hämnd eller Upprättelse—om hämndspiralens psykologi.*

British Library Cataloguing in Publication Data

A C.I.P. for this book is available from the British Library

ISBN-13: 978-1-85575-827-8

Typeset by Vikatan Publishing Solutions (P) Ltd., Chennai, India

Printed in Great Britain

www.karnacbooks.com

To avenge is like destroying one's own house
(Babylonian Talmud, Sanhedrin 102b)

To Theodor, Minna, Anya, Adam, Elias, Samuel,
Isac and all other grandchildren in the world

CONTENTS

FOREWORD

by Vamık D. Volkan

Tomas Böhm and Suzanne Kaplan state that revenge is an essential factor in the psychological interplay between victim and perpetrator. An individual or a group of individuals initiate shame, humiliation, helplessness, and complicated mourning in a person who becomes traumatized and preoccupied with revenge fantasies. Sometimes these victimized persons commit acts motivated by revenge. The response of all trauma victims will be intertwined with what already exists within their internal worlds—what kinds of unconscious fantasies, mental conflicts, defences, and resilience they have. But this fact does not change the role of an external traumatizing event initiated by another human being, or a small or large group of them, in the appearance of trauma-related affects, revenge fantasies, or actions.

The authors remind us that the revenge motif appears in literature, such as ancient Greek drama and Shakespeare's plays, which is no surprise, as we notice it almost daily in our all-too-human individual and collective behaviour. In spite of this, psychoanalysis has not provided us with sufficient examination and understanding of this motif. I will suggest some reasons for this relative neglect.

In his early efforts to develop psychoanalytic theories, Sigmund Freud gave up the idea that the sexual seduction of children came from the external world, and instead focused on the stimuli that come from the child's own wishes and fantasies for formation psychopathology. Since early psychoanalysts followed this tradition, classical psychoanalysis accepted this de-emphasis on actual seduction coming from the external world when considering the developing child's psyche and generalized it to include de-emphasis on the role of traumatic external events for all their patients (Volkan, 2006a). This de-emphasis resulted in the evolution of clinical psychoanalysis primarily as an investigative tool of an individual's internal world, with explanations about the individual's own psychological processes in forming it. This, I believe, was a reason for inhibiting, relatively speaking, the investigation of revenge fantasies and actions in clinical practice and the targeting of the instigators of the patient's traumatizing events.

I thought of another reason for the neglect by psychoanalysis of revenge-inducing traumatizing events, this time on a societal level. It came to me in 2006 when it was Austria's turn to lead the European Union. Austria declared that year to be the Year of Mozart and the Year of Freud, and I had the honour to be the Fulbright-Sigmund Freud Privatstiftung Visiting Scholar of Psychoanalysis in Vienna at this time, which included teaching political psychology at the University of Vienna for a semester and an office at 19 Berggasse. While working in Freud's house for four months trying to organize an international meeting between psychoanalysts and diplomats to celebrate Freud's 100th birthday, I pictured him at this same location as the Nazis were coming to power. I wondered about his response to a letter written to him by Albert Einstein in 1932, a year before Adolf Hitler became the dictator of Germany. Einstein asked if there is a way of delivering mankind from the menace of war and wondered how it is possible for a small group of power-hungry persons to bed the will of the majority and make them suffer a war (Freud, 1932). Anti-Semitism surrounded Freud at that time. Was his pessimistic response to Einstein an attempt to deny the impending danger to himself, his family and neighbours? I came to the conclusion that this might be true even though, of course, he was conscious of what was happening in Europe. As Peter Loewenberg (1991) and Leo Rangell (2003) remind us, some aspects of a large-group history induce anxiety.

Freud's pessimism about the role of psychoanalysis in large-group issues and in interventions for preventing wars that appears in his response to Einstein's letter was mirrored by many of his followers.

This, I think, has also played a key role in limiting for a long time the contributions psychoanalysis can make to understanding traumatizing external massive movements and large-group conflicts such as ethnic, national, religious, and ideological conflicts, even though some analysts such as Edward Glover (1947), Franco Fornari (1966), Robert Waelder (1971), Alexander Mitscherlich, and Margarete Mitscherlich (Mitscherlich, A., 1971; Mitscherlich and Mitscherlich, 1975) tried to open doors to such investigations.

This reluctance certainly played out in the clinical setting. Melanie Klein (1961), for example, did not pay attention to the war when she treated a ten-year-old boy named Richard in 1941. Harold Blum's (1985) description of a Jewish patient who came to him for re-analysis illustrates the extent to which mutual resistances may prevail when both the analyst and the analysand belong to the same large group that has been massively traumatized by an external historical event. Blum's patient's first analyst, who was also Jewish, failed to "hear" their large group's shared trauma at the hands of the Nazis in his analysand's material.

I wonder how many Jewish analysts after the Second World War were like Blum's patient's former analyst, and how many of them, without being aware of it, influenced the application of psychoanalytic treatment in a way that tended to ignore Holocaust-related external reality. I suggest that some of them who were very influential in the field of psychoanalysis, both in the US and elsewhere, exaggerated their bias in favour of a theoretical position called "classical analysis" that focused only on modifying the analysand's internal wishes, fantasies, mental conflicts, and defences without giving much attention to external realities (Volkan, 2006a). We now know that in post-Second World War Germany as well, there has been both German and German-Jewish analyst-supported (unconscious) resistance to exploring the intertwining of internal and external wars and the influence of Holocaust-related issues on analysands' psyches (for a review, see Volkan, Ast & Greer, 2002).

During recent decades, psychoanalytic approaches to trauma studies and trauma-related affects, which Böhm and Kaplan also explore, have changed drastically, although it is beyond the scope of this Foreword to review developments within psychoanalysis during this time period that encouraged studies on individual and shared traumas, their consequences, and their transgenerational transmissions. Certainly in recent decades we have seen—and still see—many impactful events and circumstances that affect large-group identity: large-group conflicts in Africa, the Middle East, Northern Ireland, India, South America, the Korean peninsula, the collapse of the Soviet Union and former Yugoslavia, wars in Iraq and Afghanistan, widespread terrorism, divisions between an "Islamic world" and "Western world", globalization and economic difficulties. These and other realities have forced many large groups to ask "Who are we now?" Large-group regression, increased externalizations and projections that support bad prejudice, increased narcissistic investment in large-group identities, and killing in the name of such identities (Volkan, 1988, 1997, 2006) have spread in many locations in the world. These external situations have been key factors in inducing and perhaps forcing a trend among some psychoanalysts to move beyond the couch. Böhm and Kaplan, both psychoanalysts, have been among the pioneers following this trend with their work and research on societal issues, adult children of the Holocaust, extreme traumatization, and education enriched by psychological studies.

At the present time, psychoanalysis is no longer hesitant to explore traumatizing external events caused by ethnic, national, religious, or political large groups that utilize revengeful ideologies. After the 11 September 2001 tragedies, the International Psychoanalytic Association (IPA) formed the Terror and Terrorism Study Group. Norwegian analyst Sverre Varvin chaired this study group that lasted for several years (Varvin and Volkan, 2003). The American Psychoanalytic Association established a committee on the United Nations that still functions. The theme of the 44th Annual Meeting of the IPA in Rio de Janeiro in the summer of 2005 was "trauma", including individual trauma and shared trauma due to historical events, where Böhm and Kaplan presented their ongoing work on the revenge phenomenon. There has been impressive scholarship as well. Raphael Moses (1982) examined the Arab–Israeli conflict from a psychoanalytic point of view. Michael Šebek (1994) studied societal responses to living under communism in Europe. Sudhir Kakar (1996) described the revenge–filled effects of Hindu–Muslim religious conflict in Hyderabad, India. Mitch Elliott, Kenneth Bishop, and Paul Stokes (2004) and John Alderdice (2010) examined the situation in Northern Ireland. Nancy Hollander (1997) explored events in South America, and later (2010) in the United States after 11 September 2001.

My own studies on large-group conflicts go back to 1979 when I wrote about two ethnic groups in conflict in Cyprus. Since then, I have written about the Arab–Israeli conflict; psychological processes in the Baltic Republics after independence following the collapse of the Soviet Union; the Serbian group psychology after the former Yugoslavia was gone; the psychology of Albanians following the death of dictator Enver Hodxa; Kuwaiti responses to the invasion by Saddam Hussein's forces; the Georgian–South Ossetian conflict; the Turkish–Greek as well as Turkish–Armenian relationships; the psychology of extreme religious fundamentalism; and the psychology of suicide bombers (Volkan, 1988, 1997, 2004, 2006; Volkan & Itzkowitz, 1994; Volkan & Kayatekin, 2006).

Analysts' contributions to the understanding and consequences of external traumatic events have been accompanied by two other developments.

The first development is this: some analysts are leaving their couches behind and actually examining the consequences of traumatizing events in their neighbourhoods, women's shelters, refugee camps, and in foreign locations where massive murders, rapes, and other unspeakable disasters have taken place. This is very important, since it may be impossible to have a comprehensive understanding of massive traumatic events and the development of entitlement ideologies connected with affects, thoughts, and actions linked to the revenge motif.

The second development refers to some analysts' genuine interest in working with scholars and researchers from other disciplines. I believe that no one discipline can explain and attempt to find adaptive solutions to man-made, deliberate massive disasters occurring now in our globalized and turbulent world.

These two developments are rather new for psychoanalysts. Tomas Böhm and Suzanne Kaplan emerge in this book as models for taking psychoanalytic investigations beyond the couch and collaborating with knowledgeable and experienced persons who are not psychoanalysts in order to understand various types of traumas, revenge motifs, and to find counterweights against revenge-taking by individuals and societies. In 2003 and 2004, they made two research trips to Rwanda. As they remind us, in 2003, 18 of Africa's countries were either involved in or just ending armed conflicts. In 1994, genocide had already occurred in Rwanda, and in this book, they tell moving stories of people they met and interviewed there, a place where the revenge motif had gotten out of hand, most inhumane acts were performed, and within 100 days, between 800,000 and 1,000,000 Rwandans were killed.

Could the victims' wish to retaliate be considered pathological, and in what way? How could victims find self-esteem, restoration, and justice? How could outside experts who came to Rwanda and worked there for a long time, such as my old friend social psychologist Erwin Staub, whose work in Rwanda was very much appreciated by Böhm and Kaplan, deal with the unbelievable consequences of an unbelievable disaster? How do experts from different cultures learn to appreciate local customs of helping traumatized persons?

Reading this book, one quickly senses the authors' intense sensitivity about what they had witnessed in Rwanda after the genocide while keeping their professional curiosity intact. They report that their two research trips to Rwanda initiated the writing of this book in order to examine the phenomenon of revenge and bring necessary attention to it. While they provide us with moving stories from Rwanda to explain the revenge motif and related issues, this book is not only about events in Rwanda or societal trauma connected with revenge.

With references to literature, movies, history, gender issues, and psychoanalytic theories, they examine the revenge motif, share their experiences in Sweden and elsewhere with individuals, couples, teenage gangs, schools, and "bystanders" who passively watch others' misery. They refer to religious fundamentalism, examine the difference between "trauma linking" and "generational linking" among people, and deal with the concept of forgiveness and strategies for treatment. Their flowing style makes this book easy to read not only for the professionals dealing with trauma affects, but also for anyone in the general public interested in learning about these dark, as well as hopeful, aspects of human nature.

With Böhm and Kaplan's *Revenge: On the Dynamics of a Frightening Urge and its Taming*, we now have a comprehensive study of the revenge motif as well as of what can be done to tame consequences of revengeful actions and find alternatives to taking these actions in the first place.

Why a book about revenge?

"What keeps coming back to my mind is the way my sister died [...].
Someone had hit her on the head with a hammer... then they put her on
a motorcycle and took her very far away and dumped her there. What
hurts me most is that the man who killed her had been our neighbor. [...]
In those days, they were looking for young men to join the army, and,
whenever I thought about that man who had killed my sister .... I felt like
joining the army so I could hunt him down and kill him. I felt that, even
if they found me out there and killed me, I would have been able to take
revenge for my sister and that was what mattered."

—(Jean, Rwandan teenager)

Our interest in the phenomenon of revenge was spurred during two
research trips to Rwanda in 2003 and 2004. The purpose of our trips was
to try to understand more about the consequences of the genocide that
had shocked the world in 1994, more specifically, about individuals'
ways of dealing with trauma-related affects. We interviewed social psychologists who were doing research on perpetrators in the jails of Kigali,
Rwandan teachers, trauma therapists, and youths who had lived on the
street after their families had been murdered (Kaplan & Eckstein, 2004).

Revenge as an essential factor in the psychological interplay between victim and perpetrator then became stunningly apparent to us. In this way, the narratives from Rwanda became a portal for us into a closer study of the revenge phenomenon. In addition, as psychoanalysts, couples' therapists, and researchers, we have long shared an urgency to understand precisely this matter, that is, psychological elements in perpetrators and victims. We can thus say that the revenge theme has evolved into a common focus for us, based on our respective professional experiences.

How can extreme situations such as experiences of genocide function as a portal into a study of revenge in general? The thoughts and feelings expressed above by the youth Jean can seem to have few points of overlap with our everyday life. However, it is in the extreme that we can discover psychological mechanisms that can otherwise be difficult to discern, but which exist in general in different contexts and on several different levels. Our intent is to lift up revenge as a neglected and insufficiently understood psychological mechanism. In fact, there is surprisingly little written about revenge in the psychology literature, especially considering that the phenomenon immediately evokes such strong feelings—and such great interest. Revenge is often mentioned in passing in the literature and drowns in descriptions of violence and aggression. In behavioural science textbooks of our times, we have seldom found the word "revenge" in the index.

The purpose of this book is therefore to compile, share, analyse, and broaden knowledge on revenge as a psychological mechanism on the individual, group, and societal levels. We describe how revenge fantasies and revenge acts can influence everyday relationships, as well as give rise to destructive phenomena in groups and in different political structures. Through documenting the universal presence of revenge, we wish in part to contribute to a greater understanding of conflicts in other countries, which can be perceived as remote and alien, and in part to give insights into how destructive processes can be generated in our own world, for example on the playground or in couples' relationships. However, we also intend to show how dialogue, mental space, and reflection can create restoration and make it possible for us to refrain from taking revenge. In the centre of our discussions is the model we have developed to understand the mechanisms of revenge: the revenge spiral.

The psychological aspects of revenge are the main focus of this book, which means that we deal only marginally with legal, economical, political, and other angles of approach. We make only brief references to historical events or political conflicts, in order to shed light on the psychological aspects in a focused manner. This is in contrast to other books, where writers go more deeply into detail with regard to historical events while intending to touch only briefly upon the violence phenomenon.

Our psyche seems to lack the capacity to take care of and transform all of the strong feelings that are evoked in us when we meet with frustrations. We cannot flee from our feelings. It is part of our make-up to have inescapable strong feelings, but what shall we do with them? The issue of how hard it is for us to handle our strong feelings (Ferro, 2005) runs like a red thread throughout this book.

We hope and believe that this book—with the phenomenon of revenge as a point of connection for the dynamic between the perpetrator and victim—will provide insight into a part of the psychological processes that we discern behind the destructive force of revenge. Furthermore, we trust that the book will be an eye-opener, serve as a basis for discussion, and show possible ways of refraining from participation in an escalating revenge spiral.

Revenge and Restoration has been our joint project. In the following, we give an account of our starting points for our work with the book.

Tomas Böhm

My starting point is an old interest in the connection between psychoanalysis and society. Even prior to my studies in psychoanalysis, I was intrigued by Wilhelm Reich's political writings such as *Die Massenpsychologie des Faschismus* (*The Mass Psychology of Fascism*) (1930–33/1997) and *Was ist Klassenbewusstsein?* (*What Is Class Consciousness?*) (1943)—probably because I needed an explanation for how Germany, the land of Bach, Beethoven, Kant, and Schiller, could go along with the genocidal policies of the Nazis. Here, as in Poland, Hungary, and later in the former Yugoslavia and in Rwanda, people who had previously been neighbours could betray and kill each other—a course of events that determined my own family's fate. My parents grew up as assimilated Jews and socialists in Vienna. My mother was part of a family with many branches there, and her relatives were spread over the entire world as refugees from Nazism. The ones who escaped and survived ended up in England, France, the USA, Venezuela, China, Australia—and Sweden. My childhood and youth in Sweden were inextricably bound with this background of being different—dark, Jewish, multilingual—and knowing that we had been forced to come to Sweden because of persecution in my parents' homeland.

Both Suzanne Kaplan and I worked for a time as psychotherapeutic group leaders with adult children of survivors of the Holocaust, the so-called second generation, which through various circumstances led me to write the book *Inte som vi—psykologiska aspekter på främlingsfientlighet och rasism* (*Not like us—psychological aspects of xenophobia and racism*) (1993). This work was followed some years later by *Att ha rätt—om intolerans, ortodoxi och fundamentalism* (*To be right—on intolerance, orthodoxy and fundamentalism*) (1998). I was getting closer and closer to the psychology of the perpetrator, and my understanding was enhanced by my collaboration with psychoanalyst Ludvig Igra, who was looking into similar issues from his own vantage point. We refer to him in several contexts in this book. At the same time, my main professional activity has been my clinical work as a private practising psychoanalyst. My writings in parallel with my practice include *Kärleksrelationen—en bok om parförhållanden* (*The love relationship—a book about couples' relationships*) (2001), in which quarrelling and the dynamics of infidelity are depicted. In my novels *The Vienna Jazz Trio* (2000) and *Bortresta* (*Gone Away*) (2004b), I have also dealt extensively with the same areas: the destructivity wrought by individuals and groups and the consequences thereof for many other people. The revenge phenomenon has been an important component in these works.

Suzanne Kaplan

My starting points are my clinical work as a psychoanalyst with children, youths, and adults, my experiences as coordinator and interviewer within an international documentation project concerning survivors of the Holocaust, USC Shoah Foundation Institute for Visual History and Education, as well as research on children in genocide—the Holocaust and Rwanda.

In 1998, I began a research project at the Department of Education at Stockholm University in conjunction with the Hugo Valentin Centre, the Programme for Holocaust and Genocide Studies, Uppsala University, concerning Jewish survivors who themselves were children during the Holocaust. This project resulted in a doctoral thesis, *Children in the Holocaust—Affects and Memory Images in Trauma and Generational Linking* (2002). My research areas have been further developed after my trips to Rwanda—especially with regard to trauma-related affects such as the revenge phenomenon. An analysis of forty video-recorded interviews with surviving children from the Holocaust was followed by twelve video-recorded interviews with youths in Rwanda. The youths, who had lived on the street for almost eight years after their families had been murdered during the 1994 genocide in Rwanda, were interviewed about their experiences during and after the genocide. Follow-up interviews were carried out after one year. Starting about two months or so before the first interview occasion, the youths had been receiving help with a place to live and their schooling from a European pediatric surgeon working in Kigali, making it possible to carry out more in-depth interviews in a safe context.

My studies concerning the Holocaust developed into an interest in finding inclusive, generally applicable psychological phenomena with regard to affect regulation in children and youths after genocide. My research has resulted in a theoretical model that can function as an analytical tool for the understanding of trauma-related affects, presented in the article "Children in genocide—extreme traumatization and the 'affect propeller'" (Kaplan, 2006). The "affect propeller" has recently been used and further developed in an analysis of chronically hospitalized Holocaust survivors' communication of trauma which is presented in the article "Affect regulation in extreme traumatization—fragmented narratives of Holocaust survivors hospitalized in psychiatric institutions" (Kaplan & Laub, 2009). My collected studies and findings are presented in the book *Children in Genocide: Extreme Traumatization and Affect Regulation* (2008).

I come from a Jewish family that has lived in Sweden for several generations. However, my maternal grandparents and other relatives were living in Norway when that country was occupied by Nazis during the Second World War. Two young men in the family were deported to Auschwitz, and one of them, Samuel, miraculously survived. My maternal grandparents managed to flee over the border to Sweden, hidden in crates on the flatbed of a truck. After the end of the war, they got their house outside of Oslo back—a very important place for me. However, the house had been used as headquarters by the Nazis and there were bullet holes in the ceiling, the walls, and a painting. Throughout the years, members of my family have recounted memory fragments for me. Perhaps these experiences have served as a sounding board in my research work.

My studies about extreme traumatization, about genocidal processes, and about living with memories that "won't let go" have been of enormous value for my psychological understanding and for my general perspective on life. Interdisciplinary international research contacts have played a great role in broadening my interest in and my understanding of the dynamic of pain and revenge.

We would like to thank the Bertil Wennborg Foundation for the support it has given to our work on this book. We would also like to thank the USC Shoah Foundation Institute for Visual History and Education, and the Hugo Valentin Center, the Programme for Holocaust and Genocide Studies, Uppsala University. Special thanks go to Dr Alfred Jahn in Kigali, Rwanda, who helped us establish contact with youths who survived the Rwandan genocide. Researchers who have been especially inspiring for us are social psychologist Ervin Staub and trauma therapist Laurie Anne Pearlman, the latter whom we met while she was providing a programme to augment and enhance the healing and reconciliation efforts underway in Rwanda, as well as psychoanalyst Vamik Volkan. Lena Forssén and Jessica Rydén at our Swedish publishers Natur och Kultur have given us important comments on our text, as have Lennart Wolff and Angela Mauss-Hanke. We want to express our warm gratitude to Pamela Boston for translating the book to English and for the engagement she has shown for the content of the book. We are also grateful for valuable discussions with young people and adults with experiences of extreme trauma, as well as for insights from our patients and colleagues.

We want to express our warm gratitude to Pamela Boston for translating the book to English and for the engagement she has shown for the content of the book, **as well as Josephine Kankundiye who translated Rwandan testimonies into English.**

ABOUT THE AUTHORS

Suzanne Kaplan, PhD, is a practising child and training psychoanalyst, and associate professor at the Hugo Valentin Centre, Uppsala University, Sweden. She was the recipient of the Elize Hayman Prize for published work pertaining to traumatized children and adults (International Psychoanalytical Association) in both 2001 and 2007.

Tomas Böhm, MD, is a training psychoanalyst in private practice in Sweden. He is the author of books dealing with xenophobia, racism, and fundamentalism, as well as novels. He is a member of the IPA Prejudice Committee.

INTRODUCTION

Revenge is much more common than we believe and perhaps want to admit. Indeed, we are so used to the silent presence of revenge in our everyday life that we seldom give it a thought. Sometimes it slips out in its raw, unmistakable form—"he's gonna get it, that jerk!"—but since we do not want others to think that we are going too far, that our desire for revenge is beyond the acceptable, we usually find a way to transform it to justified anger.

A twelve-year-old boy, Frank, speaks about an incident on the school bus:

> Yesterday John kept picking a fight with me. He wouldn't stop teasing me. And he pulled me by the collar. There was no one there [no adult who could help]. [...] But I got him back. I wasn't out of control when I did it. I did it in self-defence! I bumped him up against the wall and pushed as hard as I could. He was lucky that the wall was made of wood and not of stone. Yeah, I pushed hard. I showed that jerk no mercy.

When we refer to revenge in this book, we usually mean various forms of outward behaviour. This behaviour has its basis in feelings of hatred and revenge fantasies, which can give us both excitement and discomfort. We can regard *revenge fantasies* as a generally occurring phenomenon. We become furious but we come to our senses through mental work and reflection. Hatred or envy is given full freedom to thrive in fantasies, but we do not go as far as to express it through outward actions.

Revenge acts are significantly less common than revenge fantasies but more common than we believe, something we intend to show with the help of our examples. In revenge acts, the persons who feel violated vent their rage more or less freely, and in such a manner avoid thinking about and working through what they have experienced. Nor can they find a constructive solution at that point, such as seeking restoration or trying to see the situation from the other person's perspective.

People can also find an outlet for their revenge fantasies through watching someone else carry out violent revenge acts while they themselves remain passive. They let their revenge fantasies thrive and then later explain to others that they were powerless to do anything.

Revenge and closely related concepts

Revenge, according to *The Columbia Guide to Standard American English* (1993), is a word known from 1375, from old French, *revengier*, from *re-*, intensive prefix, + *vengier*, "take revenge", from Latin *vindicare*, "to lay claim to, avenge, punish". To *avenge* is "to get revenge" or "to take vengeance"; it suggests the administration of just punishment for a criminal or immoral act. The noun *revenge* is first recorded in 1547. To *vindicate* means "to avenge or revenge", from Latin *vindicatus*, meaning "to clear from censure or doubt, by means of demonstration", recorded from 1635; *vindication* is recorded from 1484, "act of avenging, revenge", from Latin *vindicationem*, from *vindicare* "to set free, lay claim to, assert, avenge" (related to *vindicta*, "revenge"), probably from *vim dicare*, "to show authority", from *vim*, accusative of *vis* "force" + root of *dicere* "to say". The meaning "justification by proof, defence against censure" is attested from 1647. In summary, revenge seems to have developed a meaning closer to retaliation, implying hatred as its motivation.

We can approach the subject of revenge, or acts that are revenge in disguise, by looking at closely related concepts, such as *envy*. Envy is a grudging feeling coming from a comparison whereby someone feels slighted. That person sees that they have less than what the other person has or seems to have been given, often leading to a wish to take over or destroy the object of envy. The envier can use the "sour grapes" approach and make a *derogatory* or a *degrading* remark about whatever it is that they envy and thus avoid feeling the sting of envy. *Rivalry* is a more socially acceptable way of competing with the other person, for attention, love, honour, possessions, or anything else that is possible to compare. *A scapegoat* is the person upon whom you place blame for something when you cannot or do not want to bear it yourself (or a person you make suffer when the real culprit is inaccessible). "Don't look at me. It's his fault." *Self-defence* can be a self-controlled way of preventing someone from hurting you, but it can also be a way of disguising a more aggressive revenge attack on the other person, especially considering that the revenge act is triggered by a violation. Reports of *massive acts of vengeance* reach us from turbulent regions of the world. The avengers' response can sound moderate and "legitimate" compared to the attack that they themselves have sustained. This is as if to say that the dose they give back is of a suitable magnitude in proportion to the suffering that they have been forced to endure. However, the authors of this book do not see this way of reasoning any differently: it is still an attempt to justify revenge when it actually cannot be justified.

We see the act of revenge as a more or less primitive force, which can be understandable in certain cases, but which never actually has any moral justification. However, we are well aware that when people speak of revenge in day-to-day situations, it can be referred to as a legitimate moral act, a "reasonable" counterattack. We often give revenge other names in order to make it sound less brutal and primitive. Common euphemistic expressions are *sweet revenge, dispensing justice,* or *paying back*.

About the content

In our study of revenge, we alternate between a practical and a theoretical perspective. We are given daily accounts of the atrocities that are committed against ethnic minorities the world over. We read about violence in individual families and hear about the escalating violence between teenage gangs in our own society. Words like "genocide", "perpetrator", "survivor", and "mobbing" have become a part of our everyday vocabulary. We can learn to recognize revenge motifs, both the obvious and the more latent ones, when we examine these phenomena more closely.

As will be made evident, the factors underlying revenge can vary. The breeding ground for vengefulness can sometimes be found in the neglected dialogue between parents and children, sometimes in serious oppression. To be harmed by the people on whom one is most dependent causes wounds that never really heal and that potentially become the seeds of revenge acts in adult life.

Revenge can also have a "relational" origin. For example, two partners can suddenly find themselves having different social statuses when one of them makes a climb upward on the social ladder. If the couple does not have an open discussion about the change that has occurred within their relationship, the one who feels a frustrating imbalance can strike back in the form of mental and physical violence.

Revenge on a societal level can have its origin in conflicts between different ethnic groups, which in themselves can be based on class differences. However, so-called ethnic cleansing is usually based upon construed differences between ethnic groups, descriptions that the members of the respective groups find unrecognizable. Many are not even aware that they belong to an ethnic minority prior to the persecutions. In this book, our main example of revenge in the context of an ethnic conflict is the genocide in Rwanda. We discuss the background of the genocide and bring out the dynamics of revenge in that atrocity.

As the primitive psychic force that it is, revenge can contribute to primitive brutality in cases ranging from individual passionate jealousy to collective mass murder. The examples in the book concern both everyday life situations and large-scale political chains of events with consequences for millions of people. Some of the examples include atrocities and states of mind that we ourselves—we who have no experience of them—are hardly even able to imagine: "unimaginable primitive affects" (Grubrich-Simitis, 1984).

The perspectives of different countries

We look at revenge from both a Swedish and an international perspective. English-speaking readers may need a few words on the Swedish perspective right now at the start, even though we are careful to take up the revenge phenomenon in the context of different cultures throughout the book. People in other countries often seem to have strong feelings and opinions about Sweden. On the one hand, progressives around the world see Sweden as a pioneer to be emulated when it comes to the situations of women and children. On the other hand, conservatives criticize Sweden for over-indulgence of people with antisocial behaviour, including violent criminals, for loose morals, and for hypocrisy. We have state-sponsored day-care for the great majority of children under school age, long maternal and paternal leaves, and a law against corporal punishment of children. All the same, shocking crimes of violence with pronounced elements of revenge occur here as well.

People can rightfully say that we show naïveté towards dark forces when we let our Minister of Foreign Affairs go to a department store without bodyguards and she is murdered. We seem to believe that we are immune to acts of violence and revenge, but we are not. At the same time, we have a tradition and a desire in Sweden to promote an open society, which makes us want to feel trust and not suspiciousness. People who commit crimes of violence are therefore given remarkably lenient punishments compared with what is the case, for example, in the USA. Our prisons are often open and oriented towards rehabilitation. We could say that we in Sweden distance ourselves from blatant conscious expressions of revenge, while people in some other countries might see revenge as something rather natural, and inevitable, even necessary. When justice is administered in Sweden, we try to separate the retaliation aspect from the aspects of protecting society or setting limits to stop destructive individuals. Needless to say, this difference can sometimes seem extremely subtle. However, as we show in later parts of the book, there are sometimes tendencies in different countries' practices of justice to rule in accordance with emotional needs for revenge.

The spirit and the feeling of wanting to retaliate seem as alive in Sweden as in other countries. However, attitudes and value judgements towards the actual carrying out of revenge are rather negative compared to those in some countries and extremely negative compared to those in others.

The content of the book can be overwhelming at times. We hope that readers, just as we did when we listened, can let themselves be moved and at the same time try to reserve some space for thought and reflection about the experiences and dynamics described. When it comes to the less overwhelming presentations, the reader is certain to recognize himself or herself in everyday psychological phenomena and can think about how he or she would choose to act in a similar situation.

In the book's first part, *Revenge*, we show how different psychological phenomena, such as vulnerability, envy, and humiliation, can give rise to revenge fantasies and revenge acts on both the individual and societal levels. We also show how the mechanisms of revenge have their origin in experiences of trauma. In addition, we give concrete examples of how revenge can be a motor in destructive phenomena, such as conflicts in love relationships, abuse of women, and genocide.

In the second part of the book, *Restoration*, we describe different strategies for refraining from retaliation. We also give positive examples of rescuers and helpers—people who have chosen not to take revenge but who have instead sought various constructive solutions for dealing with violence and injustices. We tie together the presentations and discussions in the different parts of the book through our model, the revenge spiral, which is introduced in the second chapter of the book. However, we first wish to document how common the revenge motif is and has been throughout history.

PART I

REVENGE

CHAPTER ONE

The revenge motif

*T*he revenge motif appears in a number of arenas and in different *cultures. We need to be mindful of its existence in order to discover how common it is. We can then learn to recognize when destructive revenge spirals are developing. By extension, we thus gain a basis for stopping these spirals successfully before they have gone too far. We can also learn what function revenge plays and has played in various contexts. A short overview of revenge as a motif in literature, film, culture, religion, and at work is therefore given as an introduction to our study of revenge.*

Stories about revenge

The revenge motif is often prominent in the literature of the ancient Greeks. The stories of Medea and the Trojan War immediately come to mind. The Oedipus myth is another example. Oedipus (which means "swollen foot") is abandoned in the woods, with his feet tied together, when he is just a little baby in order to thwart the prophecy that he is going to kill his parents if he is allowed to grow up. In the best-known parts of the myth, Oedipus murders his father at a crossroads, without knowing that it is his father, and later marries his mother, without knowing who she is. Oedipus can thus be said to have taken revenge on his parents for their attempt to abandon and kill him. Oedipus is then punished by the gods, accepts his punishment, and becomes wiser and humbler in the two later parts of the trilogy.

Greek tragedies in general concern numerous acts of revenge between the main characters while the major revenge is exacted by the gods. Brenman (2006) writes about the Orestes trilogy and the sensitive balance between unforgiving revenge and the human understanding of forgiveness. The revenge of the gods seems to correspond to a stern superego that defies human understanding.

While we are on the subject of revenge in literature, we must of course mention Shakespeare's tragedies. Rosen (2007) makes a survey of the revenge panorama in his article. He shows how common revenge is, not least within works of literature. He points out that revenge is a central theme in at least 20 of Shakespeare's nearly 40 plays.

Shakespeare seems to have been equally as ambivalent and tormented about violence as the biblical authors. His early tragedies were steeped in revenge spirals, as though he was concerned mainly with the excitement of revenge, while the later tragedies, and especially *Hamlet* and *Romeo and Juliet*, contain speeches about reconciliation and the meaningless destructivity of violence. Hamlet wants to take revenge, but he keeps postponing it because of his primitive and uncompromising conscience. It terrifies him (as it would most of us) with guilt and remorse. "Thus conscience doth make cowards of us all." However, once he commits his first murder, he is caught in a revenge spiral that leads to more murders than he ever anticipated, including those of people he loves and his own self. *Romeo and Juliet* is a tragedy about young love that is crushed by primitive acts of revenge in the context of an age-old family feud. In addition, there are all the Shakespearean comedies, in which the characters often want to take revenge (it is hard to imagine enduring the violations forced upon Malvolio and Sir Andrew in *Twelfth Night* or Prospero in *The Tempest*), but everything ends up on the level of a joke.

Several well-known examples of the revenge motif can be found in the novels of French authors Balzac and Hugo, as well as in Alexander Dumas père's *The Count of Monte Cristo* (1844–55/2003) and Heinrich von Kleist's novel about Michael Kohlhaas (2005). The stories can involve a revenge act when someone loses control and goes over the edge or revenge taken out on particularly evil-minded people. Revenge can also be described in righteous and heroic terms, as in Dumas' novel, which we discuss in more detail below.

In the world of film, there are numerous examples that depict both "righteous revenge", actually a setting of limits according to our argumentation, and evil revenge. An example of the former can be seen in *The Seven Samurai* (1954), in which the heroes help some simple peasants whose village is being terrorized by ruthless bandits. An example of the latter is found in *Basic Instinct* (1992), in which the scorned woman lover goes to greater and greater depths of cruelty in devising methods of revenge. In action films such as the *Terminator* and in the *James Bond* films, with a clear division of characters into good and evil, we can see how the scoundrel is expected to take revenge for even the slightest setback. Revenge in such cases can be termed an automatic companion of cruelty.

Why do we find this theme all around us? Is it because it is exciting, unavoidable, a part of our nature that we cannot escape? Can we say that writers and others in the creative arts sometimes simply reflect this phenomenon and other times give us a picture with more nuances, to help us find another way? Is there something here that could make a conservative say, "You see, revenge and violence are inevitable. We can't do much about them"?

We realize that revenge is perceived as *natural* in certain cultures and situations—what we in the terminology of psychology refer to as "ego-syntonic" or "ego-near"—meaning something that the individual or the group sees as being so near the inherent way of thinking and behaving that it is not questioned. In such a manner, violent revenge in a crime of passion can be considered "legitimate" and a "matter of course", or, for example, the oppression of the North American Indians can be "explained" as a "natural" revenge against their attacks. However, what we describe in most cases in this book is a dynamic whereby people in different ways try to *conceal* their revenge motives, since such motives give rise to feelings of shame in the avenger.

We argue that it is essential to remain critical towards the seductive power of simplification. Good and evil, black and white, an eye for an eye, life as getting struck and striking back. This is precisely the conservative's simplified and non-reflective view. People are caught in the revenge spiral and see no reason—or possibility—to get out of it. The allurement lies in the easier explanations, so we have an easy definition of our friends versus our enemies. We thereby avoid having to do any further thinking to try to understand the complicated world in which we live. When the then President Bush "got revenge" on Saddam Hussein in Iraq for the September 11 attacks on the USA, it was more important for him to retaliate—"those who aren't with us are against us"—than to analyse what had happened, understand the underlying dynamics, and then take well-reasoned measures. In addition, Bush concealed the troubling facts that we know now—that his friends in Saudi Arabia were involved in giving economic support to Al Qaeda's attack on "the enemies of Islam".

At the time of writing, we have just experienced the killing of Osama bin Laden in Pakistan by US military forces. The revenge motive is discussed all around the world in the media. Some people find it hard to differentiate between justice, revenge, restoration, and victory. Terrorism has to be stopped. On the one hand, there is relief when a terrorist like bin Laden is stopped, including the need for closure for those who were affected. On the other, there is a risk to act out an excited urge of revenge.

It seems that we can never get away from a simplified fascination with revenge. We see that in one part of the world men and women are involved in daily violent revenge actions, or plans and fantasies for such actions, while in another part, where countries have had peace within their own boundaries since 1945, the majority of the youth and a great deal of the best adult minds want and enjoy their daily or at least weekly dose of violent films and video games.

> The USA is a special case, since it is the only superpower and has taken on, and has been expected by many to take on, the role of world police. Being world police could imply getting revenge on behalf of others. On the one hand the US has had peace within its own boundaries since the end of the Indian Wars and has been able to build the thriving civil and science-based society and enjoy the prosperity of peace envisioned by the Enlightenment, but on the other hand it has been involved in at least 20 wars (depending on how one counts) outside its boundaries since 1945. Most violent films are produced there, many such as *Rambo* showing the USA getting revenge long after the end of a war for what their makers

consider to be unfair enemy advantages, this time of the Vietnamese, even though the Vietnamese lost 2 million people in the war.

(Interview with American teacher, 2009)

As for other parts of the world not covered much by our news media, we can assume that they are something of a mixture and that there are countries that are working hard on finding alternatives to revenge.

Films with revenge and violence as motifs can serve as a catharsis or as a way of releasing one's own feelings vicariously. This can also contribute to the fascination with psychopaths, serial killers, and monsters who want to take over the world. Depictions of revenge can make for a cathartic release or can stimulate towards copycat actions, depending on the viewer's inner vulnerability. Certain vulnerable, unstable personalities have difficulties separating fantasy from reality. Films, games, song texts, Youtube scenes, or news of attacks can stimulate them to commit revenge acts of their own.

All of us are affected by strong scenes of violence and revenge. We ourselves can note how agitated, anxiety-filled, or relieved we feel when we have finished seeing films with such scenes, but after a short time most of us hopefully regain our sense of balance between reality and fantasy.

A weapon for the powerless

Folklore researcher Bengt af Klintberg (1996) has analysed why there are so many modern legends about revenge. He argues that revenge narratives serve as a weapon for people who are powerless to take revenge. In our modern Western cultures, we must repress revenge feelings, since such feelings are considered primitive. (This can be compared with the way certain cultures, such as the Inuit culture, see revenge as a legitimate duty for everyone who wants to be respected.) Legends offer a socially acceptable outlet for revenge urges, an outlet which also relieves us of any need to feel guilty.

In these revenge narratives, revenge is often castrating in various symbolic ways. The legends can also express a conflict between people of different social statuses in which the person with the stronger position loses it and then regains it through revenge. Moreover, in fiction, revenge is designed in a manner that serves to further minimize the guilt aspect, especially when the revenge is carried out "unintentionally" by the one who has been afflicted, as in the example below:

> A woman is driving home and stops at a red light. A car full of juvenile delinquents pulls up beside her. One of the gang jumps out and bangs her car with a chain. When the light changes, the woman takes off as fast as possible. When she gets home she discovers that the chain is caught in the bumper of her car and the boy's hand is there in the chain.

The righteous revenge? The Count of Monte Cristo

There thus seems to be a need to transform the desire for revenge into something righteous and gloss over its primitive aspects. No less so in the model for all modern stories of revenge, *The Count of Monte Cristo*. Revenge is depicted as righteous, and we side with the afflicted protagonist right from the start as he sets up his acts of revenge. He retaliates systematically.

This classical novel gives us the archetypical revenge story. Right from the start, we want the unjustly treated protagonist to prevail. He forms his revenge systematically to make others suffer just as much as he has. Reading this novel as an adult can be a rather dizzying experience, and you have to ask yourself if the hero is not a bit insane.

The young Edmond Dantès, a steersman on a cargo ship, is engaged to Mercedes. His friend Mondego is jealous of him, a jealousy dating back to their childhood. Mondego also wants to marry Mercedes. Another steersman, Danglars, feels that the ship-owners have passed him by in favour of Dantès and forges plans of revenge. Mondego and Danglars cause Dantès to be imprisoned for high treason by branding him a spy. Prosecutor Villefort also has his reasons for wanting Dantès out of the way. Just by chance, Dantès has come upon some information that could compromise Villefort's career. All of these circumstances converge to land a totally innocent Dantès on the prison island of If, where prisoners are sentenced for life to extremely harsh conditions. He ends up spending thirteen years of his life there. Mercedes receives a message saying that Dantès has been executed for murder. His father dies, partly from grief.

After several years on If, Dantès meets Abbé Faria, a former soldier and priest, who is trying to dig an escape tunnel. They meet in secret and the Abbé teaches Dantès to read, fence, and to keep accounts. Before the Abbé dies, he gives Dantès a map showing the spot where an immense treasure is hidden on the island of Monte Cristo, outside of Marseilles.

Dantès manages to escape in the Abbé's shroud and flees back to civilization. He finds the treasure, dubs himself the "Count of Monte Cristo", and starts out on his mission of revenge. He finds out that Mercedes married Mondego just a month or so after he himself was put in prison. Mondego is living in Paris, as is Villefort, who has risen to the rank of national prosecutor. Danglars is a banker in Marseilles. Dantès sees to it that the three men are brought to their knees, ruined, scandalized, and imprisoned. Simply killing them would not be enough to slake his thirst for revenge.

Most people who have read *The Count of Monte Cristo* see in the protagonist an embodiment of righteousness. His suffering was just short of unbearable and the injustice done to him despicable. Young people admire the perseverance with which he seeks out his evil enemies and metes out his "righteous" revenge. Dumas' novel builds up to a moral culmination: right conquers wrong, despite all the obstacles that fate has placed along Dantès' path. The hero feels no uncertainty whatsoever as to the righteousness of his motives, which gives him the strength to overcome all difficulties. In the end, he (and we the readers) have the pleasure of seeing justice prevail and of knowing that none of the scoundrels escaped unpunished.

Under the surface, *The Count of Monte Cristo* is, as we see it, a novel about cruelty and revenge, where a mere innocent human being can turn the tables from a position of powerlessness so that those who are powerful and guilty are reduced to helplessness. Revenge becomes legitimate through our being able to identify with the protagonist and his unjust treatment. Dantès takes the meting out of punishment into his own hands in the form of acts of revenge; in other words, he equates justice with revenge. In addition, his fortune gives him unlimited means to take revenge.

In prison, Abbé Faria says to Dantès, "What has replaced your belief in God?" Dantès answers, "Revenge!" The Abbé then wonders, "Perhaps your urge for revenge is serving God's purpose in keeping you alive?"

We can recognize the words "God shall give me justice", spoken by Dantès in another exchange with Faria, as the classic motto of revenge. The avenger in religious wars, in crimes of passion, or in the genocide in Rwanda, rationalizes his own thirst for revenge by calling it God's will to see justice prevail. (In our final chapter, we take up the concept of justice again along with the aspect of how easily it can be mixed up with revenge.)

When the Count of Monte Cristo meets Mercedes again, she soon recognizes him as Dantès. She tries to move him to refrain from revenge, but he answers: "If you ever loved me, don't take my hatred from me, it is all I have!" He adds: "We will learn from their weaknesses. They will suffer as I did."

Rather than settling for what he wants to have—the woman he loved and a comfortable life—he is determined to get revenge for the thirteen years that were taken away from him. He not only recreates a balance or seeks justice. He retaliates by achieving for himself a position of advantage similar to the one previously held by his enemies. "After my revenge all my wealth will be used for good purposes", says Dantès, as though revenge can be used in a limited and goal-directed manner and then cease.

A revenge spiral: Star Wars

The six films about *Star Wars*, by director George Lucas, have captivated millions of filmgoers. Perhaps what attracts the public is precisely the constant exchange of revenge acts between the different worlds? In this space saga, there is a dramatized philosophical treatment of "the force", a principle that can work in both evil and good directions. In the part entitled *The Space Empire Strikes Back* (1980), the young Luke Skywalker is given a lesson about the force by the Jedi master Yoda:

> "A Jedi's strength flows from the force, but beware of the dark side. Anger, fear, aggression … the dark side of the force are they. Easily they flow. Quick to join you in a fight. If once you start down the dark path, forever it will dominate your destiny. Consume you it will!"
> "Is the dark side stronger?" asks Luke.
> "No, but it is more seductive."
> "But how am I to know good from bad?" wonders Luke.
> "You will know. When you are calm, at peace, passive … a Jedi uses the force for knowledge and defence, never for attack."

In the film, the dialogue sometimes concerns the evil and good sides within every human being as well as the difference between evil and good people. Yoda thus says that the force may only be used for defence, never for attack, while the dark side includes aggression, passion, anger, hatred, envy—not entirely unlike the seven deadly sins. It is easy to fall for the dark side's temptations, but if someone indulges in them, he will be stuck on a course of evil. Luke starts using dark forces when his sister is threatened, but when he injures his father, the evil Darth Vader, in a fight, he sees how much he has come to resemble his father and realizes the danger. Luke had previously idealized his father at all times, but Vader had been seduced by the dark force some time in the past. Luke tries to break with what happened in the past by saving his father and getting him back to the good side. In the end, Darth Vader does in fact go over to the good side and saves Luke before he dies. "Tell your sister that you were right, that there was goodness inside Vader."

Luke was brought up by foster parents, who were murdered by Vader. Luke knew that he himself was meant to belong to the good side but his thirst for revenge drove him to search for Vader. His master Yoda admonished him for being reckless, for wanting to rush into battle before he was mature enough for it. In this sense, he lets revenge take command over him. If he had been more mature, he would have found another way to cope with the fact that Vader was his father. Instead, he makes a series of tragic mistakes, and nothing good comes out of his lust for revenge.

We ask a young man, Shams (interview Jorjani, 2006), who has long been fascinated by *Star Wars*, to explain the effect of the story. Does it encourage a working-through process or does it encourage more violence? He was nine years old the first time he saw a *Star Wars* film. What struck him most was that Luke wanted to be a fighter for the side of light and that he has developed into a wise man by the last film. He has learned to assert himself through words instead of actions because he has achieved a better understanding of the force. After seeing the films in school, Shams came to identify with Luke and began to take in people and things around him in a calm and reasoned way. In addition, the force became important for him as a spiritual idea with its dark and light sides.

In a prelude to *Star Wars*, we find out what made the growing boy who would become Vader go over to the dark side. He is unable to save his mother and she is murdered. When he wants to avenge her death, other Jedi knights try to hold him back. He feels that they are stopping him from realizing his potential. When he gets married and his wife is expecting a baby, he is afraid of losing her. The evil emperor tricks him into doing evil deeds as a price for keeping her safe. In short, the story depicts a typical revenge spiral, where victims become perpetrators, who create new victims and who—like Luke—struggle not to become perpetrators again!

Revenge in different cultures

It is not entirely uncommon in certain cultures to see revenge as a legitimate form of vindication, something that naturally also affects the general sense of justice, as well as the court system. This is the case, for example, when it comes to crimes of passion. A man whose wife has cheated on him murders her lover and receives a relatively mild punishment since people "understand" him and consider him a victim of extenuating circumstances.

The occurrence of "honour killing" among immigrants in Sweden and elsewhere seems to be related to a complicated cultural pattern whereby certain members of these groups get the idea that it is legitimate for them to take revenge on a woman who has departed from their traditional rules on how females should conduct themselves. However, we can also see how revenge in these cases takes place in primitive, regressive situations. It is in all likelihood not a part of the culture *per se* to murder one's own family members, but when certain men feel powerless, ignored, and insignificant in the complicated integration process in a new country, primitive revenge mechanisms come to the fore. These mechanisms are perhaps more an expression of desperation than of culture. The act of murder also indicates envy towards members of the group who seem to succeed better in adapting themselves to the new country and therefore are regarded as traitors.

We can see examples of ancient revenge patterns in certain cultures. Here again, it can be useful to mention extreme examples as an illustration of something more general, namely that cultural differences can be pronounced, but also more subtle, and they become part of the dynamic when a society is shaken by a crisis. A Swiss documentary film (Dones, 2004) about clans in northern Albanian mountain villages shows how these clans are still governed by a justice system from the 1400s (!) that includes blood feuds. According to the system, called Kanun, blood must be avenged with blood on the male side from one generation to the next. Certain families can keep a male member of their family inside for years since he risks being killed if he goes out. In the film, we see a little girl with a toy gun who says, "With this I'm going to kill the ones who killed my dad."

In other cultures, revenge can be an ever-present element in a culturally accepted way, as though it is natural and unavoidable, something that cannot be or does not need to be questioned, like the sun that rises in the morning. However, we ask ourselves if it is not the case that such a cultural acceptance can always be connected to a society in crisis, where people react entirely too rigidly and too primitively. We return to this matter in a later discussion of large group reactions.

Revenge and Judaeo-Christianity

Biblical authors obviously thought that revenge should be treated as a dangerous force. In Leviticus 19:18, the Third Book of Moses of the Old Testament, it says, "Thou shalt not avenge nor bear any grudge against the children of thy people but thou shalt love thy neighbour as thyself." Here the exhortation to refrain from revenge seems to apply solely to one's own people. However, later in the same chapter, it says, as pointed out by Head Rabbi in Stockholm, Morton Narrowe, that the stranger should be treated just like "one born among you … for ye were strangers in the land of Egypt".

In the New Testament (Romans 12:19), the apostle Paul instructs, "Revenge not yourselves, my dearly beloved, but give place unto wrath, for it is written: Revenge is mine, I will repay, saith the Lord." This is often assumed to be based on a strict Judaeo-Christian code called *Lex Talionis* (the Law of Revenge), better known as "an eye for an eye and a tooth for a tooth". Interestingly enough, this phrase has come to symbolize the dynamics of revenge, even though it is controversial to interpret it unequivocally, notes Rabbi Morton Narrowe, since it could also be referring to fair pricing in business transactions.

However, we have no difficulty whatsoever in finding other statements in the Bible about the vengeful or raging God. God punishes disobedient humanity with a vengeance when He banishes them from Eden, when He puts plagues on Egypt, and wipes out Sodom and Gomorrah. He orders those loyal to Him to obliterate certain groups of people without mercy (Deuteronomy 7:16). The revenge element is stressed in the text, where it is made clear that God is not in a rage for things in general. He seems to feel violated because the disobedience or the sin has been directed against Him specifically. From this sense of violation, His rage seems to grow so intense that He has to teach those who have committed acts against Him a lesson or even crush them.

Such sections of the Bible can make the reader stop and think. If it is legitimate for the Judge of all Judges Himself to let loose a revenge-thirsty rage, why should it not also be the same for us lesser beings when we are violated? Indeed, if we see religion as a human creation, God then becomes the very image of a raging, violated, and vengeful human being. So we can hear someone taking this as a pretext for the attitude, "If he can, we can, too", and revenge becomes legitimate.

At the same time, biblical texts bespeak a stark awareness of the complexity of revenge. In a newly published edition of the Haggada—a book for the Jewish Pesach festival to commemorate the Exodus from Egypt—the authors have put together a discussion about the ten plagues that God rained upon the Egyptians (Burstein, Narrowe & Rubinstein, 2006). On the one side, we see the craving for revenge, "When the wicked perish, there is shouting [for joy]" (Proverbs 11:10). "... and Israel saw the Egyptians dead upon the seashore .... Then sang Moses and the children of Israel this song unto the Lord .... Thy right hand, O Lord, hath dashed in pieces the enemy" (Exodus 14:30, 15:1, and 15:6, respectively).

On the other side, we see attempts to rein in vengeance, "Rejoice not when thine enemy falleth, and let not thine heart be glad when he stumbleth" (Proverbs 24:17). "When the evil stumble, God does not rejoice over it. [...] By the Red Sea the angels wanted to break out in a song of praise to the Lord, but God silenced them, 'My creations, my human beings drown in the sea and you want to sing my praises?'" (Rabbi Jochanan, the Babylonian Talmud, Medgilla, 10b).

We can imagine once again how this shifting picture might reflect human ambivalence towards revenge. On the one hand, humans have fantasies about and cravings for revenge, and on the other, they have the insight that the revenge act destroys their own house.

Insight about the destructive nature of revenge is also found in Jesus's Sermon on the Mount. "Resist not evil: but whosoever shall smite thee on thy right cheek, turn to him the other also" (Matthew 5:39). The Christian Peace Movement in Sweden (bibleserver (Internet), 2004) points out on their website that Jesus's exhortation to turn the other cheek has been used as an argument not to resist your oppressor at all. In actual fact, they point out, Jesus's words were a way of encouraging non-violent resistance.

In a fight in the days of Jesus, a man struck his equal with his fist or the flat of his hand. If a man struck someone with a lower status, he used the back side of his (clean right) hand in order to degrade the other and make him obey. If a man struck someone on the right cheek with his right hand, he had to use the back side of his hand. Jesus advises us to turn the other cheek. In such a case, the back side of the hand would strike the other in the middle of the face, which at that time would mean shame for the one who did the striking. The message could be—either strike me as an equal or don't strike me at all. What Jesus could be suggesting is thus non-violent resistance in the same spirit as that later practised by Gandhi.

Revenge and Islamic fundamentalism

When it comes to terrorism in modern times, the special role of religion, and in particular Islamic fundamentalism, has been discussed. Islamologist Jan Hjärpe (2005) has written an article in which he analyses a concept that Osama bin Laden had taken from the Islamic justice tradition, namely "qisas". He writes that "it means retaliation as retribution and is based on the idea that a person has a right to retaliate like for like, combined with the conviction that retaliation serves as a means of deterrence. The idea of retaliation as retribution is part of terrorism's (pseudo)-rationality." Following this view, the attacks of 11 September in the USA are depicted as retribution for events in Lebanon in the 1980s. Similarly, other attacks are seen as retribution for other historical events.

Hjärpe also describes another pair of concepts that are taken from the Koran and used by Islamic extremism. These are "mustak-birun"—people who see themselves as great, the arrogant ones—and "mus-tad'afun"—people who are regarded as weak, the scorned ones. The extremists see the USA as the arrogant side while the Muslims are the scorned ones. The primary goal of terror attacks is therefore to humiliate "the arrogant". This is an example of a worldview that divides people into high positions and low positions, a vertical relationship, which is central to all revenge mechanisms. Hjärpe refers to anthropologist Nasra

Hassan, who has interviewed Palestinian radicals. They return time and time again to the feeling of humiliation, of not having been respected, of being scorned and disdained by those who have power. To commit acts of terror, Hjärpe stresses, is a desperate way to gain respect.

Revenge at work

We conclude by briefly touching upon a revenge motif that perhaps has a more direct connection to many people's daily life. In work situations, people tend to be observant of hierarchies, of being appreciated, of reaching a certain position, and of being treated in accordance with that position. If they are not, they easily feel humiliated. Persons who have insight into their revenge fantasies can handle the aggressivity that is thereby awakened without putting it into action. It is harder for people who are easily humiliated, who perhaps have been humiliated early in life, and whose wounds are easily torn open. Among these people we can find many bosses, who need constant confirmation in order not to feel hurt or questioned. However, we can also turn the matter around and ask ourselves if it is not the case that leadership positions can create narcissistic self-absorption. It is turbulent at the top, a person feels alone and exposed, and it can be tempting to close oneself inside a narcissistic fortress. However, this fortress is vulnerable to violations—and therewith to revenge.

According to an article in *Dagens Industri*, a Swedish daily business newspaper (Dyberg, 2008), a craving for revenge is often predominant in the business world. However, greed can be even more predominant, and thus many people refrain from taking revenge lest it jeopardize their own business dealings. Instead, they direct their energy towards vindication through comebacks. The wife of an industrial leader who had been removed from his position got revenge by exposing embarrassing information about another industrial leader in the press. Her husband chose instead to make a comeback and get vindication through achieving a high position again, in another branch.

In the book *Antonias Revansch* (Ericsson, 2009), Swedish business magnate Antonia Axelsson Johnson tells how the Swedish SE Bank tried to crush her empire in the 1990s. The housing bubble in Sweden had burst and interest rates were rising. At the most, the Johnson conglomerate owed SE Bank seven billion kronor. All of the conglomerate's bank accounts were frozen in 1993. However, the bank ultimately decided that the Johnson group was too big to fail. To be sure, Antonia Axelsson Johnson won the battle that she had waged against the bank for several years, but she felt so violated that she vowed never to do business with them again. In the book—which perhaps in itself is a comeback or a revenge(?)—she uses secret documents to describe how the bank intrigued against her.

On the more ordinary levels in work situations (and in academic contexts), we can find intrigues concerning careers, favouritism or opposition towards colleagues, as well as crises in connection with downsizing or a competitive rush to get new assignments. All these contexts hold ample opportunities for more or less blatant acts of revenge, which can be explained away in terms of "reasonable competition", "the prerogative of the strong", or other pretexts that can legitimize or conceal what is in reality a desire to do damage to a colleague or competitor. Revenge can fuse with the system's way of functioning and thus conceal itself from clear view.

CHAPTER TWO

The psychology of the revenge spiral—revenge or restoration

*I*n this chapter, we take up the psychological mechanisms that can explain the emergence of both revenge fantasies and actual acts of revenge. We also present the revenge spiral, the model that we use to describe the mechanisms of revenge and also the opposite—to focus instead upon the restoration of the self. Can ordinary people become perpetrators? Is the human being a potential avenger? There is a destructive potential in all of us, a shadow from our forefathers that can be brought to bear if we lack counterbalances.

Subjected to humiliation

Revenge fantasies and revenge acts

Thoughts and fantasies about revenge generally arise out of the anger that is awakened after we have been put in an inferior position in some humiliating way. We can say that thoughts of revenge have their basis in a *traumatic event* built up by *external violations* and our *internal vulnerability*.

We are humiliated when our sense of self-esteem is hurt and our integrity is threatened. Most of us know how this feels. We feel misunderstood, upset, and to make it plain and simple, hurt. We are convinced that the other person wishes us harm, even if he excuses what he has done by claiming that he is just trying to be sincere. He might even claim that what he did shows thoughtfulness and concern for us. We do not believe him. *Revenge fantasies* start to form in our mind. Sometimes we misunderstand other people's remarks or actions in a way that makes us feel humiliated. "Isn't he trying to put me down with that tone of voice? Well, I'll show him a thing or two."

Revenge acts are a way for us to avoid thinking and instead give rage more or less full rein. We behave in a way that is destructive both for the one who is acted upon and for ourselves, even though we do not think in such terms. As soon as we put fantasies to work, it is as though we become "another person". We do things we perhaps never thought we would do. The result is that our self-image is changed: we see ourselves as an avenger. There is thus an immense anger behind revenge fantasies and revenge acts, a rage that is awakened in connection with a perceived humiliation.

"The role and significance of humiliation for traumatic experiences have long been overlooked" (Lindner, 2001), and feelings of rage and murderous revenge fantasies are normal reactions to abuse (Herman, 1992). In interviews conducted with Rwandan youths, such as Jean, who survived the genocide of 1994 (Kaplan, 2006, 2008), the picture of how feelings of humiliation and shame are enacted in revenge fantasies has been given more depth. Such revenge fantasies risk being transmitted to the next generation, who receive the "relay baton" of unresolved traumas.

Envy and derogatory remarks

An important point in this context is that we can feel humiliated even if we have not been dealt an actual attack. There is a desire, a striving, in us human beings to be like others are and to have what others have, in other words, not to be in an inferior position compared to others. We therefore carry with us a fundamental inner vulnerability connected to our notion of what we have or have obtained compared to others. This situation means that we constantly risk being stricken by envy.

> Two friends are talking on the phone. The one tells the other about her new apartment, which is roomy and has lots of green space

outside. She mentions how lucky she was to get it through an exchange and to have had her phone installed so quickly.

–We got such a good telephone number, too, 22 30 40.

–Oh, is that so? Well, you won't have it very long, you know. All the telephone numbers are being changed to seven digits.

The friend who was so happy about her news a few seconds ago becomes silent and shrinks a little inside from this subtle expression of envy.

A common way to deal with envy is to make a derogatory remark. We try to rescue our own self-image by putting the other person down. A special form of envy can be found in social condemnation, according to author and sociologist Francesco Alberoni (1991). The person doing so makes a judgement as though he is speaking for people in general and not just for himself. An example can be seen when an actor says of a fellow actor, "He *is* a bad actor" instead of saying, "I *think* he's a bad actor."

Both envy and derogatory remarks can be seen as primitive defence strategies that come close to revenge (Lansky, 2007). There is, however, a difference between lust for revenge and envy, as pointed out by Alberoni. Envy is not a feeling that people find desirable. A person who is envious feels tormented and does not wallow in his feelings of envy the way he would in lust for revenge.

Individual vulnerability, shame, and the vengeful character

Shamelessness is shown when one individual, without honour and without conscience, forces their way into another individual's most private sphere. What has taken place is an assault, and there is a "victim" and a "perpetrator". The victim is left with destructive wounds while the perpetrator goes free.

Shame-free means that a person has feelings of shame but also the ability to bear them—has the capacity to feel discomfort and pain without acting them out. Shame can also be denied and concealed and lead to depression.

Shame can strike all of us—in the form of a box on the ears, a telling off, a scornful laugh—or silence and the absence of acknowledgement. Shame makes us feel unclean and unworthy. Intense shame that strikes us during childhood and that we cannot protect ourselves against can be downright catastrophic. It can lead to suicide.

(Beck-Friis, 2010: pp. 35–38)

Allan Schore (2003) describes the disturbed affect regulation in children with early attachment damage, which can develop into pronounced aggressivity after adolescence. He stresses that failures of early attachment invariably become sources of shame. He gives an account of studies showing that towards a baby of 10 months of age, 90 per cent of maternal behaviour consists of affection, play, and caregiving. In sharp contrast, the mother of a 13- to 17-month-old toddler expresses a restriction on average every 9 minutes. In the second year, the mother's role changes from caregiver to socialization agent, according to Schore. The child continues to explore the objects and the environment in his mother's vicinity but in doing so he brings a period of intense stress upon himself. *"Face-to face encounters that at one time elicited only joy become the principal context for shame experiences"* (our italics). The infant unexpectedly encounters a facially expressed affective misattunement (p. 17). Early experiences of being with a psycho-biologically dysregulating other who initiates but poorly repairs shame-associated misattunement are also incorporated in long-term memory as an interactive representation, a working model of the self-misattuned-with-a-dysregulating-other. Further, these representations are stored in memory "largely outside conscious awareness" as a prototype for all interactions (Schore, in reference to Lachmann, 1988a). The result may be chronic difficulties in self-esteem regulation.

Against this background, it seems probable that parents who impose harsh limitations upon their child, based more on their own needs, create experiences that make it harder for the child to cope with feelings of shame and humiliation in a constructive way in the future. Limitations are specifically manifest in recovery deficits of internal reparative mechanisms. A good example of this process occurs in the rapid escalation of rage seen in response to humiliation and in aggressive eye gaze, a very common trigger of interpersonal rage. Exposure to shame-humiliation is an all too frequent accompaniment of early child abuse, and it may serve as an interpersonal matrix for dissociated rage, Schore stresses (2003).

Thus, the degree of vengefulness in an individual can often be traced to wounds in self-esteem that were caused early in life by parents who were too controlling or too self-absorbed. Revenge fantasies are primarily directed towards such parents, as a way of trying to restore dignity. As a child, the individual has tried to adapt and repress their feeling of being exploited psychically, such as being made to satisfy their parents' needs, being neglected, or, the opposite, being too obsessively controlled. The American psychologist Mary Sherrill Durham (2000) calls "the adult heir" of this child the *repressed-exploited person*, who can take to an excessive adaptation in order to conceal their shame over not having been able to defend themselves. Their vengefulness is unconscious and is instead expressed indirectly through psychic symptoms such as excessive dependence. The *repressed-exploited person* keeps their focus on their own restoration, even though they have a hard time achieving it.

In certain cases, children are subjected to more serious maltreatment by their parents or guardians. The child grows up with an ever-intensifying lust for revenge and the focus is on the oppressor. Durham calls this person the *vindictive character*. Instead of repressing and hiding their desire for revenge, such a person wants to express it through action by putting down, harming, or destroying the other.

How, then, can we describe a vengeful character or individual? Psychoanalyst John Steiner (1996) points out the vengeful individual's typical feeling is that they are right, that they have a passion for justice, they are dutiful, and they are devoted to "their cause". When such an individual feels wrongly treated, their guilt and anxiety disappear and their legitimate need to gain redress for an injustice often runs riot and goes from benign to malign. We find an example of this in von Kleist's novel *Michael Kohlhaas*, in which an originally justified anger concerning an erroneous court decision leads the main character to burn down an entire village and murder innocent villagers. Munder Ross (Beattie, 2005) for his part argues that the unabashed and unrestrained type of revenge is more characteristic of narcissistic or perverted personalities, who can sometimes punish themselves through bringing about their own downfall.

Psychoanalyst Charles Socarides (1966) is also of the opinion that individuals who become directed towards revenge are often people who have wanted to hide psychic injuries that were dealt them in childhood. They have therefore unconsciously idealized their childhood at earlier stages of their lives. Socarides points to the "pseudo-brave" trait in people with a revenge lust. They feel no guilt. The avenger is sensitive to any eventual new injustices that are committed against them.

However, they are unconscious of their own true goal, which is to conceal a dreadful wound in the self. Revenge is a way to conceal this wound, a wound that can be traced to early abandonment or losses and to the fear that is associated with these traumas.

Psychic trauma

Psychically humiliating trauma is precisely what is central to an understanding of the revenge phenomenon and it is a fundamental theme in this book, regardless of whether the focus is on the one who has been afflicted or on the avenger, the perpetrator. We therefore describe here how traumatic experiences form and affect individuals taken as individuals and how this process is connected to revenge mechanisms.

Freud (1920) and many of his successors use the concept *protective shield* to illustrate the trauma process. The protective shield develops gradually throughout an individual's childhood and youth, starting from the moment of birth. When psychic trauma occurs, it is this barrier between the outer world and the inner psychic life that is pierced by psychic overload.

Psychic trauma arises out of single or repeated traumatic events that can evoke helplessness, fear, anxiety, and worry but also intense anger in an individual. The individual feels an intense and urgent need to regain control over his or her existence, but with personal resources at a low level, he or she lacks the capacity to cope with the intense feelings that are being aroused. Nor is there any way to make the traumatic events meaningful. There is no meaning. Primitive defence strategies, such as revenge fantasies, can be the consequence of such circumstances.

In this book, we focus on trauma caused by human beings. To be sure, natural catastrophes can also result in traumas that evoke anger and hatred. For example, on the anniversary of the tsunami catastrophe of 2004, we saw a television programme in which one of the participants, psychologist Åke Iwar, himself a survivor of the catastrophe, described how anger is a concealed feeling in sorrow. He finds an outlet for his own feelings through sports, like boxing, which help him keep the emotions tossing about inside him under control. On the one hand, there is a great contrast in as much as the humiliation aspect is not present in the same way as in traumas created by humans. On the other hand, an individual's search for an answer to why this had to happen to him can be intense and can give rise to a need to find a scapegoat. His self-image is also affected as he ponders—why is this happening to me in particular, and why now at this particular time in my life?

Both single and repeated traumas awaken strong feelings of humiliation and anger at the same time as the afflicted one "must not show that I'm afraid". Inside them is an ongoing struggle to regain an inner balance. However, the effects of the trauma depend on both the individual's own vulnerability and the degree of the violation, as well as the possibilities available to them to deal with what has happened. There is unquestionably a difference between an isolated traumatic incident after which someone is given help to work through what has happened versus repeated trauma when the person afflicted has no chance to work through anything.

> It is an ordinary Tuesday morning. Axel, twelve years old, is on his way to school with his backpack on his back. As he approaches the schoolyard, he sees three boys coming towards him. They have mean looks on their faces. Axel's heart begins to pound. He feels how fear floods his body. The boys start to tease him, and one of them kicks him to the ground. His backpack and glasses fly off. One of the boys tramples on his glasses. Then they run away. Axel tries to get up but his back hurts too much from being kicked around and he remains lying on the ground. A teacher comes along, as does a nice boy, a new acquaintance of his. They help him into the school building. The teacher sits down with Axel and asks him to tell her in detail everything that happened to him from the time he left home.

What Axel was forced to endure can be described as a traumatic incident. However, since Axel gets a chance to put the incident into words at a point in time shortly after he was attacked, he is going to be able to symbolize/represent (remember) the incident, even though it makes for a very unpleasant memory. Axel is also going to be able to put the incident behind him as a trauma that has been worked through thanks to the "psychic space" created by a caring adult, in this case a teacher.

Extreme traumas

We can now compare the Axel incident with what happens under extreme circumstances. In the case of repeated and severe attacks of aggression, such as bodily abuse and sexual exploitation, or in conditions of war and genocide, an individual can be forced to endure humiliating traumas day after day, hour after hour, for several months or more. And this happens in the absence of people close by who are prepared to listen, and without any chance to think through and talk about the loathsome acts and the excruciating pain that they are having to endure.

Any human being who is forced to endure extremely severe traumas feels first and foremost completely *terror-stricken* in the face of what is happening. Afterwards comes a period dominated by fear, and only later do feelings of humiliation become apparent. Anna, who was eleven years old when her native country was occupied by Nazis, speaks about being herded into cattle cars:

> It wasn't like we could just stand there neatly beside each other. Everyone got pushed and shoved. It was horrible. You can't imagine how it was.
> – What was the worst?
> – The dirt, the stench, and being crammed together like cattle. And the cattle car started to move. And we went from Kaunas [Lithuania] to Latvia.
> – How were you standing in the cattle car as it moved along?
> – I was standing beside a certain woman and on my right side stood my mom, my sister and my brother. Maybe two-three hundred people were standing there.
> – Did anyone tell you where you were going?
> – No, no, they said we were going to work. They tricked us. Their method was to trick us to go along for work. Their method was, keep us as calm as possible and without panic. That's the way to send people to be put to death. Everyone tried to get air. The only chance was to get close to a little hatch in the side of the cattle car.
> – Do you remember what you thought about in the cattle car?
> – [screaming] Think? Think? We didn't think, we were too scared of course. We all wanted to get close to the hatch but we couldn't ...

And then when we got to Latvia, to Riga, the cars stopped and the big doors opened. Then Russians, Ukrainians started screaming, I can't describe it … and they ran into all the cars. Get out, get out, like wild men. And can you imagine, a little girl [the pillow had, in fact, been a little girl] woke up. The woman had a daughter whom she was putting to sleep and she woke up and started to cry. Everyone was surprised. A small child! And then a Ukrainian came and pushed and shoved and wanted to know where the crying was coming from and he trampled that little baby with his boots until she died. And when we got to Estonia, the mother took her life … She took her life.

(Survivors of the Shoah Visual History and
Education Interview code 35338)

Claudine, whose family was obliterated during the genocide in Rwanda, makes a difference between being let down by people, which can be a terrible enough blow, and being "let down by life" (Hatzfeld, 2009)—which is unbearable. After extremely traumatic experiences, such as those in Claudine's life, it is impossible to speak about trauma in a traditional sense, according to modern neuroscience. Extreme traumatic experiences are asserted to lie beyond psychic *representation*. This means that the individual cannot translate them to inner images and words and thus cannot convey a coherent narrative about what has happened, as for example Axel could do in the case of the schoolyard attack. The experiences therefore do not remain in the memory in the sense that we ordinarily think about the memory.

The events are registered instead as body memories that are not possible to reach with words. Perhaps it is a visual impression or a sound, such as the perpetrator's face or voice, that has been imprinted in the body (Kaplan, 2006, 2008). As a consequence, the traumatic experiences remain as unprocessed body memories, *presentations as opposed to representations*.

According to Leuzinger-Bohleber (2010), epigenetic research can show that psychological transmission of trauma to the next generation also has genetic correlations, that is, extreme traumas can change the genetic structure in an individual. We can reflect over the unforeseen consequences this might have for children who have survived genocide and for their desire to take revenge for what their parents' generation was forced to endure. This process can come to interact with the risks that exist when political leaders try to reactivate mental representations of an historical event, which Volkan (2004) calls *chosen trauma*. Leaders can do so in order to fuel ideologies that "provide" a justification for their own acts of violence.

Dissociation

Body memories are easily aroused and can be triggered by sensory impressions similar to the ones encountered during the trauma. Memories of aggressive expressions on the face or in the voice of the perpetrator can be activated and recur during the course of the afflicted person's life, as so-called *flashbulb memories*. In Rwanda, the perpetrators whistled in the dark to keep track of each other. The survivors become petrified if they hear similar whistling sounds today, and "the body remembers" by producing a vacant stare and stiffening muscles. However, the traumatized person is usually not conscious that their fear has its origin in a special place and a special time. It is as though everything is happening now, at the time of the retelling (Laub & Auerhahn, 1993). The time aspect has collapsed. Past time and present time are located in different rooms without an associative connection, which means that the trauma has an ever-ongoing existence as present time in a part of the self. All the while, the person is living their ordinary life and from the outside can seem untouched. The traumatic experiences are stored in the memory as isolated fragments, which can also explain the fragmented nature of the narratives told by traumatized people, such as Anna's account of the cattle cars.

The one who has been afflicted thus seems to live with a kind of duality or a splitting in the self (the personality), a *dissociation*. They do not feel whole. Different voices speak inside of them. They can perceive themselves as a double (in certain cases, multiple) being, because of their difficulties in dealing with the anxiety aroused by the trauma. People who have been abused, for example, can develop this splitting of the personality (Sundh, 2003, with reference to Allen, 1993; Braun, 1998; Putnam, 1989).

Another way of describing what it is like to live with trauma has been contributed by Lena Teurnell (2002). She has worked with people who have been forced to endure sexual violence. Teurnell describes how the traumatized individuals are "perpetually on guard" as though danger could strike at any time. She points out how a trauma can be experienced as an "alien object within the psyche, which like a rock remains as it is and does not soften or become integrated in the person's inner world".

Psychiatrist and researcher Judith Herman (1992) stresses that the human being always experiences a conflict between "the desire to deny loathsome events and the desire to speak openly about them" and underscores that this conflict is "the psychic trauma's central dialectic". It is often the *secret-keeping* urge that takes the upper hand. It is important for the person to get help to tell someone what has happened and to restore the sound and sight memories that are possible to join together. A feeling of rage and murderous revenge fantasies are normal reactions to abuse, Herman asserts.

Identification with the aggressor

What, then, does all of this have to do with revenge mechanisms? The answer is that people who have been forced to endure severe abuse or other traumatic experiences often show signs of a phenomenon called *identification with the aggressor*. This concept was formulated as early as 1936 by child psychoanalyst Anna Freud (1993) and constitutes a central aspect of our model for the revenge spiral, which we shall present below. Fonagy (1998) has as a point of departure, that a universal alien self exists. This alien self is a consequence of a normal upbringing with respect to care, which has certain unavoidable shortcomings. During a normal upbringing, this self is covered over by the other self-images that a normally functioning individual can create based on good experiences. The alien self reaches its most dangerous potential when later traumatic events in the family or in the immediate environment force the child to dissociate, to split off a part of the pain he is experiencing by using the alien self to identify with the aggressor. (He takes the aggressor into himself so that he will not need to feel stricken.) In these cases, the covered-over shortcomings in the care he has been given—the vacuums—become filled with the image of the aggressor. The child experiences himself as destructive and in extreme cases as monstrous. Identification with the aggressor means that the individual takes command over stress and extreme trauma through becoming active—like the aggressor—instead of being passive and helpless: "attack is the best defence".

Psychoanalyst Caroline Garland (1998) states that our reaction to trauma often looks like this: "Someone or something has done this (to me) or has not tried to stop it from being done." When we find it difficult to use our thought processes, that is, to work through our trauma, it will instead come back to us in perpetual repetitions. Instead of thinking, we act on the basis of our ever-recurring memories. In such cases, Garland asserts, we reach out for different identities, including thinking of ourselves as the one who hurt us. Such an identification makes us a perpetrator instead of a victim.

Another identification described by Garland is to become like the dead or the injured, in other words, lifeless or depressed, in order to escape the guilt of having been one of the survivors. She bases her argumentation on Freud's classic text *Mourning and Melancholy* (1917), where he underlines the difference between mourning over a person whom one has lost and identifying with the lost person, as happens when someone is depressed.

Resistance towards mourning, which is most likely the most common reason for stagnation after a trauma, can be masked in several ways. People most often try to conceal their resistance by turning it into acts of revenge (Herman, 1992).

Strong affects

Regardless of whether identification is made with the perpetrator or with the victim, it replaces thinking. In the revenge fantasy, there is a sense that an act of revenge is our right, since we cannot think clearly concerning our own grief, loss, or injury. The feeling of righteousness is born out of rage, which organizes our inner world and gives us life in a situation in which we have felt threatened and harmed. At the same time, aggression is a reaction that is essential to life in order for us to assert our integrity, our needs, and our desires and to overcome frustration (Rössel, 2005). Let us briefly touch upon the significance of our ability to manage our feelings for the dynamics of revenge.

When we become upset and enraged, we experience many bodily reactions, for example how our facial muscles become tense, how our heart pounds, and how we almost hold our breath. If we have a chance to put our anger into words and talk about the strong feelings that are raging inside of us, we can slowly start to calm down. At that point, we gain access to our *affects*—we become conscious of our feelings and gain access to words. The neuroscientist Damasio (1999) describes how feelings constitute complicated bundles of chemical and neural reactions that form patterns. The central point is that all feelings fill some form of *regulatory function* that in one way or another benefits the individual. Ultimately, this regulatory function is patterned to help us avoid loss of integrity and threat of death. This is connected to our assertion about the way all of us strive to regain an inner psychic balance by means of revenge fantasies. In the most optimal of circumstances, these fantasies cross over into a striving for restoration in which we can stop feeling humiliated without taking revenge.

The affects, the bodily reactions in connection with emotional experiences, can be metaphorically described as glue. Our earliest psychic world is created through this process, where affective processes can be said to make up the core or the self, of the personality. We can see affects as things that give strength to the connective links within the individual. Those individuals who have limited access to their affects cannot integrate what they have gone through into a coherent narrative of their own life and their own self. As we noted in the section on individual vulnerability, the trigger for strong aggressive feelings—and thus also for revenge—can be put in place early in life, as we see, for example, in neglected children.

Rage and hatred

In order to understand the dynamics of revenge, it is important not only to understand the effects of trauma but also to understand rage and its function. The forcefulness of anger could perhaps be understood from the standpoint of our negative feelings, so that each feeling in and of itself, or taken together with others, can forge a drive to take revenge. These feelings are fear/terror, sorrow/despair, anger/rage, disgust, loathing, and shame/humiliation (Tomkins, 1995). Psychoanalyst Otto Kernberg (1992) has devoted special attention to aggression and "the psychology of hatred". He bases his reasoning on clinical work with patients in severe psychopathological states. He distinguishes between irritation, anger, and rage and shows how hatred stems from rage, the primitive affect around which the aggression drive is concentrated. The most severe affect is hatred, which also constitutes the most complex affect. Hatred can develop to the point that it takes devastating power over the psyche and is directed both towards the self and others.

Hatred contains rationalizations and distortions. The primary goal of the person who is filled with hatred is to annihilate a specific other person in his unconscious fantasies. It is a paradox that the "object is basically both needed and desired, while its annihilation is, however, equally needed and desired". Kernberg's line of thought is in accord with Schore's (2003) discussion of defective affect regulation in children with early attachment damage which can develop into pronounced aggressivity after adolescence.

As was made clear above, rage can function as a last way out, an attempt to re-establish a feeling of dignity and regain a balance in self-esteem when one is faced with extremely frustrating situations, which are perceived unconsciously as a threat from others who are in a position to persecute. Hatred is therefore not always pathological. As a response to a real danger of physical or psychic obliteration for oneself or for those one loves, hatred can be a normal development of rage. However, in most cases, unconscious driving forces consisting of earlier feelings of hatred are also activated and these intensify the degree of hatred.

As revenge fantasies begin to take form, the individual can strive to "get rid of hatred" through taking action. He wants to escape the burden of feeling hatred. Of course, the thought of revenge can also entail an endeavour to obliterate the other—symbolically or literally—in order to gain a feeling of triumph. When hatred is intense and continuous, we can suppose that the opposite might be true, that the avenger or the hater "retains and occupies himself with, downright nurses, his hatred so that he can avoid grief", as one of our friends expressed it. As Dantès in *The Count of Monte Cristo* says: "If you ever loved me, don't take my hatred from me, it is all I have."

When hatred expresses a chronic character tendency, that is, recurring behaviour, it always reflects a complex of problems with aggression. Extreme forms of hatred can lead to murder, radical disparagement, and symbolic annihilation. In certain cases, the individual directs the hatred towards himself, and in the case of identification with the hated object, suicide can be the result. In the case of sadism, there is no desire for annihilation. On the contrary, the sadist wishes to uphold the relationship to the hated other person. Causing pain gives him pleasure—an intensification of aggression and excitement. There are also cases when the person who is filled with hatred grapples with the fact that revenge is not even possible. Perhaps too much time has passed, or perhaps there is no obvious hate object at which he can direct his rage. The latter is the usual situation when there are unexpected natural catastrophes. How can you take revenge on a tornado?

Kohut (2009a, 2009b) regards shame and rage as demolition products of sound basic experiences that emerge when primary emotional needs are not satisfied. In his writings, he elaborates on this delimited "narcissistic rage", which he gradually seemed to regard in a more generalized way. We also see rage as a general human phenomenon in regulating the narcissistic balance and thereby expressions of revenge. The crux is that people may have different degrees of sensitivity, so that when they experience rage it may or may not ultimately have a regulatory effect.

Encapsulated feelings

For someone who cannot work through a trauma for various reasons, the result can be a so-called anxiety-laden trauma neurosis. Another possibility is that the individual becomes psychically and perhaps also physically paralysed, with immobility, withdrawal, and sometimes depersonalization (a feeling of standing outside oneself) as a result. Further, the individual can become excessively afraid of his own strong feelings, so afraid that he hides them from himself—consciously or unconsciously—with such force that he does not even perceive that his own anger exists. If he did so, he would feel pressured to act, but he does not know how that would end, how destructive the situation would risk becoming.

Revenge acts can thus sometimes be kept in check for a long period of time, not through thinking and working through, but instead through locking in rage, which has a stunting effect on the personality and on one's way of living and of being. The encapsulated feelings can lead to depression and psychosomatic symptoms or even to guilt-burdened self-destructivity, whereby there is identification with the dead or the injured among those close to the individual (compare the above account under "identification with the aggressor"). Or, perhaps individuals "brood" on revenge for a long time and then at last their anger explodes in actual revenge acts.

The revenge spiral

So far in this chapter, we have described how the individual becomes drawn into a "traumatic scenario", which can yield a number of different results. At this point, we are ready for a summing-up, whereby we place the concepts we have discussed into our model for the understanding of the mechanisms of revenge: *the revenge spiral*.

The revenge spiral is triggered when a person feels violated. This violation can either be factual, as when someone is forced to endure abuse, or it can have its origin in subjective feelings of having been violated. The degree of inner vulnerability plays a vital role. There is always interplay between *inner vulnerability* and *external violations* in as much as certain individuals are more sensitive to violations because of earlier experiences and/or personality disorders.

The violation leads to a *trauma*, which gives rise to strong feelings (*rage and/or fear*), even though we might call our feelings irritation, displeasure, or frustration depending on how we experience them. Since rage is a strong and a primitive feeling, it can be hard to keep it inside and not act it out.

Depending on what resources we have at our disposal to deal with strong feelings, we can find that our revenge fantasies either cross over into destructive revenge acts or have more constructive outcomes. Certain individuals and groups are thus less vulnerable and do not react as quickly on the basis of their revenge fantasies. Others, because of earlier experiences (often in childhood), are more vulnerable and need only a mild violation to trigger their revenge fantasies.

What is crucial for maintaining the capacity to function while in a traumatized state is the preservation of the ability to reflect at least to some degree. This possibility can be said to be greater if the early parental attachment has been satisfactory. It increases thereafter in relation to how far the person has come in his personal development. An adult can usually tolerate intense affects (including revenge fantasies) without becoming overwhelmed and confused.

All in all, violations create unbearable feelings in our psyche, which are hard for us to deal with on our own. We therefore try to distort them, keep them in check, or push them aside. An explanation for the desire to take revenge, to retaliate, is thus that we want to rise out of our position of weakness and regain an inner psychic balance through re-establishing our self-esteem. Revenge fantasies and revenge acts can be seen, therefore, as the individual's way of coping with or defending themselves against the strong feelings that come up in connection with being violated. Psychoanalysts have described revenge as a defence against fear, shame, loss, grief, anger, and hatred, whereby the individual directs their anger outwardly, away from their painful feelings.

Revenge fantasies and revenge acts can also be interpreted as an individual's way of projecting, loading over onto the other, feelings that they want to get rid of. For example, an individual might want to free themselves from hatred by regarding the other as evil and attacking them. In "more innocent" cases, it can be a matter of retaliating by saying something derogatory to the other. However, in many cases, revenge can put the avenger at risk of meeting violence and serious violations in return, in both the short and the long term.

In short, the revenge spiral can be described as a destructive spiral, whereby victims become perpetrators, who then retaliate with all their might, create new victims, and so on.

Dynamics between revenge and restoration

The wish for revenge is an insufficiently discussed emotion in psychoanalytic theorizing. One of our main points in this book is to clarify the difference between revenge and restoration, which has become more obvious during our studies.

We have chosen to take up restoration in order to elucidate the opposite of destructive acting out—revenge. In restoration, the one who has suffered the attack takes the focus away from the perpetrator and directs it towards themselves. What can they do to restore their own personality and what can they expect in terms of support from those around them, from society, so that they can regain their dignity? If they concentrate on restoration, they can promote their own development and go forward in life instead of striking back and contributing to an escalation of the revenge spiral. We can further underscore the dynamic between the concepts of revenge and restoration by identifying other related psychological phenomena, conceptual pairs of opposites that are central ingredients in this psychological process: humiliation—dignity, violation—respect, shame—pride. To break the revenge spiral, it is necessary for the individual to be able to create a space for reflection and dialogue, which we discuss in Part II of this book.

Can ordinary people become avengers?

In the past, nomadic groups ran into other groups who were strangers to them. They competed for the scarce resources that were available and tried to get rid of their competitors. Hurting individuals in the other group thus served adaptation goals. Conflicts with other groups were a common factor in the lives of our ancestors. In a way, we can thank our "conquering" ancestors for the fact that we exist today. This concept is now known as group selection. Most contemporary developmental biologists subscribe to Darwin's principles and assert that natural selection is especially sensitive to differences between individuals and seldom to differences between groups. However, as recently pointed out, there are nevertheless factors that lead to group selection. When an individual adapts themselves to live in a group, they also promote their own survival. True altruism can thus increase the group's chances of survival as well. It is probable that much of what human beings have developed is for the benefit of the group. This is a controversial issue among researchers, but most of them seem to agree that the group's development depends on the individual group member's capacity for adaptation.

Which adaptations increase the wellbeing of the individuals in the group? The most likely candidates are love, friendship, cooperation, ways of caring for the temporarily or permanently dependent members, communication, a sense of fairness, and even self-sacrifice. However, adaptation also includes darker sides, such as rivalry between groups in the struggle for dominance and territorial definitions, as well as fear of social exclusion. Human beings in most cultures feel that they are members of a group (a tribe, clan, or nation) and feel hostility towards other groups. What possible universal applications and outcomes can we see when we study our ancestors and their inter-group relationships? Waller (2002) suggests three developmental tendencies: ethnocentrism, xenophobia, and a desire for social dominance. These are found everywhere in the world, throughout the history of mankind, and they begin in early childhood.

We have developed a capacity to see our group as superior to all others. We can even be unwilling to see members of other groups as worthy of our respect. In ethnocentrism, a certain group sees itself as being best and as having all the right answers. Once a person has identified themselves with a group, there is no need for them to have attachments, kinship, or other bonds with members of the group in order for them to exaggerate the differences between this group and other groups.

The step from ethnocentrism into xenophobia is not a big one. When we create bonds with certain groups, we also widen the distance to others: "We are what we are because they are not what we are." Even on the level of domestic violence, research shows that non-biologically related family members run an eleven times greater risk of being killed than do biologically related ones (ibid.).

We thus seem to have an innate, developmentally conditioned tendency to seek out familiar faces, since our instinct tells us that whatever is unknown has a great chance of being dangerous and should be avoided.

With regard to the desire for social dominance, biologists assert that it is, aside from the sexual drive, the strongest motivational force in animals. In the USA, it has been shown that taller men are more often chosen for jobs, earn more money, and—remarkably—are elected president more often. The taller candidate won 20 out of 25 presidential elections between 1904 and 2000. We can see the desire for social dominance manifested in the pursuit of higher status and single-minded careerism. This desire also has consequences for our relationships, since we have the technical capacity for destruction while we at the same time lack the mechanisms of restraint for aggression that most animals still have. The species of animal with which we share 98.4 per cent of our DNA—the chimpanzee—has a similar dark side to its nature.

> Modern chimpanzees are not only fellow travelers in time and developmentally akin to us, they are also surprisingly excellent models of our ancestors ... chimpanzee-like violence took place and cleared the way for human war, which made the human being a survivor of a non-stop five million year long habit of deadly aggression.
>
> (ibid.)

This evolutionary psychological explanation of human history has obviously not gone unchallenged. It has been criticized for being ultra-Darwinist. There are, with all probability, other developmental factors besides natural selection. Nor are we slaves under the rule of our genes or our ancestors. We have the capacity to learn and to adapt ourselves to different variations of life. There is no "genocide gene". The phenomena that have been described here—ethnocentrism, xenophobia, and social dominance—are tendencies, not reflexes. They help us to understand what formidable forces we have to grapple with. To say that an individual has potentiality for something is quite different from saying that there is a determinism to make them do it. We must not underestimate our capacity for taking different approaches through the choices we make.

Nor is it acceptable to use evolutionary psychology to justify anti-social behaviour. Nothing that is created through natural selection is necessarily morally right. Natural is not necessarily good. A person may feel driven to do something, but that is not necessarily what they should do. However, if we understand these driving forces, we have a greater possibility of influencing ourselves as human beings to go in more favourable directions.

CHAPTER THREE

The grey zone between revenge and restoration

*T*hrough the many discussions that we have had with others, we have understood that the revenge theme is a loaded one and draws immediate interest. People have also said to us many times, "Come on, now, there has to be a positive revenge", or something else in that spirit, meaning that the revenge act can be justified. The one seeking revenge looks for an outlet for their intense feeling and a target at which to aim it in order to regain a good self-image. In certain cases, they offer an elegant performance in how to give someone a dose of their own medicine. They can sometimes find just the right words and thrive on a chance to be brutally honest. However, we believe that in the expression "positive revenge" people confuse revenge with other psychic phenomena such as limit-setting integrity, restoration, or other moral concepts such as justice.

We see an opportunity here to pause and reflect together with the reader on the nature of our position since—when the question comes up—it seems many people do not have a thought about alternatives to revenge. They think it would be associated with weakness. In the previous chapter on the revenge spiral, we tried to show that revenge acts never lead to a positive development (even if the act can lead to a feeling of relief for a brief moment). However, discussions can sometimes end up in confusion between revenge intended to harm the other person and restoration, where a person makes things better for themselves without intending to harm the other. We do not know how we ourselves would react in a hard-pressed situation. Would we be capable of turning into a perpetrator, or would we simply do the right thing and be a rescuer? What does a bullied child do to avoid becoming a bully himself? How can a person regain their balance in a well-considered, positive, self-assertive way?

We have a need to regain self-respect, to obtain restoration, and at the same time to find an outlet for anger and disappointment in sublimated—socially accepted—forms. This reminds us of the subtle revenge acts in everyday life. We do not give them much thought. Someone leaves dirty dishes in the sink. The other reacts by staying at work longer than usual the next day. Perhaps many little revenge incidents are accumulated over the years, and the people involved finally reach a point when they cannot remember how it started! Sometimes the feeling is even subtler—a person just suddenly realizes that a new situation has come into being because of the circular revenge spiral. Different situations differ as to degree of revenge elements. If someone says in a bossy tone, "You can't park here", in a way that sounds humiliating, or that someone who is "easily humiliated" interprets as such, the humiliated person takes revenge. A vulnerable person becomes humiliated. The easily humiliated person has probably not felt sufficiently understood earlier in life and now it seems that they are being treated the same way again! They take revenge through a disproportionately strong anger.

However, we intend to concentrate our attention here on the expression "positive revenge", which often comes into focus in the discussions generated by our lectures. Some listeners in the audience can even get so excited that they remark that "just a little, little revenge is good, isn't it?" When we listen to their examples and descriptions of the emotional implications that revenge acts have for them, it becomes obvious that there is a border area—a grey area—between revenge and restoration that needs to be analysed. These "lesser acts of revenge" ("positive revenge") have often yielded the desired result, thus the label "positive". The person in question has changed their behaviour. Those who speak of "positive revenge" are most probably referring to actions that are built up by their own aggressivity and that boost their self-esteem (they "inflate themselves") to the point at which they harm the other person, a communication where they find no words. To be able to talk about their fantasies, an individual must ascertain for themselves—and this is especially true if they are a child—that it is possible to talk about what has happened, which also presupposes a potential listener, even if the one who talks is considered to be a nuisance. We understand this as a necessary setting of a boundary directed at the milder oppressor only after repeated attempts to reach them through explanatory words have failed. We therefore see this border area as a sub-category under "restoration".

After all, we usually say metaphorically that the human being can need a second skin as a protection for his inner vulnerability. People who are entirely too thick-skinned, for example "troublemakers" in junior high school, often scare others with their readiness to resort to acts of revenge. They are not inclined to talk as a first recourse since they perhaps have lacked listeners. The harsher they are in their way of expressing themselves—both physically and verbally—the more vulnerable they are likely to be inside and the more in need of protecting themselves. Vulnerability is not the thought that first occurs to someone when confronted with such a person. So how can people in general dare to feel that it is possible to reach out to the other's vulnerability—past their armour—without reinforcing the hard surface even more? It seems to be a matter of creating trust. Dialogue is a key word, as well as the knowledge that aggressiveness is frightened vulnerability.

We see a number of themes in the *grey area* where dialogue has not worked and where the boundary between revenge and restoration can seem unclear, even if restoration dominates. In this grey area, we are looking at a sublimated way to use the energy of aggression to stake out boundaries and to restore balance.

Transformation of trauma as communication

Garland (1998) refers to Freud's theory about how the child can transform a painful passive experience (such as being left by his mother) into an active game and thereby master his inner feelings. A desire for revenge can be acted out on a symbolic surrogate for the mother rather than on the mother herself. The trauma is reversed, and the other is made into the passive recipient of the unpleasant experience. This is typical for the working through of severe traumas. The reversal of the trauma is not necessarily just an expression of revenge lust, nor just an expression of a desire to eliminate psychic chaos. As Garland underlines, the reversal can also be an expression of a hope that the other person can cope with what the traumatized person needs to share. It may be the only way available to him to communicate without words something of his intense distress.

> A man consistently comes home from work and business trips later than he has promised. His wife finally gets fed up and empties out the contents of his finest bottles of wine, which he has been saving for a long time. From that time on, he no longer comes home late.

The wife's action has an obvious element of revenge in it, but it is also an attempt at communicating. She has not succeeded in making her point with him before, and this is a way of saying, "Stop! Enough is enough!" He supposedly gets the message, but we ask ourselves, is he not also going to sit and fantasize about revenge plans of his own?

Making a comeback

The "making a comeback", or "I'll show them, just wait and see", type of revenge, which we call *revansch* in Swedish, and which has the same root as the word "revenge" in English, means achieving restoration without hurting the other person. It might, for example, be a matter of improving one's own performance in sports or at work. That we can still say that *revansch* occupies a place in the grey area between restoration and revenge stems from the fact that the one who wants *revansch* to a large extent has their focus upon the other person, to whom they want to show a "thing or two". However, they are not primarily out to hurt the other person.

In the world of sports, we sometimes find revenge as a part of the game within the game (personal communication, Matthias Engstrand, TV producer, 2005). We can hear someone utter one of the more moderate phrases for revenge, something like "Now he's going to get what he has coming to him", which can mean anything from a desire on the part of a player or a team for restoration to acts of aggression meant to put an opponent at a disadvantage. In addition, players can make use of the potential of revenge to get the other team's players in trouble and thus gain an advantage for their own team. For example, a football player might provoke one of the opposing team's most important players through rough tackling. This key opponent cannot control his anger indefinitely, and at last he retaliates with his own ugly tactics, meaning that he gets a warning or is put out of the game.

Sometimes we can see revenge-like actions in the business world in connection with competition and strategic choices, but in such cases there is often a regulatory system in place that protects against destructive extremes, keeping things from going too far.

Revenge through not taking revenge

In the following example, a new employee experiences something that most people would find humiliating. He paradoxically directs a stab at the violator by pretending not to notice what she did and thus puts himself in the superior position.

> A secretary blows up at a new employee and tells him off in no uncertain terms in front of their colleagues. He purposely does not come back at her, he does not say an unkind word about her to their colleagues. He is careful to be as friendly and polite as possible to her. She now becomes friendly, but perhaps she also feels put down and maybe even shaken up by his non-revenge. His actions mean that he does not say one single word about her behaviour.

Powerlessness

In certain poor countries where there is a generally low level of education, families can live in social deprivation for generations. They feel frustration over the humiliating actions that they have had to endure from surrounding groups in a position of advantage. The children and youth there may not have always learned other strategies than to retaliate as a way of standing up for their own interests and not letting themselves be humiliated. In this way, they are taking revenge even though what they really want is restoration, and that is even what they think they are getting.

We know that revenge in everyday language may be termed as a legitimate moral act, a "reasonable" counterattack, as when two traumatized groups are confronted and we hear statements like "act—don't think!" But we always see the revenge act as a more or less primitive force, which may be understandable in some cases, but in reality never has any moral justification.

Lindner (2001) reminds us that our present view of human rights in the West is built upon an earlier history of traditional blood-based cultures, where it was legitimate, honourable, and even obligatory, to heal humiliation by killing another human being. In Chapter One, we mentioned this phenomenon in a section on revenge in different cultures, as in the case of so-called honour killing. We now add societal history as a consideration. In a modern society with human rights, humiliation is healed instead through restoration, backed theoretically and sometimes practically by the legal system, giving the victim a chance to regain their dignity, as well as through empathetic dialogue, forgiveness, and reconciliation.

Lindner also emphasizes that structural humiliation has been internalized as something unquestionable in hierarchical societies. In Burundi, where the Tutsis governed, the Tutsis were convinced that they were born to rule and the Hutis were born to obey. In contrast, in an egalitarian society, humiliation takes on other implications. The individual experiences it as a crime against his freedom and dignity. Human rights have not taken away humiliation but instead have intensified the perception of it, making it even more explosive. In today's world, the human rights view often collides with the old hierarchical view in direct confrontations. Historical structural changes are thus reflected in people's identities and cause them to experience humiliation as a meaningful trauma.

To summarize, perhaps what people mean when they talk about "just a little revenge" or "positive revenge" is the healthy self-assertiveness that they and others use to stake out and communicate boundaries and to restore balance. We realize that this common way of thinking will be turned upside down by our definition of restoration. The sheer act of revenge does not bring restoration even if people can tell themselves that it does. It is our hope that the distinctions we make between the concepts will clarify what is ultimately and truly beneficial for someone who is suffering humiliation.

CHAPTER FOUR

The destructive group

*T*hus far, we have described the mechanisms of revenge on the individual level. Now we take a step further and turn our focus to the group. Many revenge spirals in society are connected to group psychological mechanisms. One example is the escalating violence between rival teenage gangs. The group phenomenon also plays a central role in everyday hostilities. It manifests itself in prejudices and the orthodoxy that can develop out of these. On the individual, relational, and societal levels, a complex interaction takes place between cruelty, trauma, and counterbalances. We refer to classical social psychological studies.

In order to understand conflicts and revenge-related phenomena between groups of individuals, we must first take a deeper look at how we as individuals are related to the group. It is a matter of understanding how individuals as individuals are influenced by the group and how the interaction between the leader and the group takes form.

Since we are examining revenge—a destructive phenomenon—we describe first and foremost the negative effects on an individual when they adapts themselves to a group. Needless to say, there are also good sides to adapting oneself to a group. For example, evolutionary biologists point at rational and "natural" explanations for this adaptation, which they argue has taken place because it favours the individual's survival. It is also likely that many of the features that human beings have developed are there for the group's best interest (Sober & Wilson, in Waller, 2002).

Our point of departure for our analysis is psychodynamic theory as well as various social psychological theories and experiments. Generally speaking, these studies show that the group makes the individual more primitive and extreme in his or her way of thinking and behaving and intensifies his or her feelings. The combined effect of all of this is that groups can act with greater cruelty than the individuals each on their own would be able to accept or of which they would be capable. The group is thus more dangerous and more unreliable than the individuals of whom it is composed. The American social psychologist James Waller (ibid.) calls this collective potentiation. However, Waller stresses that the group does not come up with new ideas but rather reinforces the ideas that its individual members already possess or makes these ideas more extreme. In other words, the group exposes and lifts up the thoughts that the individuals in the group have already had.

Another important part of the research concerns the relationship between the group's members and its leader. The ties to the leader (and consequently to the others in the group) are often built on idealization. Freud compared the group's relationship to its leader with the individual's relationship to a hypnotist (1921). In a group, the individual is susceptible to suggestion by both the others in the group and the leader. One way to express this is to say that the individual turns over their critical powers to someone else and loses their awareness. Their thoughts and behaviour are adapted to the group's attitudes.

If we look at the above conclusions in the light of a discussion of revenge, we can say that the individual turns over their responsibility for revenge acts to the group. Spectators at a football game, several years after the event, can boo at a player who "abandoned" the home team and nowadays plays for their rivals. Or, they can boo at a player on the rival team every time he touches the ball, simply because he accidentally injured one of the home team's players. Individuals would not do such things if it were up to them alone, but the group potentiates or reinforces their hostility so that they go from thought to action.

Freud and mass psychology

Freud reflected over the group's repressive vulnerability as early as 1921 in his essay on mass psychology (1921). Since then, his ideas have been the basis for psychoanalytic studies as well as for many studies in social psychology. Since many of his thoughts are still the subject of great interest, we find it relevant to summarize them here.

Freud argues that individual psychology is at the same time a social psychology since other people always play roles as inspirers, objects, helpers, and opponents. He first discusses the descriptions by earlier writers, whom he finds to have put entirely too much emphasis on the mass (the large group) as a social phenomenon. At the same time, he does agree with earlier writers that the individual can be so influenced by the mass that it is no longer possible for them to repress unconscious impulses. All of their destructive impulses can thus come forth without inhibition, since their conscience is numbed. Freud draws a parallel with hypnosis: the conscious personality disappears.

The group's members are vulnerable to suggestibility with regard to each other and to the leader in a way that resembles people in isolated villages or children. The mass is volatile, impulsive, and easily swayed. Everything is possible, the "impossible" disappears. The feelings of the mass are always simplistic and excessive, neither doubt nor uncertainty exists. A seed that could grow to antipathy grows instead to hate since the mass often takes to extremes. The mass is intolerant towards others' opinions and gullible when it comes to its own authorities. It wants to be controlled, even subjugated. It extols traditions and is conservative towards all that is new and unfamiliar.

All of the cruelties that have lain dormant in the individual since time immemorial can be awakened in the mass. On the other hand, a refinement of the individual can also take place. The intellectual level of the mass is always lower than that of the individual. In an ethical sense, the mass level can in some cases be superior and in other cases inferior compared to the individual level, owing to the intense feelings expressed by the mass. These feelings can be used to protect a person in trouble, such as when the members of a village defend a refugee in hiding, or they can be used to eliminate someone who is alien and frightening to the mass, such as in lynchings. The mass cannot separate fantasy and reality like the individual can. The unreal illusions often take precedence over reality.

Ties to the leader—idealization

Freud asks himself how emotional ties are brought into being within the group and in relation to the leader, and he takes the army and the church as examples. He argues that what we see above all in such cases are *goal-inhibited*—what he also calls *sublimated*—love-filled ties. These result in different kinds of ambivalent identifications that make up the sticking power of the group. Freud also brings up infatuation as an additional factor, more specifically its element of sexually goal-inhibited adoration of the other. This elevated admiration or idealization blurs the judgement. The other ultimately replaces the self. In a group, a number of individuals put the same person in the place of their own selves, and thus they identify themselves with each other.

Freud further argues that the group as such is a manifestation of regression, of primitive functions, even though the group's solidarity and feeling of togetherness also contain various sublimated expressions of the repressed hostility within the group. The demand to conform applies only to the group members, not to the leader. Freud sees these group phenomena as remnants of the primordial horde. The primordial father has prevented his sons from satisfying their sexual impulses. He has forced them into abstinence, and out of this have arisen emotional ties to him and between the sons. He has forced them to submit themselves to the conditions of the group and of the leader. The primordial father has become the mass's prototype, taking command over the ego of each individual in the group instead of each individual's having his own ideals to guide him. The suggestibility to which everyone is thus prone is built upon love bonds rather than upon thought-based work.

We can also make a comparison here to boarding schools, secret societies, and other contexts where there are initiation rites with elements of sadism. When the initiates have passed all the tests, they subject new generations to the same rites, which can be said to be a shifted revenge. The initiates do not take revenge on the ones who tormented them but rather on the new victims. The dog takes the cat, the cat takes the mouse … . This indirect revenge thus expresses the group's repressed hostility, which finds its outlet in mistreatment of the new members.

Freud was perhaps too caught up in his own terminology of the drives. He may also have been too caught up in his own culture's predominant view of the individual identity as the preferred one, together with a suspicion towards the way certain groups functioned. Nonetheless, the observations he describes still stand their ground. Today, it is clear that individuals can easily switch over to seeing their group identity as just as vital as their individual one. Such reactions can be seen in relatively unorganized groups, such as spectators cheering for their team, but also in more permanent groups, such as those having to do with a national identity.

Sociopsychological studies

Social psychologists have studied group conflicts to a much greater extent than psychoanalysts have done. There is thus an abundance of literature within social psychology that could be interesting to refer to. However, considering our focus on questions of revenge, we are only going to present certain classical studies that are relevant in the revenge context. The examples aim to show how otherwise well-functioning and independent individuals regress in certain group situations to a point at which they are prepared to be passive witnesses to cruelties towards other human beings or to carry out acts of revenge. The studies are from the USA, where resources have been available to demonstrate these mechanisms in a successful way. Needless to say, other nationalities, including Swedes, are just as vulnerable to these dynamics.

On the relationship between attitude and behaviour: the Good Samaritan

Darley and Bateman did an experiment (Darley & Bateson, 1973) that was entitled "The Good Samaritan Experiment". It says something important about passive bystanders and the relationship between attitudes and behaviour. Theology students in Princeton were told to prepare a sermon on the Good Samaritan, the Bible story about how a person should come to the aid of a stranger in need. Each of the students was assigned a time and a place to hold his sermon. Somewhere en route to this place, a co-worker in the experiment was lying down by the side of the road, obviously injured and in need of help. Some of the students had been given more of a time margin before their sermons, and a larger number of these students stopped to help the stranger in need. In contrast, most of the students who did not have much of a time margin hurried past in order to be on time for their sermon. In other words, they felt it to be more important to be able to hold their sermon on the Good Samaritan on time than to be a Good Samaritan in reality. This ingenious experiment seems to show that social situations exercise significant control over individual behaviour and can dominate over the individual's values, convictions, and earlier experiences (McDermott, 2004).

On the importance of social roles: Zimbardo's prison experiment

The powerful effect of the group process is shown even more clearly in experiments on socials roles, such as Zimbardo's experiment at Stanford University from 1973 (1996). Volunteers were sought who would participate as subjects in a two-week-long experiment on prison life. Those who signed up were tested to make sure they were mentally and physically healthy. Then they were randomly assigned to one of two groups: guards or prisoners. Zimbardo arranged for the local police to arrest the prisoners in their homes. They were handcuffed, taken away in police cars, and fingerprinted. They were blindfolded and driven to a simulated prison in the basement of the Psychology Institution at Stanford University. In their cells, they were made to strip down and let themselves be sprayed with a disinfectant, after which they were issued uniforms consisting of hospital gear that was far too small for them. The uniforms were open in the back and marked with ID numbers. The guards were also taken to the cells. They were informed about the situation and given uniforms, dark glasses, and batons. They were instructed to keep order but were not given any details on how to do so. They were allowed to do anything short of striking the prisoners.

What happened was that the guards were quick to resort to sadistic behaviour. They made up all kinds of arbitrary rules that the prisoners had to follow. If the prisoners refused, they were punished. They could lose their privileges, such as a chance to read, talk to others, sleep, or wash themselves. The guards' sadism got out of hand as time went on. They made the prisoners do push-ups, made them get into roll-call formation in the middle of the night, subjected them to isolation in tiny closets, and sometimes made them clean the toilets with toothbrushes or their bare hands. The prisoners underwent parallel changes. First, they tried to resist. One went on a hunger strike. When the revolt failed, the prisoners became passive. Their self-esteem plummeted, and some of them started to cry uncontrollably. The situation became so bad that the experiment had to be broken off after six days, instead of the planned two weeks.

No one seemed to have retained the ability to look outside the experimental situation. Not one single person quit being a part of the experiment. It was as though they believed that they were part of a real prison. The only one who objected was a student assistant to Zimbardo, and she became a heroine. Her name was Christina Maslach, and she told Zimbardo on the sixth day that what he was doing with the boys was dreadful. At first, he got angry with her and told her the guards' sadism was not his responsibility. After that, he was awake all night thinking about it and decided to break off the experiment. Some time later, he married Maslach!

In 2004, the scandal involving torture and humiliation of prisoners at Abu Ghraib prison in Iraq made the headlines. The American army lost no time in blaming what happened on a few rotten apples in the barrel rather than on the system itself. However, an assessment of thousands of psychological studies in this area made by a research group at Princeton University came to the conclusion once more that ordinary people can disconnect their normal control mechanisms in a prison system under certain circumstances (Fiske, Harris & Cuddy, 2004). The prison guards lived in an environment that evoked death anxiety in the prisoners. The prisoners were regarded as enemies. In addition, the hierarchical system seemed to legitimize torture—especially since the supreme commander in Iraq, General Ricardo Sanchez, had personally authorized a number of "hard-handed" interrogation methods. Zimbardo himself made a statement on Abu Ghraib and made the same assessment as the research group at Princeton, namely that it was not at all a case of individual sadists. Human beings fulfil the social roles they have, without reflecting over the destruction that their actions can bring about.

Carnahan & McFarland, among others, have carried out a study (2007) that shows that people who sign up for prison experiments of the kind that Zimbardo initiated have more issues with authority and aggression than test persons who sign up for other types of experiments. Taking this into consideration, it seems all in all that a combination of person and situation is required to unleash perpetrator behaviour.

It turns out, however, that the prison guards at Abu Ghraib were not there by choice at all, but rather were most often ordered to take the tasks in question (Gourewitch, interview 2009). The prison was situated—in total disregard for the Geneva Convention—inside a battle zone, where fierce battles were being fought. The prison guards can reasonably be expected to have felt an anxiety of their own, considering their vulnerable situation, a foreign country and culture, a task that was unusual for them, and new, confusing rules about "softening up" prisoners by means of torture. The guards' anxiety played itself out on the prisoners, and an indirect revenge took place on the new victims for the guards' vulnerability. Moreover, guards who are frightened become more primitive in their thinking and more susceptible to group mechanisms.

On the effect of group pressure: Solomon Asch's experiment

In 1956, Solomon Asch carried out an experiment that has become a classic because it was so successful at showing group conformism, or the influence of group pressure on individual behaviour.

Asch let a group of male college students believe that they were going to participate in an experiment regarding visual perception. He put them in a room together with some other students who were secretly his co-workers. They were all shown a card with a line of a certain length on it and then a card with three lines of different lengths. The test persons were now instructed to say which of the three lines was closest in length to the line that was alone on the first card. In the first three rounds with different cards, both the false and the true subjects gave the right answer. In the fourth round, the false subjects had been instructed to give the same wrong answer. The true subjects found themselves in a dilemma: should they say what they thought or say the same thing as the others had said and were in agreement on? This procedure was repeated several times and the true subjects became more and more astounded and unsure. Should they dare to believe their own perceptions? The result was that about one-quarter of the subjects maintained their independence and gave the right answer every time. However, between 50 and 80 per cent adapted themselves at least one time to a wrong answer and one-quarter adapted themselves to a wrong answer every time! A conclusion is thus that conformism takes hold quickly, even among strangers, and is much stronger than could be expected.

The last chapter of Sebastian Haffner's book *A German Man's Story* (2002) gives a fascinating account of how he, as a young law student, was forced to attend an ideological Nazi training camp in order to receive his law degree. To his surprise, he realizes that extremely little ideological training is going on at the camp. Instead, it is the togetherness in itself, the "comradeship" with all these men, most of whom had had their doubts about Nazism when they came to the camp, that creates a group atmosphere and changes them as individuals. To adapt themselves to one another and to make their time at the camp as tolerable as possible become more important than sticking to their own opinions and values. They undergo a gradual change whereby they become more positive towards Nazism. And before long, the camp members were psychically prepared to commit crimes and to murder. They became just like the reserve policemen when there was no substantial counterbalance to black-and-white interpretations of reality, to the idea that Jews and others had grabbed more than their due in an improper way.

On obedience and group norms: Milgram's electric shocks

And finally, the most famous experiment on obedience: Stanley Milgram's studies from 1962 (1974). His basic question was—would people follow orders even if these orders clearly contradicted their moral values? The set-up was such that the subjects came in pairs to Yale University. They were greeted warmly and given instructions by the experiment leader, a man in a white lab coat. He told them that the experiment was designed to find out about learning and memory, the main question being whether punishment could have an effect on memory. One subject would act as the teacher and the other as the pupil. The experiment leader informed them that he would stay with the teacher in order to supervise the experiment. The pupil's task was to learn and to remember pairs of words. The pupil would give the second word in the pair when cued by the teacher with the first. If the pupil gave the wrong answer, the teacher was to give him an electric shock. The shock was to increase by 15 volts for every wrong answer. After the rules of the experiment had been described, the two subjects drew lots to determine their roles. However, the drawing was actually rigged so that the true subject would always be the teacher. The other subject, the pupil, was secretly Milgram's co-worker. Before the pupil was connected to his electric chair, the teacher got to test how a shock of 45 volts felt. After that, he was taken to another room and placed beside an electric shock machine that had a dial with voltage settings all the way up to 450 volts.

At first, the experiment went smoothly, but after a certain point the experiment's designers had decided that the pupil would start to answer incorrectly according to a pre-arranged pattern. The teacher started to apply electric shocks, not knowing that in reality nothing was happening. The experiment leader encouraged the teacher to go on if he protested, saying, "The experiment requires that you continue ..."

The results were extremely alarming. In the first version of the experiment, all of the subjects gave up to 450 volts. There was no variation whatsoever. So Milgram made a new version with certain changes. The three highest voltage settings were given new labels saying "Danger for deadly shock". The pupil was instructed to state that he had a heart condition. He was also instructed to show certain reactions: at 75 volts he should give a sigh of pain, at 150 volts he should ask to have the experiment stopped, at 180 volts he should scream that he cannot take the pain any longer, and at 300 volts he should scream out about his heart condition, beg to be let out of the experiment, and refuse to answer any more questions. The teacher was then instructed to count refusal to answer as an error and to increase the voltage. This new version gave rise to extreme stress on the part of the "teachers". They begged, threatened, and screamed at the experiment leader, who replied that he would take responsibility for whatever happened. But even though they got upset and protested, most of the teachers carried out the experiment to the end. Most of the subjects continued up to 300 volts, while two-thirds went all the way up to 450 volts.

Prior to the experiment, 40 experienced psychiatrists had told Milgram that most subjects would not continue past 150 volts and that no one would go all the way up to 450 volts. They were convinced that only people with psychological deviations would go above 300 volts. But this was obviously not the case, and this alarmed everyone who found out the results of the experiment. The subjects were not even people lacking a will of their own; they were not passive or bad people. They were, rather, people who were actively engaged in what they were doing, who did want to relate to their fellow human beings, and who did not have any evil intentions. However, the structure, with the authoritarian and at the same time convincing situation, the scientific approach, the white coats, the experiment leader who said he would take responsibility, who kept everything calm and encouraged the subjects to go on—all of these factors made for a deadly obedience situation.

However, Lars Dencik, a social psychologist in Roskilde, came up with a slightly different interpretation of the test subjects' behaviour (Dencik, personal communication, 2004). He underscores that the experiment showed that people want to stick to a group norm more than it directly showed an expression of obedience. He argues that it is extremely important for us to follow the norm and to be a part of the group to which we believe that we belong. If another person is there in addition to the experiment leader (which Milgram did test in a later experiment), and this person says that the subject is free to stop the experiment, the subjects will act much more independently, and most of them will refuse to continue. This probably says something about the significance of counterbalancing and opposition, active bystanders, and democracy in general, as safeguards against destructive group processes. More is said about these matters in the second part of the book.

As a general and compressed conclusion regarding the above mentioned studies, it can be said that we are much more susceptible to, and less aware of, the influence of group situations than we are perhaps inclined to believe. This is true for all three: social roles, conformism, and obedience. We believe that we make our own decisions based on our own observations and considerations, although in reality we are often influenced unconsciously by the group.

Prejudices and orthodoxy

We have thus far shown how the group can influence "normal" individuals to carry out destructive actions. What about individuals who are already non-reflective and aggressive? When these individuals meet with group pressure, their destructive tendencies can be enhanced. They can easily be enticed to adopt the particular group's prejudices and hatred towards other groups. Through outlining this process, we argue that prejudices and orthodoxy are interesting to study as breeding grounds for group-based revenge. The rigid mindset that is typical for individuals with extreme attitudes offers simplified conflict solutions and thus carries with it a grave risk for revenge actions. Orthodoxy can lead to a fundamentalist way of thinking. Prejudices that are not held in check can lead to violence.

Prejudices

Every day, all of us work with our notions and prejudices in a way that usually gives us sufficient control over the ordinary hostilities that come up in relation to others (Böhm, 1993). Prejudices seem to make life easier, but, at the same time, they run into opposition from our sense of reason, which tells us that tolerance is better and makes it possible for us to keep prejudices within manageable bounds. However, even when we are relatively aware, something happens to our unconscious notions when they are transformed into prejudices:

- Instead of being *my notions*, they become impersonal, projected onto reality.
- Instead of being *flexible*, they become rigid and less susceptible to influence and dialogue.
- Instead of being *notions or value judgements*, they become quasi-objective facts about reality: "This is not just what *I believe*, it doesn't matter what you say, this is the way things *are*."

Prejudices are unconscious. We can be conscious in general that we have prejudices but we are unconscious as to what the specific prejudices are. Prejudices thus do not differ from other unconscious notions, even if they are more rigid and more difficult to reflect over.

As we see it, prejudices stem from a special split-ego position, the little child's way of dividing the world into good and evil, a position to which we tend to return in crises. In this split position, we do not need to suffer from uncertainty and ambivalence. We are sure of what is right or wrong. Prejudices contribute to this simplification by giving the illusion of solving problems concerning guilt, conflicts, and moral questions.

The allure of simplifying things into black/white (right/wrong) also brings with it thoughts of purity (Volkan, 2004). Most extreme political or religious ideologies express this need. According to these sorts of utopian fantasies, a group can make a complete projection of all its evil parts and then root them out in order to reach a form of paradisiacal harmony. The Nazis, for example, projected all evil onto the Jews and other non-Aryans, and not even the risk of losing the war could stop them from clinging to their projection and destruction.

Orthodoxy and fundamentalism

Orthodoxy can lead to fundamentalist mindsets. Some years ago, we interviewed three people who were orthodox in their religious beliefs, and we found it striking how these three, a Muslim, a Jew, and a Christian, appeared to have more in common with each other than with other, more moderate members of their respective religions. The Christian said so explicitly. The orthodox mindset, that is to say, a thought structure featuring absolute truths, as well as a certain degree of contempt for the lukewarm relativism of their own non-orthodox fellow believers, seemed to unite them (Böhm, 1998).

The movement towards orthodoxy seems to begin with a basic ideology or an ethical/religious mindset that is apparently beyond questioning because it is regarded as sacred, or absolute in some other sense. This goes along with the closed mind's black/white argumentation. Whatever is not right according to the particular orthodox principles is wrong. This leads to a disinclination to accept different but equally valid interpretations (multiple meanings) of ethical/religious texts or beliefs. Gradually, the orthodox believer comes to regard other interpretations as inimical to all that is sacred and thus feels that it is legitimate to fight against them. This struggle to eliminate the unorthodox begins to supersede all other human and religious ethics, since it is regarded as sacred.

As Waller and Volkan, among others, have described, we can note how people are changed in a destructive way by the process itself. Orthodoxy moves towards a more and more radical and intolerant position with regard to other beliefs. The orthodox followers see their beliefs or texts as literal and concrete, as telling them to take action (such as eliminating their opponents), rather than as symbolic, open to multiple meanings, and abstract. In the final step, they let an authoritarian, fundamentalist worldview dominate their thought processes. Purity and simplified single-mindedness distort their view of reality and crowd out its pulsating and complicated multidimensionality.

In summary, we assume that prejudices can constitute the basis for the development of a perpetrator's violence, and with that, also for acts of revenge, which are not necessarily seen as such by the perpetrator. In the next chapter, we take a look at what can happen in a society when prejudices, orthodoxy, and xenophobia are allowed to thrive.

CHAPTER FIVE

Revenge on the societal level: large groups, ideologies, and political systems

W*e are painfully aware and informed of the violence that exists in our own and others' societies. However, we are perhaps not equally as aware of how often this violence contains aspects of revenge. In Sweden and in other countries, we see gang showdowns in the underworld that seem to be pure and simple acts of revenge. In our presentation, we switch back and forth between individual and large group levels since they affect each other. We will see this, for example, in traumatized societies, where revenge is given a place as something unquestionable.*

A violent revenge spiral can involve even larger groups than discussed in Chapter Four. Antagonisms sometimes involve different ethnic groups within the same country and sometimes entire countries. There are many examples. The violence that broke out after Tito's death in the former Yugoslavia has obvious signs of the revenge dynamic, where the avenged injustices were either real or historically distorted. The genocide in Rwanda was also marked by revenge motives. For many years, we have seen the unresolved revenge spiral in the Middle East between Israel and Palestine.

The Palestinian film *Paradise Now* from 2005 portrays a suicide bomber and some of the background for his thoughts. When he has a discussion with a woman who opposes violence, she says, referring to the suicide attack, "It's not a matter of self-sacrifice—it's revenge." He answers, "What they're doing—is annihilating us." He alludes to the humiliation caused by the Israeli occupation, to be deprived of one's dignity. He does not seem to find any other way out of his desperation than to blow up himself and others.

In this destructive spiral, we can imagine that the Israeli is saying, "We can't trust the Palestinians, they want to throw us into the sea, they want to blow us up, they have to be kept under control, our survival depends on it." We can imagine the Palestinian countering, "They occupy us, oppress us, they rob us of our dignity, they degrade us. This is the only way we can get revenge, using our bodies as weapons."

All this mutual animosity, which leads to acts of destruction on both sides, is going to take a long time for those involved to resolve, especially since the flames of hatred are fanned by every political incident, suicide bomb, missile attack, razed olive grove, humiliating border control, harassment, militant orthodox settler, anti-Jewish textbook, and the list goes on.

Many years ago, our Israeli friend Haim had a good relationship with his Palestinian car mechanic, Yossef. They used to sit down together for coffee and a chat whenever Haim brought his car in for repair. However, when the tension escalated, Yossef said that he unfortunately could no longer have Haim as a customer. It was too risky for both of them.

Israelis and Palestinians could actually be close neighbours and friends, but instead they are pitted against each other by historical circumstances so that even the world outside is affected and becomes pro-Israel or pro-Palestine. Meanwhile, there are attempts in the right direction, such as joint kibbutzes for Palestinians and Israelis, football teams in which they play side by side, and orchestras with musicians from both groups. However, so far these are only islands of resistance and will remain so as long as political leaders cannot do anything about their irreconcilability—and their anxiety that they will not be re-elected if they go too far in their peace initiatives.

In Part II of the book, we will analyse ways of bringing about reconciliation in a society. At this point, we would first like to go through different background factors when it comes to violence in society. Why do long, drawn-out revenge spirals such as the ones in the examples above come into being? How can it be that not only small groups of people but also sometimes an entire nation can sanction violence against other groups of people or against the population of another nation?

Important background factors pointed out by many researchers concern societal structure, leaders (political systems), and collective psychology. In this chapter, we present some of the theories that we have found useful. We begin with the theories of the Turk-Cypriot American psychoanalyst Vamik Volkan.

Traumatized societies

Vamik Volkan has devoted a great part of his life to understanding international conflicts through psychoanalytical studies of what he calls traumatized societies, for example in Afghanistan, the former Yugoslavia, the Middle East, Albania, and the former Soviet Union. He has been involved since 1979 in a series of unofficial political negotiations at various places around the world. He is also one of the founders of the International Society of Political Psychology. Some key concepts in Volkan's analysis are *large group identity*, *large group regression*, and *transmission of trauma between generations* (*transgenerational transmissions of trauma*).

Large group identity

> Our relationship with our large group identity, in ordinary times, is like breathing . We breathe constantly, and we are unaware of it unless someone reminds us of the fact that we need air to survive.
>
> (Volkan, 2004, p. 12)

The large group's identity is like a tent over all the thousand or million members of the group, Volkan explains (ibid.). We people under the tent do not pay any attention to the tent canvas under normal circumstances, nor do we notice the poles (the leaders) that are holding up the canvas. We are much more preoccupied with subgroups such as the family, the tribe, or our professional affiliations.

However, as soon as our large group identity is attacked in a crisis situation, such as war, terror, or some other external threat, we behave as though we were in a house on fire. We become acutely aware that we belong to this particular large group. Our basic sense of security is shaken up and our priority is to uphold the integrity of our large group identity. Normally speaking, the prejudices that we harbour are kept under control in democratic countries by an ambient culture where it is our custom to reflect over complicated phenomena, but in countries in crisis, or in undemocratic countries, a threat to collective identity can be exploited by a strong leader or group of leaders, who appeal to primitive tendencies. Our basic trust becomes perverted and distorted in order to make it fit into a blind trust in the group. We follow our leaders' instructions, regardless of whether they are constructive or destructive.

Seven strands in the large group's identity

Volkan defines seven "strands" in the large group's identity, which we can translate into elements of a national identity, as illustrated here with Swedish examples:

1. Shared store of images associated with positive feelings: summer cottages, summer piers, breathtaking waterways, accordions, sailboats.
2. Shared good identifications: sports stars, Nobel Prize ceremonies, Volvos.
3. Acceptance of others' projections as the group's own negative self-image: chilliness, shyness, melancholy.
4. Identification with the leader's inner world: are we like the Prime Minister or other leaders in our values and views?
5. Chosen glorious moments: such as when "we" won the gold medal at the Olympics.
6. Chosen traumas: the murders of Anna Lindh, Olof Palme, and Gustav III.
7. Symbols for the group's unity and independence: the flag, the Swedish language, Swedish culture and traditions.

Large group regression

The individual identity is to a great degree coiled around the group identity. We can note how susceptible these strands are to pressure from the outside, especially to violations and humiliations. Consequently, large groups can easily regress, that is to say, go back to a more primitive way of functioning, and even resort to acts of revenge. Volkan goes on to describe a number of signs of large group regression, of which we can note and illustrate some of the most common and easily recognizable. Here we use examples from different countries and different epochs:

1. The group members lose their individuality: the masses make the Heil Hitler sign at Nazi parades.
2. The group backs its leader blindly: the people back President George W. Bush and his black-or-white analysis of terrorism after the September 11 attacks on the USA.
3. The group is divided into good citizens, who follow the leader, and evil ones, who oppose him. "Those who join the war on terror are with us, those who don't are against us."
4. The group creates an unequivocal "we versus them", where "them" is seen as the enemy (usually neighbouring groups): "we Christians" as opposed to "the others, the Muslims".
5. The group's morality and belief system become more and more absolute and punitively spearheaded towards its enemies: the Jews must be punished because they are not supporting the Nazis' goals.
6. The group argues that it has the right to do whatever it finds necessary to preserve its identity: "We aim to kill anyone who poses a threat to us."
7. The members of the group plunge more and more deeply into magical thinking, which is a sign of a disturbed sense of reality: "We must keep our blood pure from the contamination of foreign peoples."
8. The group reminisces over past glories and triumphs, and especially over chosen traumas, resulting in a time collapse: such as when military campaigns that took place several hundred years ago started to be celebrated anew in the former Yugoslavia.
9. The leaders create a break in historical continuity by fostering new nationalism, ideology, and ethnical emotions, and sometimes "new" history, as in the former Soviet Union.
10. The group focuses on minor differences between itself and enemy groups: "Those Norwegians, they're not like us Swedes."
11. The group becomes preoccupied with thoughts of "pure blood" and other purities: "We must preserve our own culture and keep out alien influences."

To sum up, we can see how revenge can be legitimized through the large group's regression. The division into good versus evil, we versus them, the black-or-white, either/or thinking, and the embracing of an ideal of purity and so on—everything is possible to use in order to defend the group and incite primitive feelings of vengeance, all in the name of totalitarianism and for the sake of the large group. If we compare the individual's projections or externalizations with the reactions of the large group, we discern, furthermore, a group mechanism that Volkan calls *purification* (see point 11). The tent is shaking and the group has to find a new, modified identity in order to keep it in place. Volkan gives several examples of this phenomenon, one of them concerning the Greeks, who have revised their language by ridding it of all words borrowed from other languages. (Ironically enough, they still have not been able to shake off words for food that have Turkish and Persian origins.) At this point, we can also recall the striving after purity that we have seen in authoritarian societies and in prejudiced people. The purity ideal means that there is no place for the great integrated variety of life.

Transmission of trauma

When it comes to the individual, Volkan underlines a number of psychological phenomena that are of special significance for his understanding of how trauma (and revenge urges) can be transmitted between generations. He refers to so-called *deposited traumas* and *depositing*. Here is an example. A woman gives birth to a child who dies. Later, she gives birth to a child who survives. This child naturally has no experience of its own of the deceased older sibling. However, a representation, an image, of the dead child exists in the mother's inner psychic world, and she deposits this image in the inner world of her present child, whereupon this child perceives itself as a *replacement child*.

Between generations in a family, or in a larger constellation of relatives, there are often unconscious trauma transmissions, *transgenerational transmissions*, which manifest themselves as symptoms in children (such as carrying something dead or damaged inside oneself). These transmissions have within themselves a hard core of resistance towards change. The transmission of trauma between generations is not limited to the affects, Volkan points out, but also includes *unconscious fantasies*.

We can now see what this transgenerational transmission process looks like on a societal level. In traumatized societies, the same group of people have suffered many losses that they have not been able to work through (such as after a persecution or a genocide). These traumas risk being deposited in the next generation and risk fuelling a vicious revenge spiral. If the people in the stricken group do not get a chance to work through their humiliation, to grieve over their losses, and to transform their passivity to activity, a victim-identity will be shared and will be spread within the group, Volkan underscores. This identity, and most probably an urge for revenge, will then be transmitted, without having been worked through, to the next generation.

Volkan's theory can thus explain how a revenge spiral can continue generation after generation in a society. Leaders can exploit the strong feelings of grief and anger that are rampant in the society in order to awaken the revenge potential of the regressing group.

No country is immune to large group regressions with their built-in elements of revenge, even if democracies can be relatively better protected owing to their more transparent and flexible structures. An issue in Sweden, for example, is the neo-fascist political party, the Sweden Democrats, which at the time of writing have come into parliament. When people participate in radio call-in programmes, they can be upset in the name of freedom of speech about the way the Sweden Democrats are being counteracted. There is a political forgetfulness or ignorance about what fascism stands for, what it looks like, and how it disguises itself. The simplified worldview of such parties as the Sweden Democrats, if they are not counteracted politically, can be seductive, which can set the stage for large group regression.

As was made clear above, all the individuals in a large group share the same mental pictures of certain historical events, what Volkan calls *chosen trauma*, as a sign of a large group common identity. Destructive political leaders often try to reactivate these chosen traumas in order to exploit the energy in the large group phenomenon and thus promote their own ideological interests and, as is sometimes the case, justify ethnic cleansing. The leaders in this way can more quickly establish the credibility of their motives for acts of aggression by exploiting the group's potential to take revenge and its inability to grieve. For example, in the former Yugoslavia, old stories of humiliations against the Serbs were exploited to exhort people to take revenge on other ethnic groups.

Background of genocide

The colonial genocides against native populations in various parts of the world might not look like the revenge phenomenon at first glance. Nonetheless, we argue, revenge is there all the same, albeit as a hidden motive. When the Native Americans were forced off their land in the USA, the European-American settlers called their massacres of Native Americans by the name "Indian Wars", even though the only thing the "Indians" were doing was, naturally enough, defending themselves. By blurring the way the conflict started, the settlers could bring revenge into the narrative afterwards as a legitimizing explanation and a power factor in the massacres: "We have to take revenge on the Indians for their violence." Through the subsequent escalation and displacement of guilt, the violence was accelerated, as was the dehumanization of the Indians, who were being hunted down. The consequences were devastating. It is estimated that there were about 15 million Native Americans in the sixteenth century. Around 1890, this number had been decimated by 98 per cent to slightly below 250,000 (Waller, 2002).

Ervin Staub is one of the foremost of the present-day researchers who investigate the sociopsychological conditions for, and circumstances around, genocide. His first book, *The Roots of Evil* (1989), has been followed by a number of articles and new books. It is interesting to see how Staub, with his sociopsychological terminology, describes similar phenomena to those Volkan describes in psychoanalytical language. Here follows an attempt to summarize some of his most important observations and theories (Staub, 2000).

Group conflicts and difficult life conditions

Staub argues that there are two main starting points for massive group violence, which function either on their own or together: group conflicts and difficult life conditions (1989). Examples of group conflicts are the disappearances in Argentina of people who opposed the government, the mass killing in Cambodia, and the genocide in Rwanda. These conflicts can be explained by the loss of wellbeing, threats to basic life conditions, as well as the feeling of injustice or deprivation in certain groups in comparison with other groups.

Difficult life conditions frustrate fundamental human needs. People turn to their own group when their identity and their context are threatened. They elevate their own group and look around for scapegoats. As a link in this chain of events, they also adopt an ideology with a vision of an ideal society. This ideology almost always includes an alleged enemy group against whom hostile actions are directed. The group and its members are *transformed* in connection with their hostile actions against the other group. The development of escalating violence can lead to mass killing.

Respect for authorities and unhealed wounds

Furthermore, respect for authorities is of significance for the extent to which the group members go along with the destructive development. People who are used to following strong authorities turn to new leaders, often to leaders who represent destructive ideologies that are expressed through simplified slogans. When things go this far, if there are no democratic structures that provide opposition and discussion, the risk for mass killing will increase. In contrast, it is worth considering that functioning democracies have never been participants in mass killing.

If there is already a victim identity in place in a certain group, as well as unhealed wounds in this same group, the risks for destructivity are substantial. As long as the wounds are unhealed, the group sees the world as a dangerous place. It is likely to respond to group conflicts with violence of its own, since its members interpret conflicts as a threat against which they must defend themselves. Staub illustrates this point with the conflict in the former Yugoslavia where there are numerous examples of earlier experiences of victimization and unhealed wounds.

Even if economical problems in a society exacerbate a conflict, Staub emphasizes that these problems alone are not an explanation for why the revenge spiral keeps on going as it does in a genocide. He contends that psychological and cultural factors are of great importance even when the group conflict centres fundamentally on material interests and territorial questions. The psychological factors, such as demonization of the other, often render those conflicts "unsolvable". In addition, a territory is often associated with a certain identity, as in the Israel–Palestine conflict.

Passive bystanders

There are bystanders who can look on without reacting while groups in their own society are being treated badly. They might have every reason to be afraid of doing something that would lead to a severe punishment by the people in power, but this does not suffice as an explanation for their passivity. In Nazi Germany, the German people protested against the euthanasia programme and the stench from the institutions of death, which led to their being closed down. However, they did not protest against the way the Jews were being treated, and the execution of the Jews was also moved away from Germany. Other countries assumed a similar bystander role when they participated in the Berlin Olympics in 1936, despite their having no need to fear the German regime at that point. The USA did not include Jewish sportsmen in its Olympic team, even though Germany had not made a request along these lines.

Extreme political movements thus seem to create a large group of passive bystanders who unintentionally—through passive acceptance or active complicity—play a supporting role in the oppression of parts of their own population. The bystander denies what he sees in order to be able to stay on the outside. To get away from his own fear, he avoids feeling sympathy for the victims and identifies instead with the oppressor. His own aggressivity—which is exacerbated owing to the political oppression going on around him—is directed towards the persecuted victims: "They must have done something since they are being killed." And in this manner, the psychological distance towards those who are being persecuted is also increased. Many bystanders distance themselves from their earlier political involvement and turn to cocooning or an individualistic lifestyle to avoid the anxiety that is evoked by the killing (Staub, 1989, 2003).

People are thus changed by the new values that are upheld in the oppressive society. They focus on themselves and turn to individualism in order to gain advantages. They react concerning their own situation, withdraw, and feel no social responsibility for what is happening around them, leading to political ignorance on their part. In addition, the totalitarian regime defines all opposition as unpatriotic and disloyal. People feel powerless as individuals and go into denial or psychic muteness, so that they think they cannot have any influence on anything. Perhaps another factor is a hidden envy towards the group that is being targeted, a chance to see them lose whatever advantages it is considered they have and therewith a chance to take revenge through passivity?

Summary

Here is a list of some of the phenomena that Staub points out as background factors for genocide in a society:

- disparagement of minorities—promoted by leaders;
- destructive ideology—denial of complexities, shared belief that there is one truth and only one truth;
- unhealed wounds;
- uncritical respect for authorities—shared one-dimensional view of history;
- monolithic society (one-party state);
- social injustice;
- passive bystanders—regarded as support for the perpetrators;
- superficial contact, with a limited number of common interests between different groups.

Other perspectives

In the previous sections, we have seen how the structure of a society, the form of government (the leader) and group psychology are often used in order to understand the background of genocide. Someone who has criticized this approach is Benjamin Valentino (2000). He writes on the background for mass killing from the standpoint of a political scientist. Valentino argues that the above mentioned factors are important but that further explanations are needed, since there are many undemocratic governments and social crises that are not associated with violence against parts of the population.

He underscores that the most important factor that is missing in the discussion is that high-up political or military leaders include mass murder as an element in specific goals and strategies. The decisive background factor for genocide is thus, according to Valentino, that powerful leaders can see mass killing as the most practical strategy for achieving certain radical goals (even if they base this choice on irrational notions of their own).

It is not even necessary that broad elements of society take part in the persecution. A small, well-equipped minority can cause great harm to innocent victims, as was the case in Nazi Germany. All that is needed is a combination of a small group of true believers, a larger but still relatively small group of somewhat less passionate adherents who nonetheless are willing to participate in the violence, and finally, a large, indifferent majority of passive bystanders.

In addition to all of the above, we would like to point out an additional aspect of significance. A relentless disparagement of certain minorities or ethnic groups over an extended period of time, with collectively cherished destructive values as a result, can make it easier for leaders to gather followers and passive bystanders. In Hungary, SS-*Obersturmbannführer* Adolf Eichmann, eight SS officers, and forty ordinary Nazi soldiers could deport over 400,000 Hungarian Jews to Auschwitz—with the help of a large indifferent majority of Hungarians who were willing to cooperate or remain passive bystanders (Staub, 1989).

Significance of collective ideologies

The destructive potential of collective ideologies has been discussed in some detail in the previous chapter. At this point, we would especially like to stress that several researchers have also studied the significance of the collective ideology as a background to violence in society—and even to acts of revenge. The revenge aspect is present in the message of the collective ideology to the effect that *the persecuted minority has grabbed too much of the power and resources or other good things in the society in an improper way*, which has created unacceptable injustices for the majority. The following words of Hermann Goering can serve to illustrate the destructive force that the collective ideology can exert on society:

> It's always a simple matter to drag the people along whether it's a democracy, a fascist dictatorship, or a parliament, or a communist dictatorship. Voice or no voice, the people can always be brought to the bidding of the leaders. That is easy. All you have to do is tell them they are being attacked, and denounce the pacifists for lack of patriotism, and exposing the country to greater danger. It works the same way in any country.
>
> (From an interview with Goering during the Nuremberg Trials, 1946, in Gilbert, 1963)

The now classic study *Ordinary Men* by Christopher Browning (1992) tells about reserve policemen from Hamburg who were assigned to murder Jews on the Eastern Front during the Nazi period. In that context, group reinforcement was shown to be a crucial factor. None of these ordinary men was a committed Nazi. Granted, they were more or less drenched in the ideology's disparagement of Jews, but as individuals they would have preferred to stay away from the killing. Most of them thought that the murdering was unpleasant or repugnant, but they saw it as a necessary duty. Being part of a group strengthened that feeling.

A correlation has also been found between the degree of anti-Semitism existing in a country prior to the Second World War and the number of Jews who were later murdered in the same country (Fein, in Staub, 1989). In Rwanda, there had been a collective Tutsi-hostile ideology dating back to the beginning of the 1960s that permeated the entire society, which consisted of 85 per cent of Hutus. Massacres of Tutsis were unleashed several times in a manner that was similar to the anti-Semitic pogroms in Eastern Europe prior to Nazism.

Why did the Nazis continue to kill Jews when the war was already lost? Or perhaps it was precisely because the war had been lost that the Jews also had to die? Königsberg (2004) accounts for a discussion positing that Hitler wanted the Jews to be sacrificed—as revenge?, we can ask ourselves—because German soldiers had been sacrificed in the First World War. In the psyches of Hitler and the Nazis, such a retaliatory revenge needed to be carried out on the Jews. "If we died, they shall die!" (by being gassed to death, in mass graves, and starved, just as the German soldiers who were humiliated in the trenches in the First World War).

Norwegian psychoanalyst and trauma researcher Sverre Varvin (2003, 2004) stresses the necessity of an interdisciplinary approach in order to understand complex phenomena such as terror and societal violence, where revenge is an ingredient. Studies of the individual perpetrator's character, for example, a suicide bomber's, shed light on individual aspects of vengeful violence. Social dynamics that predispose people to violence—terrorist mentality, religion, political conflicts—consist of collective psychological phenomena that influence individuals. Analyses of smaller groups can give us an idea of the pressure that is exerted when group contexts become larger and still larger. These different levels are always intertwined and have consequences for each other.

Is there a breeding ground for revenge spirals in the Swedish society? Do these theories have any relevance for those of us who live in Sweden today? The answer is yes. To be sure, Sweden is a democratic country, but we nonetheless have tendencies here towards group conflicts as well as an increasing degree of xenophobia. We should stay alert to these tendencies lest they result in an escalating revenge spiral.

The Forum for Living History in Sweden asked the Council for the Prevention of Crime to carry out a survey on the school youth population to find out their attitudes, whether they had been victims of violence, and their self-profiled criminality. A little over 10,500 randomly chosen lower and upper secondary school pupils answered a questionnaire given to them in their classrooms. The results have been presented in the "Intolerance Report" (Ring & Morgentau, 2004). They show that a clear majority (72 per cent) of the country's pupils are generally positive towards minorities, but that there does exist an intolerant group. For example, 8 per cent of the pupils are intolerant towards Muslims, and 6 per cent intolerant towards Jews.

The more intolerant the attitude the pupils express, the greater is the probability that they report having used violence against someone because of their origin or religion. When it comes to the intolerant group (5 per cent), 1 out of 5 report having assaulted someone because of their origin or religion. The stronger prejudices bear with them an increased tendency towards violence, perhaps because prejudices and denial of guilt go together.

The intolerant pupils are predominantly boys, and their parents more often have a low socioeconomic status than parents of more tolerant pupils. They have more adjustment problems of their own in school, a more male chauvinistic view, a poorer relationship with their parents, and a greater feeling of being an outsider. Half of them also express sympathies for extreme nationalists, race ideologues, and national socialists.

On the questionnaire, 6.6 per cent of the pupils with a foreign background state that they have been targeted with violence because of their origin, while the corresponding figure for the pupils with a Swedish background is 2.2 per cent. The same patterns, but even more pronounced, can be discerned when it comes to threats and verbal violations. The majority of the incidents have taken place outside of school time. The boys who feel threatened state that they go to counterattack with words or actions.

Young muggers

Revenge and violence are not synonymous. All the same, there is often an element of revenge present in violence, especially if there has also been a significant degree of humiliation in the perpetrator's life history. Sociologist Petra Åkesson has published an essay (2005) analysing the behaviour of a group of young muggers who attack other youths in a large city in Sweden. She has interviewed eleven young muggers, all of whom turn out to have been born outside Sweden, which seems to be of significance in this case. Her starting point encompasses theories about how youths from lower socioeconomic classes, where many foreigners are found, have trouble reaching up to the middle-class ideal that they confront in society. They are attracted to criminality as a way of obtaining status and of taking themselves out of their disadvantaged position where their revenge fantasies thrive. They form subcultures where spur-of-the-moment thefts give them excitement and where they have a strong loyalty towards each other. When they succeed at stealing, they see themselves as winners and their self-confidence is boosted.

Comments from Åkesson's interviews can be enlightening, for example: "It's easier to steal from Swedes because they get so scared and they are wimpy and stupid." The world outside their homes is seen as a battlefield: "When we're out in the city and mug people, we're fighting a war, a war against Swedes!" They feel an attraction and an excitement in carrying out muggings and in knowing that they can scare their victims: "Swedes gotta look at me and get down on the ground and kiss my feet." "It's all about the money and the cell phones ... money is power ... Swedes don't like us."

The youths speak relatively openly about the humiliation they feel when Swedes do not show them respect but rather come up with accusations, "even though we haven't done anything". They want to turn their humiliation into victory by "winning the war".

Our impression is that subcultures such as these are a serious symptom of a failure to accept and integrate groups with a foreign background into Swedish society. Unless something radical is done to make these groups feel less humiliated, their need to retaliate can take on even more dangerous forms.

In December 2005, all of the municipal executive chairmen in the administrative province of Stockholm, 26 in all, called for everyone to join in a broad effort to counteract violence and xenophobia. They published their appeal in the daily morning newspaper *Svenska Dagbladet* under the heading "The Foreigner can be your Friend". In the appeal, they call on all citizens to become involved in this important effort to shatter the sounding board of prejudices that exist in the

Swedish society. "We accept no violence in our society. This is ultimately a question of democracy and democracy can be fragile."

This manifesto is impressive in many ways. However, the reader might justifiably be somewhat critical when he or she sees that the factors that contribute to prejudice, such as unemployment, segregation, policies for immigrants and refugees, asylum-seeking families with children, and children sent to Sweden on their own, are not mentioned in this passionate appeal.

We can also observe how the intolerant words in the appeal are juxtaposed with the tolerant ones in an intolerance towards intolerance. On the one hand: "undemocratic elements", "whip up a hostile atmosphere", "extreme activists", "increased polarization", "we and them". On the other hand: "good value system", "security", "respect", "responsibility", "moral fortitude", "defence of democracy", "be vigilant towards".

The attitudes and actions of leaders are important, since leaders are models and lodestars, but these are not sufficient. There must also be a value system built on tolerance. The unjust factors in a society fuel the flames of envy, indignation, and feelings of humiliation. They keep prejudices alive, and the result can be more violence. As we have observed, prejudices are to a great extent rooted in envy and can ultimately lead to revenge.

CHAPTER SIX

Why does the revenge spiral continue? Among victims and perpetrators

*I*n *the previous chapters, we have seen how revenge fantasies and revenge acts can be explained on the basis of real or perceived violations and our difficulties in handling our strong feelings. We have also seen how our human inclination to adapt ourselves to the group can make otherwise empathetic and well-functioning people commit destructive acts. Added to that, if we happen to live in a totalitarian and violent society or in a society at war, we are even more susceptible to primitive drives, such as revenge mechanisms. Now we swing back to the individual again in order to discuss shame and persecutory guilt as driving forces in the revenge phenomenon.*

Though we might have a great awareness of atrocities in the present and the past, it is perhaps still hard for us to imagine being forced to endure savage cruelties, as in genocide, or even harder to believe that we would be capable of violent acts. Can any person whosoever become a part of a destructive revenge spiral? How does a perpetrator function, and how does he or she legitimize his or her violence? What is it that makes it so difficult to stop an escalating violence?

Can ordinary people become perpetrators?

Social psychologist James Waller has made a critical survey of what he considers insufficient and untenable explanations for evil in ordinary people in his book *Becoming Evil—How Ordinary People Commit Genocide and Mass Killing* (2002). These explanations often offer us a way of distancing ourselves from the supposed madmen instead of looking at our common destructive potential. For example, after the Second World War, people tried to pinpoint the "craziness" or "typical personality" of the Nazi. The "authoritarian personality" was in focus. However, a careful study of the research in this area shows that what first and foremost unites perpetrators is their normality, not their abnormality.

Sociologist Zygmunt Bauman (1989) has studied the mass murders of the Holocaust and argues that the cruelty found there is more social than characterological in origin. In other words, a destructive chain of events is determined more by the situation than by the individual personalities of those carrying out the actions. Author Hannah Arendt, who has written about the trial proceedings against Nazi war criminal Adolf Eichmann, also emphasizes that ordinary people can show examples of extraordinary cruelty under extraordinary circumstances (1963/2006). In Chapter Four, we saw how social psychologist Stanley Milgram (1974) could show that individuals who were obedient towards authorities were ready and willing to hurt others with electrical shocks. His experiments show our potential for blind obedience and/or for doing anything whatsoever to follow the group norm.

Perpetrators are changed by their violence

Psychiatrist Robert Jay Lifton (1999) has studied personality fragmentation in the Nazis. This manifested itself in the way they murdered during their workdays and were normal family members in their spare time. However, Waller sees this fragmentation as a consequence of cruelty rather than a precondition for it. He argues that such cruelty cannot be explained by extreme group pressure, the influence of ideologies, psychopathology, a specific personality type or a split ego. Instead, he points out how the perpetrator is changed by his own cruel act, both during the preparatory stage and during the act itself. An ordinary person becomes something else and the extraordinary cruelty becomes a part of his personality. This process is spurred into being when there are sufficient preconditions combined with a lack of counterbalances. Waller describes mechanisms in genocide, but we can have as a possible hypothesis that this process also takes place in other, more limited contexts where violent behaviour escalates, such as in the abuse of women or in the development of a psychopathic personality.

The answer is thus yes, ordinary people can become perpetrators or avengers. There is a potential for inhuman acts in every human being. We do not always have the capacity to handle the strong feelings that are awakened in us. We often have residues of cruel impulses of various sorts. This phenomenon can also be described in terms of our having "pockets of cruelty" (Igra, 2001), which we are not always able to manage, if we do not have effective counterbalances. The outlet for our impulses often bears the characteristics of revenge, as if it is always possible to find an injustice for which we can retaliate. Perhaps we are actually fighting a different injustice from the one that we have before our eyes—a more hidden one that we have stored within ourselves. However, the question is whether perpetrators always need to be avengers, in the sense that they act on the basis of a perception of a disadvantaged position or violation? A simple answer is that the victim does not always become a perpetrator, but that the perpetrator often has a perception of himself as being a victim (Varvin, 2004).

Why is it so hard to stop the revenge spiral?

A revenge spiral thus easily goes into effect when a victim later becomes a perpetrator who targets new victims—unless there are counterbalances to prevent this. The victim may have encountered a real perpetrator—someone who abandoned, threatened, or harmed him—or he may have perceived someone as being that way, such as when a child experiences a parent's deficient care as cruelty. In both cases, the victim will entertain fantasies of revenge. An actual act of revenge might be held back by social inhibitions, but it might continue to brew in the victim's potential cruelty pocket and be unleashed when a further violation is experienced. In other cases, the victim will go to counterattack right away, since this victim, who now has become the perpetrator, has come to see revenge as justified and heroic. The difficulty in stopping a revenge spiral for those who partake in it can be summarized in the following way:

1. Revenge in itself is driven by primitive fantasies with underlying feelings of violation, rage, and magical hopes that the "film will be

rewound" and that the evil that has taken place will be negated by the avenger's committing an equally evil act. These forces are so strong and irrational that they do not allow for self-reflection and rational considerations.

2. The avenger also constructs pseudo-moral arguments to legitimize the revenge: it is rightful, driven by what is perceived as a passion for justice, social equality, political values, human dignity, and so on.

Revenge is legitimized

Just how revenge is legitimized is an area that has interested—among others—Swedish psychoanalyst Ludvig Igra (2001). He presents an argument stemming from the war crimes in the Balkans, where the myth about the "necessary revenge" played an important role. After Tito's death, a chaotic and uncertain societal climate arose that made it easier for leaders with paranoid slogans to gain ascendancy. These leaders preached simplistic ideas that were aimed at giving an illusion of security to the citizens. "We are the targeted ones in a hostile environment. We have to defend ourselves."

Igra shows how the paranoid rhetoric drew nourishment from history and national legends that distorted history. Partial truths about the enemy became demagogically magnified. When the enemy professed their innocence, the distrust towards them was only increased since paranoid systems are especially on guard against what they regard as a deceptively friendly façade. Innocence among neighbours and colleagues of another religion was interpreted as a sign of their actual hostility.

Out of all the myths and the paranoid system, the myth of the "necessary revenge" gradually grew, according to Igra. It was as if the dead, or the self-esteem or the honour of the living, demanded revenge. Igra shows how people, obsessed with their own self-righteousness, did not shy away from even the most brutal violence. The warring parties found urgent reasons to continue to murder, despite the fact that the majority of the people in the affected ethnic groups wanted the killings to stop.

Psychologist Michael Harris Bond (2004) has also studied how perpetrators legitimize their violence and he presents his findings in an article about the genocides in Armenia, the Ukraine, and Rwanda, the Red Khmer's political slaughters in Cambodia, and the military massacres in Nanking, Song My in Vietnam, and El Salvador. An important factor that he emphasizes is the same factor to which we have previously drawn attention: the perpetrators claim that those whom they are persecuting have received unfair advantages in the past. Violence is then legitimized as revenge, writes Bond.

Shame and persecutory guilt

Psychoanalyst Léon Wurmser (1981) speaks of the shame experience as a family of emotions from the mildest twinge of embarrassment to the searing pain of mortification. Shame is often confused with guilt. Shame is about the *quality* of our person or self. Guilt is the painful emotion triggered when we become aware that we have acted in a way that has brought harm to another person or has violated some important code. Guilt is about *action* and laws, as underscored by Nathanson (1994). His concept of the "shame and pride axis" has parallels with our "revenge or restoration dynamic" in as much as we see revenge being used to try to conceal feelings of shame while restoration can instead foster feelings of pride.

When we have come this far, we notice that *the revenge spiral is an inner process that is built up inside the avenger himself.* And when you have started taking revenge, you have to continue for several reasons, among others because of the persecutory guilt that grows—if no external force brings the revenge process to a halt. Psychoanalyst Sverre Varvin sheds light on revenge by pointing out two different psychological mechanisms.

On the one hand, there is *shame/narcissism* (humiliation) where the perpetrator projects the parts of himself that he experiences as shameful and degraded onto others, so that he or she can behave in a dehumanizing way towards them (2004): "I'm not the one who is inferior and violated; they're going get a taste of what they're trying to do to me!" Most shame conflicts have traumatic origins, where the trauma or the defence against it is repeated time and time again (Wurmser, 1981).

On the other hand, there is the *projective-persecutory mechanism* (persecutory guilt), more precisely, the consequences of becoming an perpetrator. This tormenting primitive conscience becomes too heavy to bear and is instead projected onto the victim of the aggression, who is hated for reprimanding the perpetrator for his criminal actions, which in turn leads to even more violence. In both dimensions, we see the central role of projection, and we see how the spiral of revenge receives nourishment when a person is not able to endure mentally, work through, or reflect on his own psychic condition, but instead has to transfer it over to someone else.

Persecutory guilt is something other than conscience, namely a primitive guilt feeling. The perpetrator perceives it as if his victims are being resurrected in his or her inner self and in their turn are vengefully persecuting him. He perceives the people he attacks, and not his own acts of violence, as the cause of his inner discomfort (Igra, 2001). An example from our own everyday life takes place when someone gets attacked on the street. The perpetrator does not admit to any guilt, but says instead, "He was asking for a beating. He looked so ridiculous." Perhaps the victim has to be kicked one more time so that the perpetrator does not feel persecuted by guilt.

In 2005, a person was beaten to death on a main street called Kungsgatan in Stockholm after he had pointed out to some young men that they should not urinate against the wall of an apartment building. Those who are urinating know it is wrong, but they cannot stand having it pointed out by a stranger. The stranger merges with their primitive sense of guilt, which has to be attacked, since it cannot be handled in any other way. The avengers thus perceive the reprimand as having put them in a humiliating position of inferiority. When no conscience is accessible that can negotiate with this humiliation, they must turn the relationship around and put themselves in the superior position. In this case, the tragic outcome was a deadly beating.

Ludvig Igra, who was quoted above, has also described how the perpetrator's change leads to an escalation of violence. In his book with the telling title *Den tunna hinnan* (*The Thin Membrane*) (2001), he starts his chapter on revenge with two proverbs: "He who plots revenge keeps his own wounds open"; and "Revenge is a sword that strikes the person who draws it."

Igra emphasizes how revenge eats the avenger from the inside and is never satiated. Revenge can only lead to demands for further revenge. In order for the avenger to blot out the anxiety of his guilty conscience, he has to perform the act of revenge in a special state of excitement where he can deny the values he has previously embraced. Igra describes a psychic manoeuvre that corresponds to the legitimizing of revenge that we outlined above.

Going back to the analysis of antagonisms between different ethnic groups, Igra states that people in the one ethnic group cannot visualize how those in the other group can be as vulnerable as they are. Therefore, they want to afflict their enemies with their own terror. The guilt that is inevitably awakened—which we have mentioned earlier—is a persecutory guilt. This escalates to increased violence, since it does not lead to regret, empathy, amends, or reconciliation. The perpetrator hates the one he is tormenting since he is convinced that the victim is tormenting him.

Furthermore, revenge carries with it the illusion that one's own suffering can be alleviated and one's own losses recovered if the enemy is made to suffer, the illusion that we earlier referred to as "rewinding the movie". Revenge also promises, as Igra puts it, that by destroying it is "possible to recreate something that was lost". Paranoid leaders such as Milošević, Stalin, and Hitler had the ability to attract followers through their childish fantasies of triumph. Their projects of revenge combined paranoid notions with demagogic abilities. The followers who joined them immersed themselves in the illusion that they could heal their own psychic traumas by destroying other people's lives.

However, Igra reminds us that the avenger never achieves peace of mind this way. The pure, ethnically cleansed, utopian, classless society is never achieved. The dead give rise to an unconscious guilt in the avenger. He does not hear this as the voice of his conscience, but simply perceives it as yet another persecutory attack. Therefore, he must hate his victims even more, and he sees his own cruelty as justified. As we can note, this line of reasoning connects to Volkan's theories in the preceding chapter about the primitive way in which large groups use any means at their disposal to save their crumbling group identity (Volkan, 2004).

And finally …

A unique depiction of *the crime* can be found in Martin Pollack's book— *Der Tote im Bunker: Bericht über meinen Vater* (*The Dead Man in the Bunker: Discovering My Father*) (2008). This father is the same man whom Richard Swartz (2004) has written about. Pollack is an Austrian author, Slavicist, and translator. In the book, he seeks his Nazi father among fragments of documents and personal effects. His father, who grew up in Slovenia, later became a *Sturmbannführer* within the SS and worked with the Gestapo in Linz. He was murdered right before the end of the war, at which time there was a warrant out for his arrest for war crimes. He was on his way to flee to South America.

Pollack describes his boyhood, spent with his paternal grandparents, where the men in the family had opinions set in stone on each and every issue. A number of them bore mensur scars, which were gruesome facial scars left by honour-upholding fencing duels in their youth. Pollack's grandmother spoke of the Czechs as "swine". The Third Reich lived on in these people's notions and convictions despite the fact that it had been defeated in reality. There was no will or ability to settle with the past, which was stowed away in silence. Pollack shows how vulnerable and "blind" we are as humans, how easy it is to take steps that lead to a point of no return, and how we forget our responsibility for our own lives in the intoxication of the group.

CHAPTER SEVEN

Revenge in everyday life—relationships in couples

*T*hrough our studies of extreme relationships between perpetrators and victims, as well as of large groups' regression, we have gained insight into the way in which revenge is much more common and destructive in everyday relationships than we are ordinarily aware of. Therefore, we now take a step over to couples' relationships. We aim to clarify the common underlying theme of what can result from the strong feelings of which we humans are capable.

Revenge is often concealed in subtle actions or in ostensibly legitimate responses to perceived attacks. A negative revenge spiral is created and neither of the parties is aware of it until it is too late. In a recent case in Sweden (summer 2009), strong feelings led to an overt action when a sixteen-year-old boy and his girlfriend of the same age murdered another girl their age in an act of revenge related to a jealousy drama. It is clear that perpetrators have a vulnerability within them that causes a dissolution of the difference between fantasizing about an action and carrying it out in reality.

Revenge in the context of infidelity

As therapists in couples' therapy, we have seen how infidelity arouses extremely intense feelings. Finding out that one's partner has been unfaithful usually leads to reactions such as intense pain, dismay, confusion, and anger, but also to self-reproach, "How could I have failed to notice what was going on?" "What have I done wrong?" The faithful partner also wants to turn back time, "This hasn't happened, it's a mistake, things have to go back to being like they were before." The path to revenge can be opened as a way to fend off pain.

The one who is unfaithful can in turn be convinced that he or she has a right to his or her own self-fulfilment. "Life is too short. Why should I deny myself something like this?" Infidelity can be a way to get out of a relationship one no longer wants to be a part of. But it can also be an egocentric act whereby the unfaithful party disregards the feelings of the partner (whom he or she at the same time wants to keep) and denies to himself or herself that the element of trust in the relationship is at risk. Infidelity does not necessarily have anything to do with the partner: it can be a manifestation of the unfaithful one's own dissatisfaction with life, a middle-age crisis, dejection, discouragement over career or other point-of-no-return choices in life, or a character-based restlessness with incessant demands for new confirmation (Böhm, 2001).

As a result of infidelity, partners become strangers to each other, "Is this my Nick, the man I've known for 20 years?" Everything that has been taken for granted in the relationship disappears. Let us take a typical case where a man has been unfaithful to his wife. When the man becomes interested in another woman, he also begins to see his wife as a stranger, someone seen from a distance. If he decides to return and patch up the relationship, he must also take upon himself a "psychic task" in order to piece together different parts of himself: the part that was with the other woman and the part that has been and is now again with his wife. The strain of this task can make it hard for him to feel empathy for his wife to a full extent. He normally just wants everything to go back to the way it was before. The woman can gradually come to recognize her "previous" husband when this unfaithful but repentant one has been back awhile. But when something happens in their daily interaction that reminds her of the time he was with the other woman and her pain is triggered, she again sees him as a stranger. Words can be hurtful, like when trust is abused. How does she then carry out her grieving process over what has happened? It takes time to get the restoration she needs. In addition, she may perhaps retaliate in subtle ways to make him aware that "it's not as simple to come back as you think it is".

The nature of the way in which the breach of faith came to light has great significance for the couple's chances to find a pathway back to each other: was it through a candid, sincere conversation or was it an unintended discovery? The grieving process is also different for the one who has been unfaithful compared to the one who has been deceived. The former wants to avoid guilt feelings and the latter wants to avoid the shame of being deceived as well as the shame of others' knowing about it. As couples' therapists, we often find that the one who has been deceived is frustrated because the unfaithful partner has a hard time sharing his or her feelings about what has happened as well as his or her present feelings about the relationship and the return home. The difficulty is to be able to share grief in a common project, since the feelings and interpretations about what has happened are so much at odds.

The strong feelings in infidelity involve both the unfaithful one, who has fallen in love anew with someone else, and the one who has been deceived, who wants to get revenge for the violation. We can even go as far as to speak of psychosis-like qualities in these types of feelings. Falling in love is often regarded as something resembling insanity. The lover loses his or her sense of reality and sense of proportion between different parts of his or her life and is engulfed in an explosive psychic experience (ibid.). At the same time, we can also see a psychosis-like quality in the intensity of the avenger's primitive way of functioning. An illustration of what this can entail in reality can be seen in the example of Eric and Marianne.

> Eric becomes more and more agonized about being in the company of his wife Marianne. He has recently fallen in love with another woman and has been unfaithful for the first time after fifteen years of marriage. He fights against the great resistance that he feels and finally tells Marianne about his strong feelings for the other woman. It becomes apparent before too long that he wants a separation. Marianne comes back with an intensely negative reaction approaching a psychosis. She becomes destructive towards Eric and towards herself and realizes that she wants to punish him. She wants to make him feel the pain he has made her suffer in what

she sees as his attempt to destroy her life. She seeks out Eric at his gym and threatens to commit suicide if he does not return to her. After saying that, she runs out of the gym in front of him, crying and screaming, tears off most of her clothes and lies down on the hood of his car.

There is an understandable despair in Marianne's reactions. At the same time, we can sense that she has a deeper problem complex around abandonment that perhaps has its roots in earlier close relationships and has less to do with her relationship with Eric. These remnants from childhood make it more difficult for Marianne to look clearly at what is happening between her and Eric and to see how she could best deal with the new situation. During the course of the therapeutic discussions, it also comes to light that Marianne *actually* had been wanting a separation from Eric for a long time, but she is not the least bit in touch with that feeling now when he is taking the initiative. Her predominant feeling is instead that she has ended up in a position of disadvantage and her inability to cope with intense feelings makes her try to punish Eric. Her fits of anger, self-destructive actions, and suicide threats are her revenge.

> Martin and Sara have been married for 30 years. On a charter trip to Cyprus, Martin happens to see the name of the love of his youth, Louise Nilsson, on the list of participants. His curiosity is aroused. Can it be his Louise? Does she still have the same last name? Has he lived a 30-year life in which he has not been "his true self"? His head is spinning with questions. He and Louise bump into each other in the hotel lobby, and their meeting could most accurately be called ecstatic, mind-boggling, being caught in a standstill of time. Memories of his passionate love for Louise are revitalized. Back in Sweden, Sara finds out that Martin has had a sexual relationship with Louise during the month that has passed since they returned home from their trip, a relationship that Martin has now terminated. Sara is dismayed but gradually understands from Martin's narrative that he did not actually fall in love with Louise again. Instead, as he had begun to understand more and more, he had wanted to pay Louise back (be the one to break up) because she had broken up with him in the past in a brutal way. It was his anger and his urge to get revenge that had been sparked into life.

Martin and Sara's story describes a rather common situation heard about in couples' therapy. What comes up might be a relationship with a teenage love or a former husband/wife. Reviving the relationship for a period of time and then being the one to terminate it the second time around can be a way of satisfying the need to pay back a former abandoner.

The act of infidelity as revenge

We are more accustomed to seeing revenge fantasies and revenge actions *after* a discovered infidelity. It is easy to understand the violation that a person feels after experiencing infidelity and understand the motivating force behind even the more dramatic attempts to retaliate. However, we are not as well acquainted with how the act of infidelity in itself can be motivated by unconscious desires for revenge, that is to say, how the revenge act consists of infidelity. For example, a man can pay his wife back for being entirely too busy with her own activities, or, as in the example below, for being entirely too controlling.

> Steve has a daughter from an earlier marriage. He and her mother got divorced when the daughter was little and he met his present partner, Hanna. He and Hanna now have two children of their own. In the family Steve comes from, people were rather reserved and spoke mostly about practical matters. Steve thinks that Hanna dominates him through her extreme talkativeness and he notices that he avoids her and goes to the children. Hanna has many thoughts and feelings that she wants to share with Steve, but he feels that she is too demanding and finds himself at a loss for words in her presence. One day, Steve meets a woman at work who is just as quiet as he is. Contact with her makes him feel relaxed and they start a relationship. When Hanna discovers his infidelity and reacts, Steve has a hard time putting himself in her shoes, since his thoughts are on the other woman. He deceives Hanna and says it is over at the same time as he continues to see the other woman. Hanna ultimately discovers what he is doing again, whereupon he suddenly becomes afraid of losing her. He wants to repair his relationship with Hanna and seeks couples' therapy.

Hanna is angry, despairing, and suspicious. Steve is frightened and dazed and still does not appreciate to a full extent the problems that he has caused. He has no guilt feelings but just says that what he did was understandable. His ambition is to patch his relationship back together, but at the same time he is unable to communicate genuine empathy for Hanna's situation since he is entirely too caught up in his own confusion, which he needs to sort out. In couples' therapy—as he begins to understand the revenge process—he is gradually able to see that many of his actions with the other woman were actually directed at Hanna. It became clear that Hanna had made him feel frustrated in various ways by being controlling and demanding and primarily by trying to take over the upbringing of his daughter. To meet someone else was the only solution he saw, a survival strategy. He was unable to get in touch with or to talk about his own feeling of frustration. However, he finally understands that Hanna's suspiciousness has to do with his withdrawn manner and that it is a misdirected way of trying to reach someone.

More common that men get revenge through infidelity

When a person in a relationship falls in love with someone new, he or she often splits himself or herself up—dissociates—in his or her psyche. Falling in love concerns *one* person and the other becomes uninteresting. The way of letting the other person down, that is to say, the revenge, is to cease to exist for him or her. What was formerly a close togetherness based on trust no longer exists since the one partner's innermost feelings are directed towards another person.

Men are often sensitive—perhaps more sensitive than women—about losing the interest of their partner, of feeling taken for granted. This can be traced back to the feeling of abandonment that the boy child experiences at the point in his development when it is time for him to identify with and align himself with the man/the father. He therefore bears within himself a tendency to let a woman down if she makes him feel unimportant. He is then reminded of his experience of being let down by his mother. In order not to be abandoned, men can therefore tend to want to control their partner, and many macho men feel that they are victims if they cannot control their woman.

In close relationships, men can believe that they are more equal than they actually are. They often want to feel that they are in a position of "supervisory authority" towards their partner. When a woman becomes occupied with her children, her profession, and her own interests, the man can feel that he has been put at a disadvantage and can behave so that he places the woman in a similar position of feeling ignored.

Monica feels crazy with doubt about whether Paul is telling the truth. Is she excessively suspicious or easily hurt? She thinks that something about him has changed. He has withdrawn himself from her. Perhaps it has happened since she has become more and more occupied by the new gym she has started, a project that he at the same time has encouraged her to pursue! She finds several harmless sms's in his cell phone to a woman that he has ended with "hugs and kisses, Paul". He says that this is just his style of communicating with this woman, who has become his pal at work. But when Monica confronts him, he discovers a growing desire for revenge within himself for what he experiences as Monica's abandonment of him, that she has become "obsessed" with the gym.

In Monica's and Paul's case, the revenge urge is discovered before anything serious has happened. This is not the case with George and Lena.

George has been unfaithful over a period of two years. Lena found him out when she was getting a pair of his formal-dress trousers ready for the dry cleaners and came across a note with an unknown telephone number in the pocket. She is reduced to despair. He wants to make up and immediately leave the illicit affair behind him. He tells Monica that his affair may to some extent have been his way of getting revenge because he and Lena had too little in common.

George's infidelity sets off a revenge spiral. Lena has a hard time making up, even though that is what she wants. In her body, there are still memories of his absence. When he is away at his new evening job, she is reminded of the trauma, old memories come up and are replayed in her inner self. Her tolerance for painful feelings is tested time and time again. These memories lead her to refuse to talk to George, especially when he wants them to return to a good relationship as quickly as possible. "It's not going to be that easy", she thinks, with a mixture of sorrow and revenge feelings that are difficult to keep separate.

Her years of grief cause her to find herself in a border area, a grey area between revenge and restoration, where she communicates, works through, rebuilds, and takes revenge in what often seems to be emotional chaos. Infidelity is always an enormous challenge for a couple. It takes time to heal and calls for a great deal of tolerance for emotional fluctuations. The one who is frustrated over feeling neglected and turns to someone else can also be the woman, needless to say.

Sophia and Carl are married and have a son. Sophia is dissatisfied with their sex life and sees no way out, even though she has tried to talk to Carl about it. He usually brushes it aside and says that her expectations are too high: "Our sex life is no better or worse than most other people's." Sophia happens to run into her old boyfriend Joe in town and is reminded of the passionate sexuality that they shared. Before long, she exceeds the limits and gets involved in a secret sexual relationship with her former lover. However, it is clear to her that she does not want to lose Carl and she cannot keep things secret from him. Carl is beside himself and in the couples' therapy that follows, they begin a serious effort to work through their sexual relationship and the differences in their views of sexuality. Carl starts to listen and, even in the midst of his humiliation, he is able to change and to be more open to Sophia's needs.

Women seem to have a greater tendency to blame themselves when a relationship feels unsatisfying. They keep trying as long as they possibly can to make themselves even better in order to meet their partner's expectations. It therefore indicates that the relationship is in worse shape when the woman gives in to the temptation to be unfaithful.

Fluctuation between equality or domination/submission

Leonard is angry because Sylvia comes out to the car too late when they are going to go somewhere. He thinks that she has made him wait too long. He tells her how disappointed and frustrated he feels, but he also takes revenge by speeding and being sullen and silent as he drives. He knows that Sylvia does not like fast driving. When she tries to get him to slow down, he says that it is her fault that he has to drive so fast. She should have thought of how important it was to be on time so that they would not have had to rush.

Most couples in relationships—even the ones built upon equality—seem to be able to cross over into an interaction characterized by domination–submission positions whenever strains and irritations become too great. It is as though frustration always lurks there wanting to make equal relationships into authoritarian ones. Anger unites with the need to dominate: "Now you will do as I say!" We thus confuse our anger with the need to dominate the other. And in order for the one to dominate the other, revenge mechanisms inevitably come into play.

Emotional oppression

When the one partner's need to control the other partner becomes more constant, revenge manifests itself in what we can call emotional oppression. The list below gives some examples of how emotional oppression can work in practice. Both women and men can subject their partner to such stress, but as we have seen earlier, it is more common that men believe they need to control and dominate their women because of their fear of abandonment. We therefore use men's oppressive acts for our examples (Jukes, 1999). Note that the man's behaviour triggers a revenge spiral in which the woman also participates, since she becomes more and more desperate in her search for a way to retaliate or to flee from the relationship.

- He puts her under constant pressure, insisting that she make quick decisions.
- He rushes her, blames her for everything that goes wrong, it's her fault that he cannot find things, etc.
- He does not keep his part of their agreements, manipulates the children against her, looks at pornography though he knows she does not like it, and shirks his share of responsibility for the household and the children.
- He is emotionally inaccessible and refuses to give her emotional support. He sees his problems and feelings as more important than hers.
- He does not take care of himself, does not learn how to fix meals, abuses alcohol or drugs, does not make friends of his own who could give him emotional support, and tells his partner that she is a bad mother.

Quarrels and revenge

Conflicts in relationships are unavoidable. When we are two, we cannot help but irritate and find fault with each other. With time, the irritation can become harder and harder to hold back and we take action: raise our voice, make spiteful comments, or do something else that we associate with gearing up for a quarrel.

To show anger and irritation can be necessary. The problem is that we often transform anger into a demeaning of our partner or a determination to find fault with her or him (Böhm, 2001). The ideal quarrel takes place when the instigator can keep the focus on his or her own feelings, in other words, on his or her own sensitivity, and at the same time maintain his or her ability to put himself or herself in the other's shoes as an equal human being. However, only in an ideal world are such things always possible. In reality, we often try to put the other person down, rise up from our feelings of humiliation, and retaliate. We let go of our self-control and self-criticism and just want to cause the other person pain and distress.

The quarrel can proceed into more destructivity or into reparation of the relationship. Attacks on someone's most sensitive and most vulnerable points often trigger a destructive spiral. The spiral has within it the avenger's desire to hurt the other person for the sake of revenge, to escape what he or she sees as a humiliating and disadvantaged position.

Below is a presentation of some sensitive points in men and women that can both arouse a craving for revenge and be used as the actual revenge in an attack on the partner. And, these issues are commonly present when quarrels degenerate into revenge. (Needless to say, there are many other variations on these sensitive points in different individuals.)

Ambivalent and tense relationships to parents-in-law. A person can say that he or she hates his or her own parents, but it is another matter altogether if the partner hates those same parents and compares the other partner with the hated parent or parents' worst sides.

Confrontation with social failure. An individual can harm his or her partner by pointing out how much he or she is disliked by people who are important to him or her. In this way, the partner's self-image is undermined.

Inability to get pregnant or sexual problems. Men can be attacked for being impotent or infertile and women for being frigid or unable to get pregnant for various reasons. Criticism and disparagement here call the partner's identity as a man or a woman into question when the partner instead needs empathy and shared responsibility for the problem.

Denied substance abuse. There is a great difference between confronting a partner who is trying to deny substance abuse and doing so in a constructive and helpful way as opposed to using it as a guise to hurt and oppress the other. "You're lying about how much you drink and about everything else as well."

The other's children from earlier relationships, where the step-family theme is used to hurt the other by criticizing or disparaging his or her child. In the revenge act, the one partner sometimes forces upon the other partner an impossible choice between the child and the partner: "If you want to live with me, you have to give up seeing your child so often." Or the one partner criticizes the other partner's child, "Can't you make your lazy, good-for-nothing son behave?" "You don't set any limits for your daughter."

In the destructive quarrel, the aim is not to reach the other with feelings but rather to "quarrel the other out the door". When revenge takes over, the goal is to hurt the other person, not to repair the relationship or to achieve restoration.

Psychodynamic couples' therapy

The couple is not always conscious of how the revenge motif is functioning in their relationship. Moreover, they often do not attach the significance to the revenge motif that is perhaps motivated. The *pas de deux* of the couple's relationship consists of intricate patterns, strong feelings, and a risk that these feelings are being expressed in more or less discernible revenge acts. Our way of working in couples' therapy encompasses several aspects that affect the couple.

To start with, there is the early attachment between parent and child that each and every individual takes with him or her in various complex ways into adulthood and into a partner relationship. Attachment theory can constitute an essential basis for an understanding of the relationship between partners, including the two individuals' ability to regulate strong feelings (Schore, 2003). Other aspects are life history and the possible traumas that remain alive in the inner life of the couple, as well as the mutual relationships of the couple's own parents, which can be described as a sounding board.

In couples' therapy, sensitive areas often come to the surface for one or both of the partners. A quarrel about some trivial matter, as for example how important it is to do the vacuuming, can provide a gateway into something more emotionally profound in the relationship. The couple's therapist might ask: "Is there anything that comes to your mind that can shed light on why this is so emotionally charged for you?

Something that happened to you at some earlier time?" At that point, the individual might make associations with some incident or scene from his or her life history, something that shows the more profound dimension of whatever at first seemed trivial.

One way to bring to life and summarize common themes in couples' therapy is to give a fictitious and compacted account of a couple living in an extremely complicated relationship. The account is based on themes we have encountered in different couples we have worked with but the details have been changed.

> Alice and Bob are just under 40 years of age. They both have several relationships in their past. Alice has a son, Bob has a daughter. They have no children together, even though they have lived together for five years. They are both active professionally in creative, stimulating jobs. They quarrel incessantly about who is going to look after the children and about getting time of their own. In addition, Bob has many conflicts with Alice's son, whom he regards as slack and ill-mannered. They have hardly any active sex life since Alice has lost her desire and Bob feels rejected whenever he tries.

Alice says something cutting about how Bob begs for sex the way a child begs for candy. She does not want to have another child until he becomes more of an adult and takes more responsibility. Bob is tense-jawed and silent. Alice speaks more spontaneously and mentions Bob's infidelity, which she discovered after some months. She cries, does not know how she is going to regain her trust in him, and points out that of course he does not say what he is thinking, either. She wants to trust him, but it would be false to do so if the feeling is not there. Bob mutters that he cannot get a word in edge-wise. Sure, he'd say something if he didn't get interrupted all the time.

Both of them had a painful childhood and adolescence, with numerous elements of abandonment, loneliness, and breach of faith. Bob has a younger sister with severe psychic disorders. Alice has an older brother with drug problems. Her parents have been divorced for many years. Bob's parents live together but quarrel incessantly. Both have authoritarian fathers, who imposed their will on the other family members. Both speak of their low self-esteem. Bob says with a mournful smile that maybe they would not have been able to get anybody else. Both of their former partners left them. "I'd rather be with Alice than be alone, even though things are not so good between us." Alice gets upset when Bob says so. She believes that his infidelity was an act of revenge because she was occupied with her job and her son.

They have a hard time putting themselves in each other's shoes. Instead, they make sarcastic remarks at each other, which are humiliating for both of them and trigger retaliation. It is as though they are playing on different teams instead of being team players, where they would be able to negotiate and discuss taking care of the children, getting time for themselves and time together. However, they cannot negotiate, but instead try to impose their wills on each other or dominate each other in various ways. They are different and do not find these differences enriching but instead regret them.

Sometimes when we meet couples similar to Bob and Alice, we ask them explicitly, "Why are you together?" The couple is sometimes shaken up, takes the question as an eye-opener, and can see the tragi-comic in their predicament. However, most often, they are so entangled in their destructive behaviour that this simple question mystifies them.

In Bob and Alice's relationship, there is an absence of trust. Perhaps it was there even before the infidelity, but it is even more pronounced now afterwards. They are pulling in different directions without finding a mutual project. Furthermore, they have completely separate economies. Bob tries to dominate through his silence, Alice through her words. Alice tries to make contact through words; he tries to get peace and quiet or contact through sex. These tendencies are also accentuated by earlier traumas, based on which Alice's anxiety is evoked by being shut out and Bob's by being questioned in a way that he finds altogether too intrusive. He takes no responsibility for the relationship, does not share his thoughts, perhaps does not actually know what he thinks or feels, except that he thinks she is difficult. He wants a nice woman who gives him affection and sex. She wants a man who makes her feel loved, who shares his feelings and thoughts with her. She keeps going on at Bob in a harsh, accusatory way and does not understand that she thus achieves less and less. Neither of them has the strength to be empathetic with the other. They both think, "I'm the one who deserves most of the sympathy." They are not in a position to take on the issues concerning their respective stepchildren since they can hardly discuss or negotiate anything without taking to the trenches.

They have both accommodated themselves to an unreasonable extent to emotionally disturbed siblings in their childhood and adolescence, and they have unconsciously internalized an authoritarian posture and power struggle through their parents' quarrels. The result of all these unresolved themes and conflicts is a never-ending stream of revenge acts, labelled euphemistically with other names, but which aggravate their antagonisms and nourish the revenge spiral.

In efforts to bring about a dialogue in couples in therapy, a general difficulty for the therapist is how to avoid getting caught up in questions such as "how the whole thing started" and "whose fault it actually is". The history is important but not as a tool in the power struggle. For the couple to be able to put such questions behind them in the long run is a precondition for a developmental dialogue.

CHAPTER EIGHT

Revenge from a gender perspective: abuse of women

*I*n men's violence against women, there is an individual perpetrator perspective that has connections to group ideologies pertaining to control of women. However, we can also see how psychological factors in individual men indicate the emotional background behind their development into perpetrators. We can observe the extensive element of revenge in this background. We describe several interviews with abusive men and discuss ways of understanding the phenomenon of men who abuse women. Absences of attachment and empathy seem to play a central role.

Men's violence towards women is a male capsizal (Eliasson, 2000) and more common than many can imagine. In London, one in three women has been forced to endure severe violence by a male partner. Two of three men interviewed in a British survey say they use violence on their women in "conflict situations" that can be as minor as her not having dinner ready on time (!). In England, two women are murdered every week by a male partner or lover (Bloom, 2001). Approximately 12 per cent of all men, according to an American survey, have committed acts of violence on women at some time in their lives, such as punching, kicking, or striking them with an object or using sexual violence (Strauss, in Fonagy, 1999).

Most violence in times of peace takes place between people who know each other well: 88 per cent of the murdered women in one study knew their murderers, who were often their partners or former partners. Of those who are arrested for acts of violence around the world, at least 80 per cent are men (ibid.). Every week, a large number of women in Sweden are also abused by men they know well. According to the Swedish Council for the Prevention of Crime, there were over 22,000 crimes registered in 2003 as abuse of women, of which approximately three-quarters constituted abuse carried out by a perpetrator known to the victim.

In order to analyse men's violence, we concentrate primarily on psychological factors. We take this approach in part because it is our area of expertise, and in part because we believe that such factors have a crucial significance for the understanding of men's behaviour. It is their experiences, impulses, defence mechanisms, rage, guilt, sense of having been violated, and inability to grieve that take the upper hand when they resort to violence. The psychic phenomena also have relevance for the nature of the treatment.

To understand the emergence of violence in couples' relationships, we look primarily at the interplay between positions of advantage and disadvantage. As we saw in the previous chapter, feelings of being at an advantage or a disadvantage are often connected to revenge mechanisms. When someone in the relationship feels humiliated or at a disadvantage, the quick solution might seem to be retaliation through verbal or psychic violence. In its most destructive form, revenge can be manifested in physical violence towards the partner.

Woman can exercise violence, but it is far more common that men abuse their female partner. Men are more outwardly aggressive, whereas women more often turn their aggressivity inward in the form of guilt feelings and self-reproach. In larger, collective contexts, there are fewer differences between men and women when it comes to committing acts of violence. For example, there were large numbers of female perpetrators who took part in the genocide in Rwanda.

Explanations of violence against women

According to a psychoanalytic view, violence emerges primarily as a masculine pathology (Chodorow, in Varvin & Volkan, 2003). Masculinity in this respect is defined as not being a woman, since a boy becomes a boy by liberating himself from his first and early identification with his mother. Psychoanalyst Nancy Chodorow has described the double humiliation that many men experience and that makes them extra-sensitive if someone calls their masculinity into question. As a "non-girl", a man is sensitive to accusations of being unmanly. In addition, he is sensitive about being dismissed as "not man enough" by other, older men. A man who feels threatened in his ethnic-religious-national identity can also feel threatened in his masculine self, something that awakens a fear of the feminine and of a loss of the self. This fear resembles the fear felt by homophobic men, who worry about seeming small and feminine.

We can also refer here to our original inclination towards a splitting of the ego (Igra, 1983), where painful experiences are often deposited and "locked in" in one of the compartments. Researchers have traditionally regarded abusive men as having impaired ego functions, which cause them to overreact and become violent. In the specialist literature of psychology, we get a description of men who are repeatedly abusive as being afraid of weakness and dependency and as being awkward when it comes to emotional problems. Morality, empathy, and reason are knocked out by violence, since these values cannot function simultaneously with aggressivity.

However, certain authors caution against seeing violence as an expression of severe emotional disturbances, since such a view might remove responsibility from these men in the present and facilitate their excuse-making (Eliasson, 2000). At the same time, they point out, bad experiences in childhood lead to increased vulnerability and reduced power of resistance towards acting violently.

Those taking a feminist perspective argue, however, that childhood factors do not explain violence and the deliberate use of violence and others actions meant to control women. Certain violent men are mentally ill, but all mentally ill men are not violent. Cultural factors can also uphold violence towards women (Raakil, 2000), especially in the case of unequal gender roles, as when women in many cultures are brought up to obey and men to dominate.

In a culture that legalizes the right of men to oppress women, the risk for violence towards women increases, since the imbalance between men and women is not questioned but instead is seen as legitimate. In societies with (a) violence in the media, (b) state violence exercised through capital punishment, (c) acceptance of corporal punishment in schools, and (d) a high degree of participation in legal violent activity, such as use of weapons, women run an eight times greater risk of being raped than in societies with a lower degree of legal violence (Bloom, 2001). This most likely has similar consequences for the occurrence of other types of abuse of women as well. In addition, oppression is a phenomenon that can easily take on different forms, one of several important reasons to emphasize that abuse of women is a problem for everyone. A society that is sufficiently authoritarian to allow it to ensnare women in an unbearable position of simultaneously being put on a pedestal and being degraded carries within it the capacity to exercise other forms of oppression as well—against people with a certain skin colour, a certain sexual preference, or with certain opinions (Hydén, 1995).

A combination of different views

Psychotherapist and researcher Margareta Hydén emphasizes that abuse of women is a problem for all of us and not just for women. She combines the two traditionally most described perspectives—the individual psychological and the feminist—and views the act of violence as a social process. This means that the act concerns private individuals but has a significance that transcends the private. A social process is also changeable and composed of several phases: in this case, a prelude to violence, an act of violence, and the consequences of that act. In order to understand repeated acts of violence, it is important to study the entire sequence of events. The act of violence itself is regarded quite differently by the woman and the man, respectively, Hydén shows. In contrast, the descriptions of what led up to the violence do not differ, surprisingly enough, to any significant degree between men and women.

Victims become perpetrators

In general, we see that one of the most important factors for determining whether or not a person resorts to violence is the presence of dehumanizing experiences in childhood, experiences that are triggered by events in the present. We recognize this phenomenon from the discussion on violation and rage. A violated and traumatized victim becomes a perpetrator himself. The phenomenon called identification with the aggressor can thus function as the "motor" in a revenge spiral that includes abuse of women.

Men who resort to violence are always vulnerable in close relationships, since they have a poor understanding of possible alternatives to violence in frustrating situations. They have unhealed, non-worked-through traumas, and perceive the world as dangerous. Arriaga has divided male perpetrators of violence into three different groups according to their personality characteristics, their degree of violent behaviour, and the incidence of violence manifested outside the home (Arriaga & Oskamp, 1999):

Group 1 refers to men who *only resort to violence within the family.* They have the lowest incidence of obvious underlying factors that can explain their violent behaviour. They can give the outward appearance of mental health, making them difficult to distinguish from men who do not use violence. Nor does their violence seem to escalate.

Group 2, depressed/borderline, have a traumatic background that often includes abusive and rejecting parents. Research shows that men in this group have experienced sexual violence as children to a high degree and have had mothers with health problems. It is difficult for them to form trusting relationships and they are highly dependent on their partners, whom they are afraid to lose. They are often jealous, have deficiencies in their capacity to relate, a hostile attitude towards women and a positive attitude towards the use of violence. Frustrations can often unleash violence towards persons to whom they have an attachment.

Group 3, the *generally violent/antisocial*, have a pronounced inclination towards aggressive behaviour. They have experienced a great deal of violence in their family background and they hang out with deviant and violent peers. They have obvious difficulties when it comes to being dependent on and empathetic towards their partners. They are impulsive, poor at coping with relationships, show hostile attitudes towards women and positive attitudes towards violence, and they also use violence in social contexts outside the home.

Deficiencies in attachment and mentalization

The British psychoanalyst John Bowlby's *attachment theory* can also be used to help us understand aspects of violent behaviour (Holmes, 1996).

Attachment is a way for the child to obtain security from the adult. Through attachment, the child also learns to mentalize. Mentalization is the ability to understand and interpret human behaviour on the basis of the mental states that underlie it. The groundwork for mentalization is laid when an individual himself is understood in that way as a child in a close relationship. When attachment is impaired, the ability to have a mental perception of oneself and others as subjective beings is obstructed (Fonagy, 1999).

Fonagy shows how abusive men have a high incidence of early attachment traumas. In his interviews, they are also consistent in not commenting on their own or others' mental states, which indicates that they lack a tangible theory on how human beings function mentally (that is, the ability to mentalize). In childhood, they have become bewildered when they have sought physical closeness and consolation, since they at the same time have been forced to create a mental distance between themselves and their threatening parents or guardians. They therefore have difficulties thinking and feeling when it comes to intimate relationships. Nonetheless, their psyche can be split in a way that allows other parts of their personalities to function. They are even able to put themselves in other people's shoes, provided they are not dependent on them.

Fonagy shows that attachment impairment in these violent men has a double background. On the one hand, they have had mothers with their own attachment impairment and, on the other hand, fathers who have shamed, violated, and punished them in an arbitrary way. The impaired relationship to their mother makes these children unable to deal with the violations from their father. The father's animosity is perceived as coming from inside their own selves.

Fonagy argues that the man's need to control the woman is also a manifestation of his need to have the woman as a container for his own unbearable feelings. When the woman is perceived as altogether too independent, this mechanism is threatened and she must be put down once again. We recognize this as a complicated revenge mechanism and as racism's extermination dynamic: the frightening part of one's own self must be re-created and re-experienced in the other person and then be destroyed in the hope that it will never come back again. When the perpetrator sees terror in the eyes of his victim, he feels assured that he himself does not need to feel terrified. When the man asks the woman for forgiveness afterwards, his remorse can be genuine. He needs the relationship so that he can use the woman as a container the next time his feelings become unbearable.

Disadvantaged position–advantaged position: the dynamics of violence

In the book *Kärleksrelationen* (*The Love Relationship*) Böhm, (2001) describes how the quarrel between a man and a woman contains the seed to the power struggle that can later develop into violence. As pointed out earlier, the quarrel according to this definition is an inflammatory and angry attempt to put the other person down in order to put oneself at an advantage. "You don't understand anything. Let me tell you a thing or two!" If the two can set aside the quarrel and go over to negotiation, the situation becomes more balanced again, "I let my anger get the best of me. We need to talk about this and see what each of us thinks."

However, men who are abusive cannot negotiate. Margareta Hydén has interviewed twenty couples where the woman has reported the man for abuse (1995). All of the couples except two stated that the violence usually started with a quarrel about something that in retrospect seemed insignificant. The quarrels and the prelude to violence often concerned an expression of disapproval by the woman, comments on the man's way of being, which the man interpreted as insults and provocation. In other words, the man sees the woman's comments as an invitation to a quarrel and not to a discussion of common concerns. What the woman and the man had different opinions on might be, for example, the man's drinking or his way of handling money.

The man then tries to re-establish the balance by completely overpowering his wife. His difficulties in verbalizing his situation make him regard the woman as verbally superior and impossible to talk to, which in turn makes him feel frightened and powerless. The fear of appearing weak prevents him from showing consideration and thoughtfulness. Instead, he calls the competence of his complaining wife into question and derides her for her low status or deficiencies in her personality, habits, or appearance. It is not the content of what she says but rather the way she says it that he does not accept. He repudiates his wife as a person in the early stages of the quarrel. When the man cannot acknowledge the importance of trust, care, and solidarity in a relationship, what he has left are power and control (Hydén, 1995).

Important factors that are common for couples with violent men have been described (Arriaga & Oskamp, 1999). There are often defects in *social competence*, such as the ability to negotiate, listen, perceive one's own and others' feelings, and to be self-critical. In conjunction with these deficiencies, there is a strong notion that the man's need to *control the woman* is not to be questioned. The poor *emotional climate* in the relationship is perceived as unavoidable and natural, even though it makes violence and infantile dependency possible and promotes projection between subjects, unpredictability, and emotional explosiveness. The constant sense of frustration becomes habitual when the climate in the relationship is bad. These factors lead to a *deficient interaction* in the relationship, which bears with it a rigid communication, and, in the woman especially, negative feelings, withdrawal, resistance, and fear.

We see how the theme superior position/inferior position takes over at the expense of an equal relationship. It is in such a vertical relationship that primitive revenge mechanisms thrive. We saw in the previous chapter how quarrels and verbal violations can either be the beginning of a constructive dialogue or an escalation towards more destructivity, in this case violence.

All in all, men who abuse women see conflicts as threats instead of opportunities to negotiate. Violence can therefore be understood as a sign of weakness that is concealed by the force accompanying it. The man perceives himself as being taken advantage of, misinterpreted, and misunderstood. Abusive men try to explain away their violence in a manner reminiscent of that of substance abusers. When they finally arrive at the point of seeking help, it is more because the woman has set the conditions than because they understand their own predicament.

Escalation of violence

In relationships where the man strikes the woman, we can often see an escalation of violence in parallel with the man's increasing feeling of being in a disadvantaged position. Dismissive and rejecting remarks towards the woman counteract empathy with her and are a prelude to violence. The risk that violence will break out increases the more the woman makes the man feel that a separation is imminent since the man then sees that he is in danger of losing his chances of controlling her.

The risk that violence will be repeated increases if the man does not need to be held accountable or if the consequences are not of a sufficient degree to be taken seriously. The boundary for what is possible is moved and the man's personality changes in the destructive process if witnesses do not intervene. In other words, this is a concrete example of how the perpetrator is changed by his own "perpetrating", as we described in the chapter on the revenge spiral.

The woman's behaviour does not seem to have any correlation with whether or not the violence continues. Even those men who reduce their physical violence seem to continue with emotional oppression. At the same time, there is often a sadomasochistic *pas de deux* wherein both partners in an unconscious way keep the revenge spiral alive. Needless to say, woman can provoke and hurt men, but our intention here is to put special emphasis on men's difficulties in finding alternatives to violence. In almost all instances, men are the ones who will turn to violence instead of setting limits or getting out of a relationship in another way.

Interview study with abusive men

In 2002, one of the present authors, Tomas Böhm, together with Ludvig Igra, made an interview study with men who abused women. In the eight interviews that resulted, we can find most of the familiar factors that we have referred to above from the literature on the psychological dynamics in relationships where abuse of women takes place.

Approximately 10 per cent of the women abusers who are in contact with the Men's Center in Stockholm go to group therapy, which indicates that they need a more secure context and help from each other in order to be able to verbalize their experiences, thoughts, and feelings. Böhm´s and Igra´s interview subjects came from this "more difficult" group, which can be one explanation for why violence was common in their backgrounds. Here we describe three typical cases (compare Arriaga's introduction):

> Chris has struck his girlfriend on one occasion in an incident involving jealousy, alcohol, and a pub environment. His parents got divorced early in his life and he became a mamma's boy. He has always found it hard to talk about conflicts. His father was away much of the time and was authoritarian. He re-married and Chris called his new wife a witch. As an adult, he has taken on a non-verbal approach to life and has a hard time talking about feelings. He gets his feelings hurt easily and the women in two of

his relationships have left him. He has low self-esteem as a man and a hard time exercising self-criticism. He feels that women are always accusing him of something and dismisses them as nags. At the same time, he is terrified of losing his woman. Alcohol triggers his jealousy and unleashes sudden violence.

Chris belongs to a group of men who lack both an emotional language and an ability to reflect over their behaviour and their thoughts. At the same time, he seems to belong to the least pathological group, whose personalities are not deviant as far as outward appearances are concerned. Violence occurs only within the family and in his case on only one occasion thus far.

Walt bears with him a number of risk factors from childhood. His mom was often unfaithful and his parents, who did not show love for each other, ended up getting a divorce. He has never met his biological father, who, as far as anyone knows, seems to have passed away. His stepfather beat him and his mother never intervened to stop the abuse. As an adult, he has become a man of few words who tries to be a tough and strong big brother. In a traditionally male way, he has a hard time showing and talking about feelings. He often got jealous of his wife's real or imagined contacts, especially when he drank large amounts of alcohol. On such occasions, he also became paranoid in an overly excited way and was determined to get her to "confess" to infidelity. Only the answers he wanted could be accepted, whereupon he "let the pressure-cooker boil over" and struck her. His violence was also triggered by his wife's making light of what he saw as her blatant flirtation with other men. The marriage situation got worse and he felt that she was not taking him seriously. After going through therapy, he has a greater tolerance for his wife's contacts with other men and he can get in touch with his own feelings of grief.

Walt can be said to belong to group 2, depressed/borderline. Part of his pattern is his need to dominate women and his desire to see them submit to him. If the woman does not immediately satisfy his pent-up need for empathy, he becomes overwhelmed by rage. He drinks to dull his senses, but by drinking he also unleashes the split-off, raging part of himself, which seems to be connected to the way his parents let him down. A constant and propulsive revenge fantasy and desire to repair the damage he suffered as a child govern his behaviour.

> Harry is a violent man who suffered harm at an early age. His childhood contains all the factors that generally underlie a violent/ antisocial personality. His parents quarrelled incessantly, his father beat his mother. He himself was physically abused by his father and his older sister. His father was a heavy drinker. Harry moved to a new part of town as a child and was bullied all the way up to the ninth grade, at which point he started to drink and get into fights to impress others. He joined a gang that cruised around in big used cars, committed burglaries, and beat up people. As he was growing up, he developed a personality characterized by callousness in fights and regular abuse of alcohol. He was brought to trial and sentenced for assault and battery. He could not listen to women, but instead used verbal violence against them. Nor could he feel any empathy for others. Whenever he felt backed into a corner, he sought a solution in violence. He describes it as though he was overcome by tunnel vision. The blow came from behind, as though he had nothing to do with it. This often happened in connection with the intake of alcohol. In his contact with women, he became more and more explosive and split. Later, he had a girlfriend with a healthier lifestyle who called his lifestyle into question, but he could not meet her half-way or discuss the issue. He feels nothing for the people he has assaulted. As for women, they deserve to be degraded. In his eyes, the ones he has beaten are not human beings.

Harry has gone through treatment but still makes somewhat of a frightening impression. He lacks language skills as well as ability to mentalize. Control and domination of others seem to come to him as a matter of course, as does an intrusion of the past through his fragile defence in the form of a desire for revenge towards his sister and other women. Violence has always been accepted as a means of contending with powerlessness.

Analysis of the men

We tried to understand why these men were violent and not just "crazy" or disturbed in a broad, general way. Seen from the outside, they resembled thousands of other men, but their inner self was in a great imbalance. In several of them, we saw how guilt feelings were projected onto the woman and converted into an attack on her. It was apparent that what we were dealing with here was precisely the *persecutory guilt* that we described in the chapter on the revenge spiral. In other words, the men did not experience their guilt as their own inner bad conscience but as something that someone else had inflicted upon them.

Furthermore, the men were often overwhelmed by feelings and primarily by what appear to be feelings of shame—feelings of worthlessness—that could neither be verbalized nor contained within them. *In the attack against the other*, we could therefore sense that the revenge was also based on shame, together with envy and persecutory guilt (Nathanson, 1992). In our analysis, we also found that the men suffered from a lack of a mental space for working through experiences and feelings as well as a lack of conviction that feelings are something that can be changed with the help of words.

We can also note that these men had little space for ambivalence or multi-meanings or for a so-called *integrative position*. The last mentioned means that an individual perceives human beings, himself included, as both evil and good. This fact can most likely be related to early traumas that split the man's inner self into different parts. As we described earlier, there is a tendency towards splitting as a potential in all of us. As babies, we seem to live with separated pictures, where good and evil exist in different places. This potential is always there inside of us, as pockets of frustration and cruelty, but our integrative ability helps us to resist a splitting. In these men, the ability to resist is absent.

When the men describe how they do not know what is happening with them when they strike, they are thus telling the truth in terms of what they experience, even though they are obviously the ones carrying out the action. Alcohol consumption is used to explain away everything, but it also helped them to get in touch with the destructive part of themselves. In other words, the men drank in order to feel more whole and to go beyond their own splitting of their personalities.

It was hard for them to question their craving to be the number one decider or their need to dominate over women, since these postures unconsciously functioned as vital defences against fear and powerlessness. Aggression came as an unpleasant surprise for them, since the split part of them did not seem to be perceived as belonging to their own person. To them, life seemed to be playing itself out behind a powerless shell, a façade, devoid of emotional language. They were often preoccupied with fending off emotional memories of parents who let them down, of their father's violence or alcohol abuse. All in all, they often seemed to have had a weak father relationship, a defensive attitude towards women, and an absence of factors in their background that could have served as a counterbalance to violence.

Unconscious revenge on other women

In their use of violence, these men also had difficulties distinguishing past time from present time. The women towards whom they were violent were often perceived to be distinctly similar inner copies of mothers, sisters, or other frustrating women. The difficulty in verbalizing their situation made it so, as noted, that the men regarded their female partner as verbally superior, envied her, and insisted that she was impossible to talk to. This seems to stem from their undeveloped intermediate area, another term for Winnicott's (1971) cultural transitional area, which is based on the child's having had possibilities of working through separations early in life in a favourable manner.

These men also had more difficulties than what is usual in tolerating the "aesthetic conflict" (Meltzer & Harris Williams, 1988), to love, to be dependent on or bonded to someone whom they cannot control, an ability that is essential for the development of a love relationship. This can also be described as a lack of trust grounded in their poor, shame-related self-image. Since dependency is more primitive, every manifestation of independence from the woman will be interpreted as abandonment and a breach of faith that must be stopped.

Violence has changed them

Their brutality was fomented by earlier incidents of violence, where the boundary to crime has already been crossed over and their personality has been changed through "learning by doing". It can be said that their non-worked-through traumas make the world a dangerous place, where conflicts are perceived as threats and must be fended off with violence. Granted, their violence is kept secret from the outside world through a split-off, socially vigilant part of themselves, but at the same time, another part can become more and more numbed and habituated with violence as a way of addressing problems. When violence is exercised on a repeated basis, the ability to feel guilty that normally accompanies it is lost. Dehumanization comes to fruition as a consequence of this gradual splitting off and numbing.

Other angles of approach

Something that we do not know is how many men there are who have had similar traumas in childhood, but, even so, do not resort to violence. Most likely, there is a fairly large number of such men. However, the factors that stand out in the men we have interviewed are violence and shame in childhood along with the absence of both attachment and a secure adult's genuine empathy with their situation. Precisely as in the study by Fonagy referred to above, the men we interviewed have a high prevalence of early attachment traumas. As a consequence, many of them also had difficulties when it came to verbalizing feelings.

It is as though the mental intermediate area is missing or has shrunk to such an extent that it cannot be used. Instead, it has been replaced by a splitting between a violent part and a social part. This, in effect, seems to be a diagnostic sign of a traumatic childhood that has only been possible to cope with through splitting. Violence serves as an accepted way of exercising control in a secret, shut-off world, where the man sees himself as ruling over the woman and seems to want to force into being the empathy that he has missed. What he wants most of all is to control a fantasy mother, who should be infinitely patient and empathetic and always there to meet his needs. In addition, he expects her to function as a container for his own frightening feelings. In the light of his wishes, an independent woman is perceived as provocative, a "nag" and a "blabber".

These violent men become like caricatures or stereotypes for the patriarchal society, where men exercise control over conquered women. The strong strike those under them in the hierarchy. The men hide their own weakness, indulging in their belief that women, children—and perhaps other weak groups such as foreigners—are even weaker. They find themselves in a predominantly split and closed position, which consists mostly of polarities, superiority versus inferiority, control versus obedience. Their veneer of vocational or professional education and adulthood truly seems to be a thin, easily broken, layer. They have hardly any capacity for ambivalence and uncertainty. Depression—grief and guilt—come up instead during treatment. First comes denial, then appeals for indulgence, followed by attempts to make light of every-thing and externalization, then depression and confusion, followed by an accepting—which can require an extensive period of time.

CHAPTER NINE

Extreme collective violence: the example of Rwanda

*W*e return to large group phenomena after having used a revenge perspective to look at everyday situations. We take up Rwanda as an example and describe the atmosphere prevailing there ten years after genocide. The interplay between leaders and followers is a primary factor and at the same time there are phenomena that are special for the perpetrators in Rwanda. We discuss their ways of explaining what they did and how they look at it now through interviews made by a French journalist. Finally, we take up the revenge murders that inevitably followed in the aftermath of the genocide.

Rwanda is a small country of 26,338 square kilometres, not larger than the Swedish province of Småland and slightly smaller than the state of Maryland in the USA. It is an extremely poor country with a population of about eight million, situated north of its twin Burundi and wedged in by Kenya, Tanzania, Congo, and Uganda, up on a lush green plateau in the middle of Central Africa. At the point in time prior to the start of the genocide, the Tutsis made up 15 per cent of the population and had long been the well-educated elite in society. They were mainly ranchers, while the Hutus, who made up 85 per cent of the population, were for the most part farm workers.

During the genocide in Rwanda, from April to June 1994, the Hutu extremists killed approximately 700,000 people, mostly Tutsis, as well as approximately 50,000 politically moderate Hutus (Staub, 2011). About 75 per cent of the country's total population of Tutsis were murdered. The Hutu extremists had gained huge popular support for their movement "Hutu Power". It is estimated that over 120,000 people took an active part in the killing (Gourewitch, 1998).

Human Rights Watch (Rakita, 2003) estimates that 400,000 children—more than 10 per cent of all the children in Rwanda—are orphans today. This is a result of the genocide but also a consequence of HIV that was spread through rapes during the genocide.

How could such a horrendous genocide be allowed to happen? And how is this connected to revenge? We will now attempt to answer this question with the help of research and some of the phenomena that we described in Chapters Two, Four, Five, and Six. We also use material from our own studies. During our study trips in 2003 and 2004, we interviewed Rwandan researchers, trauma therapists and young people, as well as genocide researchers from various parts of the world.

Historical background

The origin of the two ethnic groups is shrouded in myth and unclear (Gourewitch, 1998). According to the dominating Hamitic myth, the Tutsis supposedly came from Ethiopia several hundred years ago while the Hutus migrated primarily from other parts of Central Africa. However, the ethnic groups are highly mixed in the present times; there have always been intermarriage and common social life.

While Rwanda was a Belgian colony during the early years of the 1900s, Hutus and Tutsis were played out against each other. The colonizers put Tutsis in direct and indirect positions of power in order to divide and conquer. In a similar fashion, people in other African countries have been divided by the colonizers into so-called *subject races*, which were then politicized, that is to say, assigned different statuses, such as coloured, Asians, or Arabs.

When the Tutsis demanded independence in 1959, the Belgians changed their tune and supported the Hutus, who seized command. Thus when liberation from colonialism came in 1962, a Hutu-run government was in power and restrictions were put into place against Tutsis with regard to work, education and equality with Hutus.

The government required everyone to obtain ethnic-identity papers, in which it had to be stated if they were Tutsi or Hutu, depending on their father's ethnic belonging. The question of ethnic belonging was thus kept front-centre in a way reminiscent of the methods used by European fascists. As time went on, this emphasis on ethnic belonging developed into racism on physiological grounds. Measurements were made of nostrils and head size just as in the Europe of the 1930s. Tall, slim people with slender noses were classified as typical Tutsis while shorter people with darker skin and broader noses were classified as Hutus. A Rwandan teenage boy says, "One of them told us to show our hands because they could judge us by looking at our palms. He said that a Hutu does not have a straight line in the middle of his hand while the Tutsi does have a straight mid-line" (Kaplan, 2006).

Massacres of thousands of Tutsis took place recurrently in different parts of the country from the 1960s up to the genocide in 1994; nevertheless, most of the surviving Tutsis remained in the country. The Tutsi-dominated liberation army, Rwandan Patriotic Front (RPF), trained in Uganda, tried to remove the Hutu dictator in 1990. They got all the way to the outskirts of the capital but the Hutu regime was rescued through a phone call to France's President Mitterrand, who saw Rwanda's French-speaking Hutu government as a part of the Francophone world (Melvern, 2000). Paratroopers, weapons, and money were pumped in to the Hutu government and the Tutsis were forced to retreat.

The Hutu extremists in Rwanda started their ethnic hate propaganda and the most important communication link was the radio. As early as 1990 and from 1993, the now so well-known hate propaganda was broadcast on the radio (Radio Télévision Libre des Milles Collines). The Tutsis were called cockroaches: they should be sent back to where they came from. Successive steps were taken to get people used to the idea of the forthcoming extermination of the Tutsis, who were defined as alien vermin (Mamdani, 2001). A number of derogatory labels paved the way for the persecution.

After four years of a campaign inciting Hutus against Tutsis, an airplane carrying Rwanda's Hutu president and Burundi's president was shot down and both men were killed. A dominating belief is that the Hutu fascists orchestrated the attack in order to blame it on the Tutsis and to use it as a reason to commit genocide as revenge. They thought that their president had shown too much willingness to negotiate with the Tutsis and the UN. It was in April, well known to be the poorest month, when the Hutu extremist leaders could count on the support of hungry, desperate people, who would join them for a chance to plunder.

The course of the genocide

The indiscriminate massacres that turned into genocide were begun. The entire political opposition was murdered within the first 48 hours and after a relatively short time 50,000 moderate Hutus were murdered as well. The genocide was not stopped by the UN or any other international organization, or efforts by other countries, even though there were a number of reports and warning signs about what was in the making. On the contrary, the French kept on supplying the Hutus with weapons. After intense pressure from the USA and France, the UN also withdrew its protection troops two weeks after the genocide had begun.

Boutros Boutros-Ghali, the Secretary General of the UN at the time, who was responsible for these troops, must bear a great deal of this fiasco on his conscience, writes investigative journalist Linda Melvern (2000). In Rwanda, the UN soldiers were first ordered to remain as passive bystanders and then to leave the country while the genocide was still in its early phases. We can ask ourselves if their obedience can be considered just as criminal as the obedience that murderers can plead. Was it not the soldiers' moral responsibility to protect the civilian population? The Canadian UN Force Commander in Rwanda, General Roméo Dallaire, has expressed his firm conviction several times that the 5,000 UN soldiers who were there before the withdrawal would have been able to stop the entire genocide if he and they had been given a mandate to intervene. However, he was not given this mandate and the several hundred UN soldiers who remained in the country could only watch while the tragedy unfolded.

Tutsis and "neutral" Hutus were sometimes shot to death with rifles but most often they were murdered with machetes, clubs, arrows and axes. The methods were bestial. What made this genocide unique was that it was carried out by over 100,000 civilians of whom many were organized in militias. The majority of the country's population is Roman Catholic. Priests and bishops took part in the genocide. Congregations of Tutsis were locked into churches that were then set on fire or bulldozed to the ground. Doctors murdered their patients, teachers their pupils, neighbours their neighbours. Gangs of Hutus hunted down Tutsis who had fled to hide in the swamps or forests and slashed them to death with machetes.

When the Rwandan liberation army at last invaded the country from Uganda, they were able to put an end to the killing. A new government was appointed, with General Paul Kagame, a Tutsi, as president and with several Hutus included in the regime. The rule that a person's ethnic group had to be stamped in his ID papers was taken away. The new leaders emphasized that they were going to unite the Rwandans at the same time as they launched into the extremely difficult task of implementing the reconciliation process, or as they preferred everyone to call it, "an acceptance" of history. As late as 2003, there were 120,000 criminals from the genocide still in jail, and to try them all through the normal court system would have taken hundreds of years.

After the war, there was a shortage of everything, including lawyers, judges, and courts. The UN set up a court in Arusha in Tanzania, where some of the most barbaric of the leaders were put on trial. Millions of dollars were spent, and so far only a small number of sentences have been set down. The new government in Rwanda instead took another approach in 1998 and brought the old village court councils, Gacaca, back to life (more can be read about these court councils in the concluding chapter of the book).

Revenge murder after RPF's seizure of power?

These are those who speak of a double genocide in Rwanda. In mid-April, the RPF succeeded in seizing power in the area of Mutete (Pagnier, 2004). The soldiers found an area devoid of life; they found only the dead bodies of Tutsis on all of the hilltops. According to Hutus who fled, the soldiers killed every Hutu in sight. However, there is great uncertainty about the extent of such revenge acts. Anthropologist Jet Pagnier underscores the complexity of this question. There is a difference between genocide and mass murder. Nonetheless, at the subsequent village trials, many people asked if these cases of revenge would also be taken up. No one in an official position of authority seemed inclined to let this happen. It was said that those people were killed by the RPF because of their own evil acts (or because of their families' evil acts).

"We are all survivors of the war!" says a Hutu on the subject of reconciliation. This attitude implies great difficulties if the desire is to create a shared view of history and of justice. According to our understanding, speaking of double genocide adds another segment to the revenge spiral, since it legitimates continued antagonism. The revenge murders that took place were perhaps seen by the parties as inevitable in the chaotic situation that emerged after the genocide, even if they are, of course, no less unacceptable in themselves.

"Africa's Hitler" and the ideology behind the genocide

One of those who set the tone for the Hutu fascists was Théoneste Bagosora, who has also been called "Africa's Hitler". He was one of those who appeared before the UN International Criminal Tribunal in Arusha, and he has been identified as the mastermind behind the genocide in Rwanda. He and his group had been planning the genocide down to the smallest detail since the autumn of 1992, more specifically two years before the genocide was actually unleashed. They imported half a million machetes and had them distributed. They built up Hutu militias. They were the ones behind the radio-broadcast propaganda that exhorted people to prepare for the final extermination of the Tutsis, "the cockroaches".

These leaders provided the genocidal process with a destructive ideology, which functioned as a driving force. How their own inner lives might be supposed to function is something we have already touched upon in earlier chapters. The manner in which they instigated destructive processes in a large part of the population was devastating. This was especially true because counterweights—such as intervention by the UN or other countries—were not in place or had been eliminated, as in the case of the opposition within the Hutu group itself.

Rwanda's history of civil obedience, whereby people tend to trust what the authorities say, also contributed to the rapid momentum of the destructive process, asserts Pagnier (2004). Violence was trivialized and normalized without any intervention by the authorities. The perpetrators used expressions like "pulling out the roots of the bad weeds" to refer to the killing of women and children. All chances for a new generation to come into being were to be eliminated. An idea of a final solution reached general acceptance. When President Habyarimana's plane was shot down, it seemed that all obstacles had been removed for the "*genocidaires*", who felt free to carry out their secretly prepared plans and start a genocide.

Expert on African history and politics Mahmood Mamdani (2001) argues that the genocide in Rwanda is a genocide carried out by those who define themselves as native Rwandans against those whom they see as aliens or settlers. In most instances, colonialists politicize the colonialized people's identity as natives of the land negatively, and then the native people themselves take over this way of thinking and politicize their ethnicity as something positive. In the case of Rwanda, the Tutsis were set up as a privileged group by the Belgians and then labelled negatively by Hutu Power as "non-native" after 1990. For the Hutu, the Tutsi was not a neighbour, but instead an alien.

We shall now return to some of the theories that we have taken up in earlier chapters, most importantly in Chapter Five, "Revenge on the societal level", and analyse the background of the genocide in Rwanda. We start on the individual level with Jean Hatzfeld's interviews with perpetrators in Rwanda. We wish to emphasize once again that genocide never develops out of spontaneous actions by a group of individuals or a population. Individual or sociopsychological factors are not sufficient. Impulse-driven group destructivity is limited in time. Riotous behaviour ends as soon as the outburst of rage has cooled down. Genocide, in contrast, requires leadership, ideology, and organization. People who participate in genocide have had time to undergo a change, to be trained in carrying out special tasks in a mechanical way, as well as in accepting a dilution of responsibility. There is interplay between ideological organization and blindly functioning group phenomena whereby the ideological leaders know how to get their supporters to rally around them blindly. Also, political power struggles are often recast as ethnic struggles in order for the leaders to gain supporters. This strategy can be a part of the leadership's ideological organization. Large-group regression can be manipulated by leaders, either to make the large group function better or to make the group members have an even more regressive, even blinder, faith in the leaders (Volkan, 2004).

How perpetrators undergo changes: Jean Hatzfeld's interviews

In Chapter Five, we took up the significance of the large-group identity. When large groups regress, often through manipulation by political leaders, their large-group identity takes the foreground and can even feel more real that their individual identity. The individual's basic trust is perverted into the group's blind trust.

Jean Hatzfeld, a veteran international reporter and author, has interviewed and followed a group of prisoners in Rwanda and has written a frightening book about his findings: *Machete Season* (2005). These Hutu boys were once ordinary sons of farm workers, a gang of friends who had known each other since childhood. They also cooperated with some slightly older men from the same neighbouring area. With the help of Hatzfeld's interviews, we see how these fairly normal boys are transformed into murderous monsters as a consequence of large-group regression, produced by manipulation, and thereafter begin their operations as murderers. In the following sections, we take up and comment upon some of the important themes that come out in the interviews.

Long tradition of fear and hatred

The tradition of fear and hatred has been there for a long time:

> "I was raised in the fear that the mwami—the Tutsi kings—and their commanders might return."

(p. 166)

There was a difference between the individual's own experiences and what was being taught:

> "I was born surrounded by Tutsis …. Still, I did grow up listening the whole time to the history lessons and radio programs that were always talking about major problems between Hutus and Tutsis—though I lived among Tutsis who posed no problem."

(p. 167)

There was an obvious envy towards the Tutsis as a group:

> "… a Hutu could certainly choose a Tutsi friend, hang out and drink with him, but he could never trust him … he had to be a natural target of suspicion."

(p. 216)

This paranoia was then nurtured for generations:

> "They would also murmur that a Hutu with a Tutsi wife, like me, was trying to show off … a Hutu child feels a natural jealousy of the other child, sees him as a show-off."

(pp. 217, 219)

In a description given by one of the Hutu boys, we also see the enticement of utopia. With the help of glorious words about total victory, the leaders in power win the potential perpetrators over to their side. The temptation in this case consisted not only of the promise that the Hutus would get rid of all their fear. The chance to plunder the possessions of the murder victims also stimulated hopes of reaching utopia.

At the same time, there was also a rivalry over the land since: "... the plots of land were not large enough for two ethnic groups" (p. 217). This feeling of unfairness was repeated time and time again on the radio and at public meetings. The party platform of the political Hutu parties had been proposing the killing of Tutsis since 1992: "They were read over the radio ... read aloud at meetings and warmly applauded" (p. 177).

Group identity and group dynamics

Comradeship laid the groundwork for ideology in the same way as we have seen in the youth camps in the fascist countries of twentieth-century Europe (Haffner, 2002). Group identity gradually became more important than individual identity. The interviewed boys did not actually have a hostile attitude towards Tutsis as individuals but their solidarity with the group took over: "I think that someone who was forced to kill wanted his neighbors to have to kill, too, so they would all be considered the same ..." (p. 224). And even when the killing was over and the men were in prison, they remained unchanged in their attitude: "Friendship is as strong as before the killing ... whatever we have to do, we do it as comrades, in every situation" (pp. 54, 55).

As we pointed out in the previous chapter, there is often a fear in men of being humiliated by other men. The group dynamic in the killing in Rwanda also included this fear: "... the jeering of colleagues is awful to overcome if it gets around your neighbourhood. It is just the same in school ... but more serious in the marshes. This taunting is a poison in life" (p. 226).

This phenomenon can be difficult to understand, that one human being through murdering another human being escapes humiliation by his comrades. At the same time, perhaps it is possible to understand the perverted logic here if we call to mind other absurd circumstances and see this as an extreme variant of the macho culture's psychodynamics.

Persecutory guilt and dehumanization

On the one hand, there is a certain degree of persecutory guilt: "The eyes of the killed, for the killer, are his calamity if he looks into them. They are the blame of the person he kills" (p. 22), one of the murderers explains. To meet the victim's gaze thus makes for difficulties in killing, while at the same time the killer must kill in order to get rid of that persecutory gaze.

On the other hand, the killer is killing an "animal": "I had never tried it on a warm-blooded animal ... killing with a gun is a game compared to the machete, it's not so close up" (pp. 22, 24).

In this context, it can be relevant to refer to the interviews with perpetrators that anthropologist Charles Mironko has carried out (2004). Through his knowledge of the local language Kinyarwanda, he was able to focus on a social mechanism called *Igitero*, "group attack". The concept is normally associated with the hunting of animals, a task for which the king originally was the supreme leader. When the new leaders used the same concept, it was to dehumanize the ones who were going to be murdered, in order to make the perpetrators see no difference between the murdering of people and the hunting of animals. The term used to designate the murdering militia, *Interahamwe*, also has a meaning that is associated with a neutral work team, namely "we who work together".

The Tutsis thus became dehumanized: "We no longer saw a human being when we turned up a Tutsi in the swamps ... the hunt was savage ... savagery took over the mind" (p. 47). The boys learned to kill through practice and repetition, "In any case, the manner came with imitation. Doing it over and over: repetition smoothed out clumsiness .... That is true, I believe, for any kind of handiwork" (p. 36), "... someone who had already slaughtered chickens—and especially goats—had an advantage, understandably" (p. 37).

Vertical relationship

The vertical relationship—that one group dominates another subordinated group—became a necessity.

> The marshes left no room for exceptions. To forget doubt, we had
> meanness and ruthlessness in killing, and a job to do and do well,
> that's all (p. 47) ... when you receive firm orders, promises of

long-term benefits, and you feel well backed up by colleagues, the wickedness of killing until your arms almost fall off is all one to you. (p. 235).

As we see, the background to the killing can be found in leadership and group phenomena, which transformed these ordinary young men into conscienceless murderers. They themselves are not conscious of this psychological and moral transformation while it is going on, and they can hardly see it afterwards, either, since their shame and guilt would be too great to handle.

Splitting and dilution of responsibility

Furthermore, the murderers in Rwanda seem to have undergone an obvious splitting (compare the analysis of men who abuse women in Chapter Eight), which allows them to feel less responsible for their actions: "… it is as if I had let another individual take on my living appearance, and the habits of my heart, without a single pang in my soul …. Therefore I alone do not recognize myself in that man" (p. 48).

Education and supposed maturity did not seem to play any role during the persecutions: "A priest, a burgomaster, the subprefect, a doctor— they all killed with their own hands … these well-educated people were calm …" (p. 68). Conscience, the decision, and the responsibility were left to someone else: "When you have been prepared the right way by the radio and the official advice, you obey more easily …" (p. 71).

> Killing is very discouraging if you yourself must decide to do it, even to an animal. But if you must obey the orders of the authorities, if you have been properly prepared … if you can see that the killing will be total and without catastrophic consequences for yourself, you feel soothed and reassured.
>
> (p. 49)

As in the case of the murderers in the Nazi concentration camps during the Holocaust, the murderers in Rwanda also seem to have had the ability to divide their existence into "work" and "home": "He [the woman's husband] left the blades outside. He no longer showed the slightest temper anymore in the house, he spoke of the Good Lord …" (p. 110).

Since the Tutsis were regarded as dangerous cockroaches or as animals that only pretended to be human beings, they had to be exterminated wherever they were: "We were forbidden to choose among men and women, babies and oldsters—everyone had to be slaughtered by the end ... anyone who lowers his machete because of somebody he knows, he is spoiling the willingness of his colleagues" (p. 120). It was thus especially important for the men to kill people whom they knew in order to show that they understood the radical goals.

Process of becoming a psychopath

Hatzfeld has the impression that these murderers never permit themselves to be overwhelmed by anything. They are more worried about their own fate and, strictly speaking, feel no pity for anyone other than themselves. They appear to be blocked off and egocentric: "I think my sleep will recover a normal restfulness when I regain my liberty and the life I used to have" (p. 159).

Some disturbing memories come up sometimes, but only because what happened really stood out even in the murderer's perverted existence, like the memory of Tutsis who were burned alive. "I had not foreseen that this memory would work at me so viciously. I'll never forget it ... I believe it is because of the smell of the burns ... I believe it is unnatural for men to kill men with fire" (p. 158).

The murderers speak of the need to be forgiven, not of being able to put themselves in the victims' shoes. Their thoughts about forgiveness seem extremely shallow. In contrast, forgiveness is a subject that the survivors hardly ever mention. They speak instead of justice.

Social psychologists use the concept "just world-phenomenon" to describe an authoritarian view of the world, according to which there is a just cause behind everything that happens. This concept also helps us to understand something about how the passiveness of the spectators seems to legitimize the murders: "... we thought deep down they were fated to die, here and now, all together. We thought that since this job was meeting no opposition, it was because it really had to be done" (p. 231).

The process of becoming a murderer corresponds to the process described by James Waller (compare Chapter Six). The boys and the men have become psychopaths by way of their actions, that is to say they have lost their capacity for guilt, empathy, and mutual relationships: "We put on our field clothes ... we made bets on our victims, spoke mockingly of cut girls, squabbled foolishly over looted grain ... we traded stories about desperate Tutsi tricks, we made fun of every 'Mercy!' cried by someone who'd been hunted down ..." (p. 244). Perhaps they had a certain degree of predisposition to become this way, but their destructive acts seem overwhelmingly to be the force behind the changes. According to Hatzfeld, they seem to have been fairly normal youths before the genocide, perhaps with the exception of a few rotten apples. Notably, they believe themselves to be unchanged afterwards.

Sociopsychological theories

James Waller has also contributed theories that can be used to analyse the background of genocide. We shall now go through and comment upon the factors that Waller underscores as important for understanding the background of genocide and connect them to the events in Rwanda. Certain factors uphold the culture of cruelty that is gradually built up, he points out. Many of the factors are dependent upon the dynamics of the group to a great extent and are frequently used by manipulative leaders as a way of achieving the participation of the general population in primitive revenge acts.

Cultural belief systems and trust in authorities

Sociopsychological research shows how religious systems of belief often increase the tendencies towards prejudice in a society, despite the fact that they are said to include the message of love. People in such societal systems often react passively towards authoritarian orders instead of redefining the situation according to their own values. Rwanda is a Christianized country through and through and consists of Catholics and Protestants, but in spite of the message of love, religion had no curbing effect whatsoever on the murdering. On the contrary, priests murdered in the name of religion.

We can find blind trust in authority in most of the cultures where genocide has been committed. In Rwanda, obedience to authority is considered essential. Power is admired. A Rwandan lawyer says: "You take a poor, uneducated farm worker, give him a weapon and say: This is your weapon. Kill! He's going to obey."

Moral change

Moral change is a process whereby certain individuals are gradually placed outside the application of moral norms through:

a. Moral legitimacy, whereby the individual sees himself as threatened, a victim, or a potential victim. Some form of moral imperative is used in all genocides: religious, ideological, economical, or segregational and nationalistic. "We must defend ourselves."
b. Euphemistic descriptions of evil actions. Language mystifies and redefines cruelties. "Bush clearing", "tea party", "dance", and "birthday party" were expressions used in Rwanda, while similar concepts in Nazi Germany were "final solution", "special treatment", and "evacuation". The perpetrators can also avail themselves of passive de-personalized terminology, such as cleansing or cleaning, which creates a psychologically secure area that is dissociative, denying, and distanced.
c. Excuse-making comparisons. The perpetrators compare their deeds with alleged cruelties towards themselves. "The others do much worse things!" In Rwanda, the Tutsis and the RPF were demonized by Hutus out of fear of losing their own social dominance.

The moral change is also not so attention-catching in the beginning, but it is a necessary ingredient in the changed view of human relationships that we find in large-group regression, from horizontal equality to a vertical power hierarchy.

Rational self-interest

Rational self-interest refers to a phenomenon whereby the individual will do whatever favours his own position. We can distinguish between (a) professional self-interest, as when the rank-and-file soldiers identify themselves with and desire to have the appreciation of the militia leaders. In Rwanda, the perpetrators felt pride over having participated in an "action", to have overcome their resistance towards killing, and shame if they had not done so; (b) personal self-interest. The perpetrators have a typical compensatory falsely heightened feeling of self-esteem, as a consequence of earlier humiliations, which spills over into rage whenever someone challenges it.

Professional socialization

Professional socialization means that people learn to murder through: (a) escalating involvement. Individuals who are hesitant gradually go further and further in their actions as perpetrators. After they take the first step, the psychological and social pressure on them to continue becomes stronger. In Rwanda, the first step was to terrorize and the second, to kill. Feelings of guilt came to be projected onto the victims; (b) ritual behaviour, which means military formations, marches, meaningless physical training, as well as forcing the victims to strip naked and tormenting, then murdering, them. This behaviour strengthens the culture of cruelty; (c) repression of the conscience, which has a desensitizing effect. Brutalization is not a cause but rather an effect of the behaviour. Inhibitions disappear or can even lead to excitement and perverse pleasure.

Effect of the group's cohesiveness

The cohesiveness of the group means:

a. Dilution of responsibility—the larger the group is, the smaller the personal responsibility becomes. In addition, fragmentation and segmentation of the task of killing take place. In such a manner, the perpetrators retain a feeling of moral responsibility for their own areas only. Through the process of distancing, people kill "during work hours" and carry on their family life during their leisure time. Their conscience is diluted and turned over to anonymous leaders. It was first when the perpetrators were placed in re-education camps after the end of the genocide in Rwanda that many understood the extent of what they had done and were shocked.

b. De-individuation, which means that the group changes its appearance before it goes into operation. They use masks, paint their faces, cut their hair, drug themselves, rant and rave, and therewith let go of their personal values. During the trials after the genocide in Rwanda, the perpetrators had a hard time explaining why they went along with such evil actions and preferred not to mention the worst crimes: "someone else did that". When the group identity has been dissolved, the individual does not recognize that he has committed crimes.

c. Conformity in the face of group pressure—friendship, "comradeship", and dependence on others in the group make it difficult for an individual on his own to refuse to participate in the killing.

Some concluding reflections

While we work ourselves into a culture of cruelty, it does the same to us. We tend to integrate the outer and the inner, what we do and what we are. The less force there is to make us join in the first place, the more we see the activity as a part of ourselves. Initial acts that bring about limited damage result in psychological changes that make it possible to go on carrying out destructive acts. We could see this process as a negative working through in contrast to the constructive transformational effect that we wish to achieve through psychotherapeutic working through. People who go through destructive changes as a result of their actions would probably take up the same actions again if the situation allowed it. The weak confessions in Rwanda are similar to those given by former Nazis in Germany. This pseudonormal personality (Igra, in Böhm, 1993) retains a compartmentalized destructive part of himself that can be released in street fights, football hooliganism, acts of terror, or acts of genocide.

Negative destructive behaviour manifests itself most easily if there is a minority group that can be identified and seen as a separate entity and upon whom projections can be directed. First, the members of the minority group are deprived of their identity and then they are excluded from the community. Dehumanization through language usage usually precedes genocide: cockroaches or insects, "they, them", "and all of a sudden they were gone". The more the victim can be dehumanized, the greater is the cruelty.

The destructive group projects its own feelings of weakness upon the other group and therewith removes these feelings from its members. The result is a mental impoverishment with more muted feelings towards others. The end goal is a "pure utopia", where all that is shameful is projected onto the others, who should then be cleansed out. Revenge is a part of this shifting of evil to the other.

What is it that makes spectators into resisters, alternatively accomplices, in relation to the perpetrators? Research on spectators shows that all of us—regardless of personality and background—are influenced by being together with others (Staub, 2003). This makes for a situation in which we as individuals have a responsibility the entire time for making conscious moral choices.

This general aspect is underscored by several authors, such as Igra, Waller, and Arendt: it is all of us, not just the pathological others, who have a choice between cruelty and caring. It is as though cruelty and caring are competing for the same space inside us and certain factors cause us to choose the one or the other.

Staub emphasizes how individuals develop tendencies to disparage others through actions or—to the contrary—to care about others, to care about the ones who are strange or different, something he calls "inclusive caring" (Staub, 2000). The individual's relationship to his own group is also of significance. A blind patriot who follows his group regardless of the issue makes choices in a different way from a constructive patriot with a self-critical distance to his own group.

Staub speaks of the pro-social value direction that characterizes a constructive patriot who dares to take the step of helping others with responsibility and empathy. The blind patriot, on the other hand, has an embedded self, according to Staub. He finds himself blindly in the self of the group, while the constructive patriot has a more coherent or autonomous self with a capacity for distance towards his own group. Staub's reasoning seems to have connections to Volkan's reasoning concerning large group identity and the capacity for taking a critical position towards one's own group in cases of large group regression.

In interviews with men who have abused women close to them, we found several unhealed childhood traumas that did not seem to have been mentally represented or emotionally experienced in the present, but instead were expressed as a destructive splitting that found an outlet in acts of revenge. The Hutus in Rwanda, who lived under the Tutsis' regime for long periods of time, can also have experienced this unhealed humiliation, which was converted to vengefulness. This vengefulness was further intensified through the long-term hate propaganda against Tutsis.

Large group regression, which developed after years of dictatorship and was manipulated by the leaders in Rwanda, led to even more regressively blind trust. The guilt that can be felt for the cruelties that were committed is primarily of the persecutory type. The enticements towards simplification and the needs for purity are powerful. The perpetrators in Rwanda harboured a utopian conviction that they could completely root out all the evil parts of themselves, such as envy, rivalry, negative self-images, traditional hatred, and feelings of inferiority—all they had to do was to project it all on to the enemy.

We see verticalization of relationships as a primary concept in the interplay between an authoritarian society and the individuals in it. The regressive society avails itself of a destructive ideology, whereupon the individual responds with splitting and dissociation concerning all sorts of imagined dangers or real humiliations. The projective processes contribute to destructivity by creating prejudices—"They're the ones— not me—who are dangerous!"

PART II

RESTORATION

CHAPTER TEN

Refraining from revenge

*R*efraining from revenge starts with a person's own resistance, which in the best case scenario can transcend into a mental realm of reflection— a dialogue, as we see in the example of Jean. We also illustrate how this dialogue expresses itself in psychotherapy. The goal now is to break the spiral of revenge and achieve restoration.

"It's amazing that they had such mercy on us. That shouldn't even be possible."
Alphonse, one of the Hutus who took part in the massacre in Rwanda, after his prison release

(Hatzfeld, 2009, p. 16)

We will now return to Jean, the youth whom we cited in the book's foreword. Jean experienced the unbearably painful loss of having his entire family obliterated during the Rwandan genocide, after which he lived on the streets until he received help from pediatric surgeon Dr Alfred Jahn, who provided a place for him to live and arranged for him to attend school. At the time of our first conversation with Jean in

2003, he has lived with Dr Jahn for a couple of months. He is dressed in a scruffy t-shirt with cut-off sleeves and he looks grim and edgy, almost a little dangerous, with his piercing gaze and powerful voice. His face is twisted in anger, and he holds his hand up in front of him in a demonstrative gesture, as if he wants to show his fighting spirit: his zeal to take revenge. However, at the end of the same interview, he suddenly looks considerably more relaxed and says:

> When I still was in that place [the street], I met a special lady who liked me and she took me to a place for people who pray. She even gave me some plastic bags to sell so that I could get a little money to live on. She was so happy when she met me recently and found out that I am now going to school and studying. I no longer think the way I used to because those who are dead can't come back to this life that we're living in. I just hope for a better future with a wife and children. I'll tell them about everything I have gone through.

When Jean is interviewed a second time the following year, he has lived with Jahn a little over a year. The particular day on which the interview takes place is 7 April, a day of commemoration, exactly ten years after the start of the genocide. Jean is wearing a beautiful multicoloured African shirt. He is calm and serious. He does not look at all dangerous. He has a friendly smile and looks the interviewer in the eye when he speaks. He is holding a blue cap in his hands, which he balances on his fingertips (during the interview of the previous year, he had had his fingertips pressed against his forehead). Ever since he has had the chance to live at the doctor's, "things have developed in a good way". What he thinks about most is school. "In this world there's a lot to do in the future", he says. His dream is to get to work at a hospital, "I hope to become a doctor." "And I want to work for my country", he adds. Jean's ability to accept both the kind lady's thoughtfulness and the doctor's help make things look bright and hopeful for him.

The concluding chapters of this book are devoted entirely to counter-weights against taking revenge. We describe in more detail the difference between, on the one hand, the temptation to take revenge and, on the other, the clearly acceptable need to find restoration and justice. Many people's spontaneous reaction to the idea of refraining from revenge is to call it cowardice. The importance of retaliating for a humiliation or a violation, and thus regaining control over the situation and strengthening one's self-esteem, is often viewed as unquestionable. The person who does not take revenge can be accused of "failing to stand up for himself". Many might ask why he should shy away from a fast counter-attack, which they see as something that would restore the balance.

The question, though, is whether or not the opposite is actually true. Is it not an act of over-simplification and cowardice to insist upon retaliation? We would argue that it instead shows strength to be able to refrain from retaliation. You become the one who breaks the spiral of revenge and who shows that you can do other things to strengthen your own integrity. Granted, you are forced to reflect on what you ultimately want to achieve—perhaps it is restoration, which in the best-case scenario also means respect and empathy for the other person's situation. This can require a great degree of courage. Someone has to start. The central ingredient, which runs like a red thread through this entire part of our book, is thus the ability to maintain your own sensitivity and empathy for other people's situations. Furthermore, we would even go so far as to assert that this ability is the prerequisite for all resistance to oppression.

Newspaper coverage of heinous acts of violence where children have been tormented and murdered gives us detailed descriptions of reactions by family members. Some parents cannot rest until the perpetrator gets the "right" punishment, meaning a long prison term (or the death penalty in some countries?). Other parents focus more on the possibility of spreading information about the criminal act in schools. Perhaps they can help prevent similar crimes in the future? They might deal with their severe feelings of loss by setting up a fund for antiviolence lectures in schools. By doing so, they also keep the memory of their loved one and of what happened alive in a constructive manner.

In the first part, we also presented a model for the spiral of revenge. The spiral showed which mechanisms trigger revenge as well as how a destructive spiral of physical and psychic violence between victim and perpetrator continues. We now want to complement our model with factors that can make us refrain from revenge. What are the forces inside an individual that can promote self-reflection and, by extension, an understanding for and dialogue with others? To explore this question, we discuss and use some of the different concepts that appear in the figure: space creation, mentalization, and dialogue/horizontal relations.

Space creation

Psychic trauma, the *perforation* of the individual's psychic shield, has been described as a prerequisite for understanding the revenge phenomenon (Kaplan, 2006, 2008). When there is a non-worked-through humiliation or loss, with unhealed wounds, there is a risk that we resort to revenge acts in order to compensate for the working through and healing that have not taken place. Accordingly, we always need to keep a space open where we can reflect on our ongoing interactions with other people, something that has been emphasized by British psycho-analyst Donald Winnicott through his concept of the intermediate area (1971). It is described as a transition area between the little child and the mother, represented by, for example, a favourite blanket, a teddy bear, the child's thumb. It creates a third area where play, thinking, and culture come into being.

Space creating is one of the author's, Suzanne Kaplan's, concept for the inner psychic process through which traumatized people try to keep threats at bay and create a space, a psychic space and/or a concrete, physical place, for thinking and taking action. In this "mental refuge", the individual can maintain a connection with important people and with events in the past and even plan for the future.

Through space creation, people in situations of war and genocide can create, despite a minimum of resources, a glimpse of a life-affirm-ing experience. Interviews with survivors of the Holocaust show how thoughts around events and meaningful objects in their lives were interwoven and made it possible for them to uphold a sense of their own existence and personal integrity (Kaplan, 2008).

Edith, a Jewish child, fantasized about a tree that she saw far away through a little hole in the wall of the freight car that was transport-ing her to a concentration camp. Alice remembered her father's lullabies when she played with the light that seeped in through a twig hole in the shed where she was being hidden. The children could thus remove themselves mentally from their terrifying situation and for a brief moment feel alive.

By accentuating these moments of fantasizing, we can get a feeling for how victims of cruel acts of revenge can use mental strategies to cre-ate links to inner pictures of meaningful people and events in order to keep the fear of being hurt or of dying at bay.

Mentalization

We mentioned Winnicott's concept of the intermediate area in the pre-ceding section. You could say that we develop our ability to reflect via the intermediate area, which has received a kindred concept in Fonagy's work on *mentalization* (Fonagy, Gergely, Jurist & Target, 2002). In the analysis of the violent men in Chapter Eight, we mentioned how British psychoanalyst and researcher Peter Fonagy (2005) has brought this concept to light in a fascinating way. Mentalization can be defined as "a form of mainly preconscious fantasy-marked mental activity, namely to understand people's actions in terms of subjective, mental states" (Fonagy, 1999). This means to be able to empathize with people and to perceive them as separate from oneself, as people with their own inner spirits, their own opinions and motives for their actions.

In addition, Fonagy (Fonagy, Gergely, Jurist & Target, 2002: pp. 4–5) underscores:

> Affect regulation, the ability to regulate emotional states, is closely linked to mentalization inasmuch as it plays a fundamental role in the development of the feeling of a self … affect regulation is a precursor of mentalization.

The psychic phenomena that are described with the help of the mentalization concept are of major importance, we contend, in order for a person to refrain from taking revenge and instead to deal with his humiliation or loss in other ways. For example, if he is able to mentalize, he can handle strong feelings and not act them out in a destructive manner. To be able to feel, think, and fantasize about the hatred he feels and about how he might be able to achieve restoration is a significant step away from the readiness to live out the revenge urge. The ability to empathize with other people's perspectives is also an important quality.

An example of how training in the ability to mentalize can reduce conflicts comes to us from a school setting. Girls in elementary and middle school can have trouble playing with each other if there are three of them. Noisy conflicts easily arise when one of the girls wants her "best friend" all to herself. An elementary school teacher, who for obvious reasons had a hard time accommodating all of the children who suffered hurt feelings during recess, found a solution. She divided the children who had been involved in conflicts into pairs and put them in different corners of the classroom. The two members of each pair had to take turns telling each other how they had experienced what had happened in the schoolyard. The child who at a given moment was the listener "was forced" to see things from the other child's perspective and then they changed places. That was all there was to it. Each child in the conflict had been shown respect for her own view of the situation. In most cases, this was enough to dispel the tension—at least for the time being.

Dialogue and horizontal relationships

To be able to take an equal position in relation to other people is also an important condition for a constructive dialogue, restoration, and ultimately for the ability to refrain from acts of revenge and destructive violence. An example on a societal level is how the conflict between the African National Congress (ANC) and the Zulu-dominated Inkatha Freedom Party (IFP) in South Africa did not result in genocide when ANC won, since the parties probably saw each other as equals.

A vertical relationship is marked by the domination of one party over the other. The dominating party uses disparagement as a way to dominate. We saw examples of that in the chapter about violence against women. A horizontal relationship (Böhm, 2006b), on the other hand, is characterized by dialogue and give-and-take, where neither party finds himself or herself in a constant position of superiority or inferiority. Good and bad are integrated and acknowledged to exist in both parties. This type of relationship also provides a basis for self-reflection and self-criticism, and makes for an equal balance between the two parties. "The other party is just as valuable as I am and any conflict I might have with the other is open for re-negotiation."

We can illustrate the difference by looking at the world of sports. Cheering for my own team denotes constructive or playfully patriotic (nationalistic) feelings: "I like my own team the best." But if I express myself less playfully, I might say: "My team *is* best." This reminds us of what we previously described as envy-inspired disparagement of the other, put forth under the guise of neutral language! Then I have transformed my position to one of blind patriotism (nationalism) and I have a more closed mind.

Constructive open patriotism, on the other hand, can be described as the integrated position. The individual here has a tolerance for differences, ambiguities, and uncertainties in relation to other people. I understand that others also like their own team the most. Even if it is difficult for me to understand what the others like in their team, I can stand this uncertainty and imagine myself or put myself in their shoes. I can acknowledge that they must have their own reasons. In addition, there is a difference between my feeling for my own team and my proneness to express it through destructive acts against other teams.

In an "open" mental space, there is thus a basis for a horizontal relationship, which in turn is linked to *restoration*. By doing something that is good for myself—without hurting the other—I pull myself up from my inferior position to an equal level. By maintaining my respect for the humanity of the other, I refrain from exchanging my inferiority for a new superiority that would lead by extension to a revenge spiral. We would also like to remind the reader here of the grey zone between revenge and restoration, which we described in Chapter Three. Actions can be inaccurately designated as revenge when they actually revolve around various attempts at restoration for the most part. The party seeking restoration uses his assertiveness in a sublime, socially accepted, way to set limits and restore balance.

Revenge in clinical settings: psychotherapy

In psychotherapy, the patient gives form to his or her inner life with points of reference in current and earlier relationships. The temptation to take revenge becomes clear, and at the same time, it becomes possible to work through the revenge urge and give it space in words instead of in actions.

A woman talks during a psychotherapy session about how her boyfriend didn't call her the evening before, which he had promised to do. She says that if that was the way he was going to be, she absolutely didn't intend to call him either. The therapist suggests after a while that the woman seems to want to retaliate in order to avoid facing how she really feels and to avoid having to talk to her boyfriend about her disappointment. The woman agrees and then takes up her general doubt that anyone would have enough interest in her to listen to how sad she is about feeling invisible.

Even children can end up with such difficulties under certain periods of their lives that they need help from someone on the outside, someone who does not belong to the family or who is not in any other way a part of the child's everyday life. It is important that the analyst/therapist is indeed someone whom the child does not know. It is only then that the child feels completely secure and can express his or her anger and take up what is experienced as the problem without having to worry about hurting someone else or getting another form of bad reaction. This often happens without words at first. The analyst, the room, and everything in it become an arena for the child, who through play and imagination can put form to what is happening on the inside. The task of the analyst is to be an attentive, accepting receiver—like a container—for everything that the child is sharing, and later be able to translate these observations into words that are meaningful for the child.

Martin has a stomachache and comes to the clinic. He plays with plastic figures on the couch and gives them a little push so that they fall from the edge to the floor with a bang. Some of the figures land at the feet of the therapist. Martin repeats the sequence triumphantly over and over again, session after session. Suddenly one day, he talks about the boys who scare him in the schoolyard. He wants to get back at them! The plastic figures and the therapist's feet get a taste of his anger. With the help of the therapist, Martin can start putting words to his feelings towards the boys and formulate possible solutions to the threatening situation.

Challenges for the therapist

In psychotherapy, there are many examples of situations that play out between the patient and the therapist that could be characterized as revenge-related:

> The therapist is going to a funeral and needs to cancel a session. When the time for the next session arrives, the patient cannot get out of a meeting at work. Subconsciously he is retaliating for the therapist's previous absence.
>
> The patient has felt betrayed earlier in his life and retaliates by not trusting the therapist.
>
> The patient has felt abandoned and abandons others—quits therapy before the sessions are completed.
>
> The patient thinks that the therapist does not give him enough time. He says that an acquaintance of his heard a lecture by the therapist and thought it was worthless.

In psychotherapeutic contexts, revenge can thus take the form of the patient's putting brakes on or sabotaging the treatment. One patient can become passive in order to express his discomfort with the therapist's advantaged position, while another patient can sabotage the treatment in order to take revenge on a parent who wants the treatment to succeed.

Therapists can take their own revenge by making exaggeratedly aggressive comments to the patient, by keeping silent too much of the time, or by forgetting until the last minute to give notice about summer breaks. Certain interventions can take on a particularly vengeful undertone, as when the therapist repeatedly points out the patient's need to control him or her—something the therapist should instead try to understand and work through in what is termed his own countertransference.

A nineteen-year-old boy, Robert, has problems with separation and closeness and is unclear about his sexual identity. He grew up in an all-too-close relationship with his single, suicide-threatening mother and goes to psychoanalysis to get help. He feels rejected at the end of the therapy sessions and during the weekend breaks he thinks about ways he could inflict harm upon himself. On the subway on the way to analysis, he feels paranoid. He thinks that people can see how horrible he is—that he has sexual fantasies and impulses to attack any person crossing his path. He is scared to death about losing control. He is sure that the analyst will see how horrible he is and repudiate him. He arrives later and later for his Monday appointments and lets the analyst wait and feel repudiated the way he himself feels repudiated and excluded during the weekends. He sees suicide as the ultimate way to abandon the analyst instead of being abandoned himself. Gradually, Robert is able to see that his wish to attack the analyst just bounds back on him (Laufer & Laufer, 1989).

The interaction between the therapist and the patient is often seen as an expression of envy and rivalry, but the obvious revenge aspect is often missed. Sometimes this revenge aspect is hidden by a begrudging stance: "What you have to offer isn't worth anything anyway, so I don't need to take revenge on you; instead it's enough that I look down on you." In this way, a "sour grapes" attitude functions as protection against too strong a feeling of envy, and as a brake against an outward act of revenge.

Envy towards the therapist can even take expression as the patient's feeling worse despite the fact that crucial questions are being dealt with, as when the patient ends the session by saying: "Today's session has been worthless for me." This so-called negative therapeutic reaction becomes a way of expressing envy towards the therapist's ability to help and at the same time blocks the patient's wish to take revenge. Through such behaviour the patient is often telling the therapist, without being aware of it, what he has been through or experienced in his life. In this way, the patient's behaviour can provide important clues to his emotional history.

The therapist is faced with several problems. Durham (2000) contends that the repressed-exploited patient (compare Chapter Two) will feel used by the therapist, while the vengeful patient will feel that the therapist want to take revenge. The process of freeing oneself from vengefulness in both cases, though, goes through grief work, where the patient must leave the sweet, exhilarating, frightening, or addictive revenge urge behind him. Grief is a matter of having the strength to realize the nature of one's past and to let go of the defensive attitudes that have resulted from a difficult childhood. What, among other things, makes this process harder is the outpouring of shame that the patient will inevitably face over having been exploited and forced to endure evil without being able to defend himself, which by some is described as feeling tainted.

CHAPTER ELEVEN

Surviving psychic trauma

A Rwandan boy pointed to his chest and said: In my heart there will always be sorrow and anger. I will not be able to reconcile myself with what happened but I accept it.

A woman who was a child during the Holocaust said: I showered for hours ... but I couldn't wash those feelings away.

The liberation after genocide probably belongs to the most painful period, paradoxical as that may seem. It is no longer possible to deny reality. The inevitable moment of reckoning has arrived. People can no longer cherish the hope that missing persons in their families will return. Their closest relatives are no longer alive. Their sense of loneliness is overwhelming (Kaplan, 2008). How is it possible for people who have experienced traumas in war and genocide to bear their wounds and perhaps their hatred and, optimally, to free themselves of them? How is it possible for them to get on with their lives and tolerate the affects that are invading their psyche?

Coming to terms with devastating experiences

We meet a Rwandan woman who is in a deep depression. She tries to imagine how her future will be, considering that the perpetrators are among her neighbours in Rwanda. She says: "To open the window in the morning and see the people who murdered my family ...". She touches the back of her hand and continues: "I feel like I have open wounds ... the wounds in my skin that had just closed ... are opening up again. I don't know how I am going to react ... now I have the power to do something."

It takes time for wounds to heal, to heal enough to make it possible to resist feelings of revenge. Needless to say, it is especially challenging for the victim's affect tolerance if she has to have the perpetrators as neighbours (Kaplan, 2008). At the same time, it is important to remember "Whoever broods on revenge keeps his wounds open" (Bacon, 1625). The individual wrestles with two opposing forces: healing/reconciliation versus wounds/revenge.

For Holocaust survivors, revenge can take on more concealed and sublimated, and thereby more socially accepted, forms, such as refusing to buy German goods. Jacob, a Polish Jew, witnessed how a German was beaten up by the allies in the final phase of the Holocaust. In a radio interview, he comments on the incident and says that it made him feel all warm inside. Samuel is a Norwegian Jew who survived Auschwitz and was one of the extremely few survivors who returned to Norway in 1945 after the war. Suzanne Kaplan met him in 2005, and he told her:

> I arrived in Oslo on the 30th of May. I was driven to the prison where Quisling, the Norwegian Nazi leader, sat in a cell. The guard didn't have the key. He opened the food hatch and I peered in. Quisling sat on his cot. Didn't look up. I said nothing. He said nothing. I felt no hatred, no revenge—I was just happy that I was a free man and that he sat in a cell.

The persons in these examples do not give any open expression to revenge fantasies of their own, but they show an obvious satisfaction in seeing the tables turned.

A Rwandan boy tells us what triggers his traumatic memories most strongly. It is the sight of two boys fighting, with the one boy on top of the other, something he accentuates through words and body movements. Based on his traumatic memory fragments, perhaps he identifies with the one in the bad position, while at the same time, in his imagination, he unconsciously puts himself in the advantaged position in order to retaliate. Both positions can be experienced as frightening, albeit in different ways.

People who have been forced to endure extreme traumatization often speak of feelings of shame, usually in an indirect way. Perhaps it does not matter—when it comes to certain aspects—whether someone is a perpetrator or a victim in a genocide. It is as though everyone has been contaminated by all the degrading and shameful acts. A Rwandan boy asks, "How do you Europeans see us? As some kind of crazy monsters?"

A person who has been traumatized also looks at himself in the same way as the other, the one who shamed him, looks at him. He takes on a self-image that resembles the other's image of him. In an interview study with psychotherapists concerning extreme trauma and shame (Klefbeck, 2004), it was shown that male refugees had a special problem with feelings of shame, which could lead to rage and take different forms of expression. In addition, these men were likely to provoke someone to violate them in order to have an outlet for their rage. It is conceivable that rage can temporarily fill a person's need for self-esteem. To immerse oneself in hatred and revenge can be seen as a way of generally postponing the mourning process that always follows in the footsteps of shame, humiliation, and rage.

Integration between psychoanalytical theories and the striving for restoration

We have referred to the feeling of shame in several instances, and we keep coming back to it. If we are neglected, rejected, or humiliated in our desires and curiosity, the basic feeling *shame* is born in us. This feeling can pass through a constructive development with phases of frustration and aggression and ultimately to a healthy assertiveness and protectiveness of our own integrity and needs. However, in contrast to the anger that is meant to lead to survival, aggression can be perverted into hatred and conscious, systematic destructivity, many examples of which we have seen in this book. The aim in those cases is obliteration or absolute power over the other/the perpetrator through acts of revenge, a futile project in which hatred breeds hatred and revenge does not alleviate the destructive rage (Rössel, 2005). Psychoanalyst Robert Rössel has held lectures to elucidate the theme of shame, using the works of

Nathanson and others as a starting point. He says, in short, that we in general can take four different positions towards shame: we can withdraw into an embarrassed feeling of worthlessness; we can direct the scorn inward and make common cause with the perpetrator; we can conceal and overcompensate our sense of shame; and finally, we can attack others and make a big point of their worthlessness at the same time as our own is masked. He further emphasizes that the naming of basic affective reaction patterns in the therapy relationship and the explanation of their function and significance in the here-and-now situation constitute the best way of helping the individual patient resolve his issues with shame.

Repressed painful experiences become most threatening when traumatic events in his family or in his immediate circle force the individual to split his ego, that is to say, dissociate, and, through identification with the aggressor, conceal from himself a part of the pain he has experienced (Fonagy, 1998). As shown in the previous chapter, the possibility of surviving psychic injury/humiliation and of refraining from acts of revenge increases if there is *support* for the development of a mental space. To be sure, afflicted individuals also need to make use of a certain splitting of feelings as a defence in order to continue functioning with the help of an undamaged part of themselves while they repress the damaged part. Nevertheless, there still needs to be a certain degree of connection between the parts. This gives the individual a chance to take a pause in his emotional chaos and reflect instead of acting out the impulse to retaliate.

In the history of psychoanalysis, we find documentation of the analysand's so-called negative therapeutic reaction in some cases, meaning his or her symptoms are worsened despite or maybe because of a genuine understanding on the part of the psychoanalyst. Applying our concepts, we could say that the analysand targets his revenge on the analyst by "not getting better". True, the analyst has a genuine understanding of the analysand's problems, but he does not understand how he himself is seen in the transference relationship. The analyst does not always perceive that he is thus re-traumatizing the analysand. This lack of insight can occur because of his desire to help the analysand, a desire that makes it difficult for the analyst to see simultaneously that he is actually being perceived as a negatively charged person. A well-known such case was Freud's patient Dora (Freud, 1905). She broke off analysis because Freud was unable to understand quickly enough that Dora saw him in transference in the same light as her uncle who had betrayed her trust. When Dora breaks off her analysis, she saves herself from re-traumatization, but at the same time also directs an act of revenge towards Freud by quitting, a form of communicative revenge. Klein (1975) has emphasized the role of envy when analysands compare themselves to their analysts along with the humiliation that comes in the wake of feeling inferior. However, she also emphasizes how important it is for the analyst to comprehend his or her role in negative transference in order not to fall into a trap whereby he or she is a helper who paradoxically re-traumatizes his or her patient.

In traditional psychoanalytical terms, the dynamic of revenge can be seen as an unconscious projection of the experienced trauma. Unconsciously, one wants to shift the trauma to the other person so that it can become undone in oneself. It is as though history is being rewound and the trauma has not happened because it has been placed over on the other person. We can also see similarities with the concept of narcissistic rage (Kohut, 2009a, 2009b), which refers to the rage that is experienced after a violation. We have previously described the shame reaction that is a part of this rage via Rössel (2005) and Nathanson (1994). One of the directions that the reaction may take is an attack on the person who has caused the humiliation, which corresponds to an act of revenge. Narcissistic rage is perhaps much more general than described by Kohut when he took up this phenomenon in primarily narcissistically disturbed people. Some people unleash their rage in actions without applying many brakes to speak of, while others are better at controlling their rage. Most probably, the patient needs to express this rage in words as a way of moving beyond the humiliation that was behind the rage. Narcissistic rage can thus be seen as a necessary step in the healing process whereby revenge fantasies are expressed and acts of revenge are avoided.

It is conceivable that successful psychotherapy, physical recovery, reparative justice, and an eventual reconciliation operate in a mutually enriching manner and bring about lasting security. These factors do not keep the flames of violence burning but instead transform them. People might suppose that hatred, revenge, and retaliation will bring them relief, but this is never the case (Weingarten, 2003).

Comprehensive research work concerning the series of traumas that children were forced to endure during the Holocaust was carried out by Keilson (1992) in the 1970s, but only in more recent years has this study received international attention. His results point out the great significance that care received after the war has had for the child's recovery, a finding that also gives hope. A good "approach" in the meeting with the traumatized, the confirmation of his or her feelings, facilitates recovery. The mental space is broadened when new thoughts break the compulsive repetition.

Trauma linking and generational linking

In the following, we present two directions that the psychic process can take for traumatized people (directions that can be discovered, for example, during a talk with a therapist or other helper): trauma linking and generational linking, concepts that have been developed in work with survivors of genocide. These concepts are described by means of Kaplan's model the "affect propeller" (2006) and are discussed at length in the book *Children in Genocide: Extreme Traumatization and Affect Regulation* (2008).

Trauma linking is the inner psychological consequence of perforation (persecution, humiliation, and violence) and means that traumatic experiences are "easily awakened" associatively during a discussion of the individual's own life story and in conjunction with events in everyday life.

Generational linking is the result of successful psychic space creating and means that the traumatized individual in discussion has his or her attention directed towards significant positive persons and things in the past and in the present and that there are associative connections between these objects. This process strengthens the feeling of living in a context and can be seen as an aspect of recovery. A good "approach" in the meeting with the traumatized (as described above), meaning that his or her feelings are confirmed, facilitates generational linking. The mental space is broadened and takes the place of a rigid repetition.

The two tendencies, trauma linking and generational linking, respectively, can dominate in different phases of life and during one and the same discussion. To say "yes" when asked to recount one's life history during an interview or a therapeutic discussion can be seen as an aspect of generational linking, for example. The individual is exposed to the risk of becoming emotionally stirred up and perhaps feeling anxiety and pain when recounting traumatic experiences (Kaplan, 2006, 2008).

The urge to live a normal life, to leave one's survivor identity behind, is strong, however, which can mean at the same time that the individual's creativity comes to the surface more and more. The individual says when interviewed that he or she *can feel freer in relation to the past* during these moments. We can say that the trauma no longer exists on the side only, enclosed in a part of the self, but is to a certain extent also incorporated in a time perspective in the individual's own life course. However, in extreme repeated traumas, the person can sometimes feel that it is only possible to live a good life in the present. As one of the surviving women in Rwanda expressed it after her wedding: "Thanks to my marriage, life does seem good now, but only if I just think of right now. Because, you know, I see that my future is already ruined by what I was forced to endure" (Hatzfeld, 2009).

The *affect propeller* (Kaplan, 2006, 2008)—a schematic illustration of the complexity and the variation in affect regulation in traumatized individuals, from revenge to restoration—can give us a picture of how quickly feelings shift. The propeller's blades represent variations in the two types of linking presented above. They rotate and at times overlap in a way similar to the fluctuation of feelings. They thereby also show the different directions that revenge can take. The hope is that trauma-linking processes, with their accompanying temptations to take revenge, will gradually be "covered over" by generational-linking processes—the latter then becoming the *dominating links*. At that stage, the individual feels a greater wholeness of being, has achieved restoration, and has regained his or her dignity, and therefore does not have the urgency to take revenge.

Listening to the narrative of the traumatized

How are we affected by the life histories of the victims and the perpetrators? As we have emphasized, the life histories concern extreme traumas and, especially when it comes to genocide, situations that we normally cannot imagine ourselves experiencing, "unimaginable primitive affects" (Grubrich-Simitis, 1984). Even so, as listeners, we can try to be as present as possible in order to gain an idea of what the person has been forced to endure. In this manner, we serve as witnesses to their painful experiences.

Our own vulnerability comes to the fore most evidently if our listening in some way touches us personally. In a way, survivors of the Holocaust can provide a special type of support to the Rwandan survivors and can have a special understanding of their situation. They can make good suggestions for actions that can alleviate pain. For example, they can point to the importance of memorial sites and memorial days. Afflicted help other afflicted, and the dynamic is most likely the same within other supportive endeavours, such as organizations through which formerly abused women help abused women and former alcoholics help alcoholics.

However, there is also a risk that people with a background of their own unworked-through traumas are drawn to this type of support work and try to use it as a way of coming out on the other side of their own difficulties. Instead of having a helpful dialogue, the two who are working together are more likely to find that their common mental space is shrinking. The one's narrative triggers the other's, and a situation of catharsis may possibly arise. In that case, there might be a feeling of temporary relief, but a re-traumatization is most likely on the way.

The international project USC Shoah Foundation Institute for Visual History and Education aims to document narratives by survivors of the Holocaust. Part of Suzanne Kaplan's task as the coordinator in Sweden was to arrive at a suitable matching between interviewers and interviewees (Kaplan, 2002, 2008). Interestingly enough, she did not find a consistent answer to the question of whether the survivor wanted an older or a younger, a Jewish or a non-Jewish, a female or a male interviewer. For example, it was not necessarily so that an elderly female survivor wanted to talk to an older Jewish female interviewer. All possible combinations of requests were found. It is not always the people who on the surface seem to resemble the traumatized individual the most who are the best listeners. The particular needs of every individual must be taken into account.

There are many people who at some time in their life will listen to another person tell about his or her traumatic experiences. The listener may be an interested and empathetic fellow human being, a good friend or a neighbour, a teacher or a colleague, a policeman or another person employed at one of society's institutions, as, for example, a trauma therapist.

A special challenge for the listener is to be attentive to expressions of emotion when the words are not there. In addition, the listener needs to be the one who stands for hope, who shows that life can be different. The trauma therapist must do these things as well as be able to "contain" the afflicted in a professional way, be a model for affect tolerance, and show that it is possible to bear strong feelings without breaking apart. No, the person will not break apart, even if it feels that way. He or she can thus begin to feel less helpless and gain more control over existence.

Vicarious trauma

In more recent years, awareness has grown regarding the stresses and strains to which trauma therapists are exposed. It is essential for a therapist to have colleagues with whom they can share their thoughts. There are obvious risks involved in working with traumatized people during too long a period of time without being mindful of one's own vulnerability and fatigue (Gentry, Baggerly & Baranowsky, 2004). Advisory sessions with more experienced therapists can be essential for noting early signals of so-called *vicarious trauma* (Kihlbom, 2004).

Vicarious trauma means that the patient's trauma is turned into a trauma for the therapist. Secondary traumatic stress refers to the effect that trauma has on the therapist as well as upon the patient's relatives and friends. This stress is also called *compassion fatigue*. Remaining in an empathetic relationship with the traumatized patient thus brings about a special strain. The difficulties stem from the daily flow of several heavy transferences that the therapist must be able to bear. Many therapists have lacked concepts for these painful phenomena. They need, but have not always had, practical experiences of how to approach a patient who seeks help for severe traumas and a support team that can contribute with an understanding of the nature of the therapist's role in the therapeutic process (Figley, in Pearlman & Saakvitne, 1995).

The trauma therapist runs specific countertransference risks, since they might develop either a feeling of omnipotence as a defence against helplessness or an identification with the patient's rage and sorrow (Herman, in ibid.). The therapist might either be elusive or over-identify with the patient.

At the same time, the therapist's countertransference is a significant source of information. To take note of the relational space between the patient and the therapist also means that we take a look at the therapist's own history, feelings, values, defences, and unconscious processes. In this context, we can ask ourselves what similarities and differences, respectively, between the therapist and the patient mean for the therapeutic process, for eventual over-identification, which can obstruct the therapist's empathy as well as the patient's working-through process.

Interview with a trauma therapist

Suzanne Kaplan (K) interviewed a trauma therapist, Wretling (TT) (interview, 2005) concerning his work with his patients, who are refugees living in Sweden. The trauma therapist says that what he finds hardest to bear as a helper are the acts of perpetrators, meaning atrocities that have been committed in reality as well as murderous impulses in everyday life. The acts are associated with a black-or-white mindset that can characterize patients with unprocessed traumas in their past.

TT: A man who comes to mind had been severely, and I mean severely, abused by his mother. His image of a mother figure has nothing whatsoever good about it. There is no cherishing, no forgiving, no understanding within him. If I guide him back to his past, situations emerge most of the time that precede his experiences in prison. In these situations he is being forced to endure something terrible or he is abandoned and he is often in physical pain. Most of these situations were brought about by his parents. It is extremely difficult to help someone who has been forced to endure a great deal of evil. Perhaps the difficulty also lies in our notion, our notion meaning the therapist's, the helper's notion, of the extent of evil. Remember, these people have been forced to endure atrocities, yet we still base our therapeutic process on the belief that there is also some good, that it is possible to do something reparative. And then we get close to a person who has not seen the good, does not have a sense that the good exists, and we see that reparation work is not relevant. What we have to do instead is build up something new, which has to be done in mid-life or perhaps even later, when there are also the problems of exile to take into consideration. In such cases it is extremely common that these patients split up reality and are either subjected to aggressive impulses again or perpetrate such impulses on others. Human contact is extremely difficult for these patients. It is tricky for them to be a good parent, in the event that they have even succeeded in becoming a parent in the first place. They have extreme difficulties finding a place in our society, including employment and the like. There can be elements in their narratives that make me distance myself from them emotionally as well.

K: Such as?

TT: Well, primarily everything having to do with a black-or-white mindset. Yes, that's it …. I think of the man I just mentioned. His basic idea is that all women are of lesser intelligence. The challenge for me was to keep from drowning in that myself … to be able to come back with something that encourages him to reflect over his own thoughts on this issue instead of just saying laconically, "That's just the way it is." But when you feel like you're up against a brick wall the whole time, it is easy to take another position and either distance yourself from the material or drown in it.

K: If you are bombarded with comments like that, if comments like that fill the session, what is your next step?

TT: It is indescribably difficult to find a process in all that hopelessness, to find a maturity that makes it possible to begin to see nuances in this massive block of negativity. Ultimately we should find a process that helps the patient relate in another way to things that happen in his or her life.

K: You told us about subtle acts of revenge, for example the episode with the daughter at school. I remember that we spoke in terms of revenge.

TT: Yes, but the issue in that situation is … the patient has a history of violence during his own school years, that is, corporal punishment by the teacher during a period of time in an authoritarian school system. Things went so far that he knocked the teacher down and was subsequently punished for it. He was put in prison and was beaten—not systematically tortured but beaten. The patient was around 13 or 14 years old at the time. And then we fast forward 25 years and here is his daughter encountering serious problems in school in Sweden. She has learning problems. She also feels frozen out by her schoolmates. He communicates to me a rage and a desire to retaliate—to attack the teachers in the Swedish school who make his daughter suffer.

K: What happens to you when you hear him say things like that?

TT: My task is to be receptive and to cope with it in the moment. My task is perhaps not to get him to pause and reconsider; no, that is a later step. But it is all too rare that we get to that later step and instead we are stuck in this position of hatred. It is hard to get to the next level, the level at which the hatred can be guided back to the patient and he is open to finding some constructive component in this situation with his daughter.

K: So in many instances you become the bearer of your patients' hatred? What does this mean for you right there where you are working? Can you sense what you need when you leave your room after the session?

TT: I must remind myself that these are experiences of reality that people are exposing to me. This is the way the world looks for these people, and they can be violated in our society as well, no doubt about that.

K: Do your patients ever present you with revenge fantasies they are having in the here-and-now?

TT: Oh, yes, I might hear things like how they want to send a mail bomb to employees of the social services, immigration or housing authorities, for example. I also have to work on responding to these things in some form that is easier for the patient to handle. My adviser helps me to set limits. I also learn new things about the various techniques that I use—my *geist* comes back as do my curiosity and my interest in the issues I work with. When we are many colleagues, there are more chances for us to help each other hold evil in check. When I am in the room with my patient I am alone with it. I might feel overpowered and not be able to hold on to my belief in the good. So that's why colleagues are crucial and it helps to know they're out there. The most difficult are the inhuman losses, inhuman behaviour. To be forced to endure things that no human being should ever be forced to endure—I mean these total breaches of everything we human beings can reasonably be expected to need in life—of how we reasonably should expect to be treated so that we can feel all right. Needless to say, everything that happens to people in prison has been set up on purpose to break them down. All forms of systematic torture have become more and more refined through the ages in order to break down individuals, I know all that but still to hear about it—it is nonetheless placed in a context—it is exercised by a state, it is there to fill a purpose, so it is possible to relate to it professionally. What is extra difficult is to hear how these individuals, in addition to being violated by a state, have been treated with just about the same methods by people who should have been on their side.

Reflections around the interview with the trauma therapist

The interview made us take particular note of the therapist's emphasis on the special difficulty when it comes to working with traumatized patients who have had prison and torture experiences. The inhuman treatment that these people have been forced to endure constituted a repetition of attachment traumas (they had been subjected to violence within their families that led to a special vulnerability). Those who "feel the worst"—or, more accurately, have had a harder time coping with torture and imprisonment—are those who, while in prison, have re-experienced difficult childhood experiences involving their family or others close to them.

Are attachment traumas the result of authoritarian systems in certain countries? Do these result in traumas being carried over from one generation to the next, with traumatized young parents who abuse their children? And in that case, how can we work with such profound disturbances?

Work with tortured and traumatized individuals who have come as refugees to Sweden places heavy demands on flexibility when it comes to the role of the therapist—an oscillation between process-directed psychotherapy and supportive help, which includes practical measures to assist the patient. The therapist role challenges one's own values. It is hard to determine when the therapist becomes a pure projection target for the patient's revenge fantasies versus when the therapist becomes drawn into the patient's revenge fantasies and perhaps unconsciously sees them as justified.

CHAPTER TWELVE

Stopping the revenge spiral

*I*n order to prevent the act of revenge or to stop it from developing into a revenge spiral, people who can provide counterbalances are needed. They can be individual helpers and rescuers or ordinary people who show civil courage and do not remain passive spectators of violence. In this chapter, we want to inspire resistance by giving examples of such helpers and of initiatives that can help prevent or stop various types of violence, all the way from violence in the home and on the street to genocide.

Passionate humanitarians, rescuers, and helpers

During the twentieth and twenty-first centuries, we have learned about a number of people and organizations that have shown civil courage and an impressive involvement, and have thus counteracted hate and revenge. Their actions usually start as private initiatives and sometimes become institutionalized in later stages.

Social worker Irena Sendler smuggled 2,500 Jewish children out of the Warsaw ghetto, and Swedish diplomat Raoul Wallenberg saved Hungarian Jews from the Holocaust. Organizations such as Amnesty, Save the Children, Doctors without Borders, and international groups against torture are other examples of forces for the good. The list is long and encouraging, although, at the same time, the well-documented strength of the destructive forces in the world is almost paralysing. The passionate humanitarians with whom we ourselves have come into contact, however, show us the possibility and the importance of individual resistance against hatred and potential revenge.

Alfred Jahn's example

"The meaning of life, in my opinion, is being there for other people, to show caring, and in doing so you get everything you need for yourself in return." This is what Alfred Jahn, whom we met in Rwanda, says to us. He grew up in the former East Germany. As a child, he had experienced the bombings of Dresden. He became a paediatrician, and was for 19 years the chief paediatrician at a clinic for children in Landshut. His social involvement led to his going to work in Vietnam in 1967, first on a hospital ship and later on land. Between 1978 and 1982, he worked in refugee camps and at 22 different hospitals in Thailand. At first, he used his vacations for this work, but eventually he resigned his chief's position in Germany. Following the genocide in Rwanda, a doctor was sought who could help build up the completely non-existent paediatric surgery capabilities and relieve the children's great suffering. Jahn was the only one who answered the ad for this position in the medical journal *The Lancet*. He is probably still the most qualified paediatric surgeon in Rwanda, even though he is currently giving further training to his colleagues on site.

The large number of begging and orphaned street children led him to acquire a house in 2002, to which he moved with seven boys. He provided for them and helped them with their schooling. Since then, the operation has grown to include 55 boys in 2009, all of whom go to school and take care of themselves. There are no additional personnel. Some of the older boys are employed as night watchmen and cooks, but aside from that, the boys manage everything on their own. They know that their survival and their home with Dr Jahn are contingent upon their doing well in school and cooperating with each other. The boys who can meet these demands have most likely had a good emotional start in life.

Jahn is a father figure for these boys, who in some cases lived on the street for several years following the genocide and became used to more or less running wild. He therefore also has to solve many conflicts, prevent violent showdowns, look for boys who run away, put demands on the boys in terms of school, and talk to downhearted boys who miss their families and have a hard time visualizing any future whatsoever—and all this while the country is in constant crisis mode.

He also helps them mentalize, since many of them, through the loss of people to whom they were attached, have lost that ability. He becomes in this way a new attachment person for them during their adolescence. He says he does not want to do anything else, even though he soon will be 70 years old and sometimes feels tired and discouraged. In addition, he has his work at the children's hospital during the day. All the same, the work is more rewarding than anything else he can imagine. He also cooperates through e-mail and regular mail with other organizations throughout the world that take care of street children, and this communication replenishes his energy (Kaplan & Eckstein, 2004).

Conductor Barenboim

In 2006, Israeli conductor Daniel Barenboim led a Palestinian youth orchestra as the members performed a concert in Ramallah (Schüllerqvist, 2006). He says in an interview:

> It's amazing to see what you can achieve by playing music together—when you're playing your own part and at the same time listening to the others. It's willpower that determines the outcome—no conductor in the world can make an orchestra play better than its members want to ... when you play together you cease being an Israeli or a Palestinian, music is universal.

Barenboim describes the horizontal relationship in musical terms, where the desire to play together makes every individual musician take care of his own task while listening to every other musician with respect. Consequently, in 2008, he toured with a Palestinian–Israeli orchestra.

Retired social worker Emerich Roth

> *You should not make more of them than they are.*
>
> *Passiveness makes you and me accomplices in the crimes against humanity that are committed around us all the time, even in our everyday lives.*

(Roth, 2005b)

Emerich Roth is a former a concentration camp prisoner who has spent a great part of his life trying to convert young men who have ended up in Nazi groups (Roth, 2005a). However, he never calls them "Nazis". He might say "so-called Nazis" or "so-called racists". He calls them instead "haters". They are members of criminal and violent gangs, but to give them a political or ideological label is to assign them a significance that they do not have or deserve, he argues. They are really just boys who have grown up under difficult family circumstances and without good male role models. The girls usually have a more behind-the-scenes role in the gangs, and often are sexually exploited (for example, in motorcycle gangs).

It is important to reach youths before they establish themselves in destructive groups. "In the beginning, logic, politics and ideology never have anything to do with it", and it is therefore futile to discuss or argue with a person who is full of hatred. The choice for these youths is between being an unloved nobody or belonging to a gang.

When Roth travels around, lectures, and gives guidance in schools, he often brings along "former baddest boys", as he calls them. They have similar backgrounds and many have been violated themselves. Roth has helped them move away from their hatred and their need to get revenge for all the wrong that has been done to them. To use our terminology, he has helped them develop a reflecting mental space, where they can find self-respect.

Roth is extremely critical of the way the media describe these youths as a threat. There are about 1,000 or so active so-called Nazis in Sweden. "But the rest of us, we're nine million. Turn your back on them and don't keep writing about evildoers all the time. Write about all the other youths who are doing good things." (Roth, 2005b).

The helper's background

How can it be that some people become helpers or rescuers? Emerich Roth, whose work we described in the previous section, is a good example. Virtually his entire family was obliterated by Hitler. He himself could have become a hater. It took him a long time to become a normal person after the camps, but he gives credit to the love he felt in childhood, which helped him choose a new path in life.

How do some people dare to become rescuers even in situations where they must have huge amounts of courage and must go against other people in their own group? In Rwanda, for example, it was extremely risky to go against the perpetrators. All members of the political opposition were executed within the first 48 hours of the genocide. Moderate Hutus were also executed, at least 50,000, during the genocide. Those who did not partake in the murders could be threatened with murder themselves. To maintain an open space for thinking (the capacity for self-reflection and for empathy with other groups) cannot have been easy, especially not in such a hierarchical society, which is built on obedience to authority and orthodox Christian religiosity. There was little room left to be a constructive patriot with pro-social values and a capacity for distancing oneself from one's own group.

However, there are people in every situation who have inner mental counterbalances, without seeing themselves as deep thinkers or exceptional in any way. There were Hutus who saved Tutsi families while risking their own lives. They expressed themselves in the same way as rescuers all over the world have done in similar situations: "We just couldn't do anything else."

In the literature, these rescuers are often described as having a pantopic identity. What is meant by pantopic is that they always have the ability to put themselves in the other group's situation. They often have to distance themselves from their own group. In Nazi Germany, some of the helpers and rescuers belonged to marginalized groups. They had another religion, had recently moved into the community, or had a parent born in a different country.

Furthermore, many of these helpers came from families with strong moral and humanistic values and thus a strong aversion towards Nazism (London, Tec, Oliner & Oliner, in Staub, 2003). People with such backgrounds and convictions include even a stranger in their own group. They are what Staub refers to as pro-socially oriented and have a sense of personal responsibility for others, along with steadfast moral principles and empathy for the suffering of others.

Helpers have also been shown to have a strong belief in their own abilities. They are fearless and prepared to take risks. Some have a streak of adventurousness (London, in Staub, 2003). Raoul Wallenberg's adventurousness, for example, had already been documented during the periods he spent in the United States, Israel, and South Africa, that is, before he started his dangerous mission in Budapest (Böhm, 2004a).

Oskar Schindler—the subject of the film *Schindler's List* (1993)—seems to have lived, as did Wallenberg, on the margins during his childhood and was also adventurous in his opposition to the Nazis. Schindler cooperated with the Nazis and was allowed to take over a confiscated factory whereby he, by using Jewish slave labourers, increased his own wealth. At the same time, he took care to protect his slave labourers and to treat them humanely. Just as perpetrators evolve through their acts, so do helpers (Staub, 2003). They become good fanatics, so to say, who completely devote themselves to saving lives.

Significance of spectators

Spectators (so-called bystanders) of ongoing, gradually worsening persecutions of their fellow human beings have a great influence on the course of events (Böhm, 2006a). Perhaps we cannot expect bystanders to sacrifice their lives for others. Nonetheless, we can expect individuals, groups and nations to intervene at an early stage when they see a chain of events taking a turn towards destruction, especially if the danger to themselves is limited and it is still possible to stem the tide of destruction.

Bulgaria was allied with Nazi-Germany, but when the Bulgarian government tried to deport Jews, many important power bases of society protested: Orthodox bishops, physicians, doctors, and writers. In the end, the king intervened and stopped the deportations, so that 82 per cent of the Bulgarian Jews could survive the Holocaust. The Bulgarian example allows us to conclude that the German Nazis needed accomplices and passive bystanders in order to carry out their genocide.

Even so, individuals, groups, and nations are often passive. Individuals can be afraid of getting involved in something that is over their heads. On top of that, bystanders are often not aware of the great significance of their actions. Instead, they experience helplessness—"what can I do?" This, however, leads the perpetrators to see their actions as legitimate. When bystanders are passive in the face of the suffering of others, they themselves are transformed. They accept the persecution going on around them, and some even join the perpetrators (Böhm, 2006a). It is difficult to remain a passive bystander while others suffer and simultaneously continue to oppose the perpetrators or empathize with the victims.

Counteracting violence and bullying in school environments

If passive bystanders fail to provide positive counterbalances, the opposite is true of bystanders who react and function to counteract violence and to stop the spiral of revenge. An example from everyday life where the actions of bystanders matter greatly is the school environment. Studies in schools show a strong link between, on the one hand, the existence of passive bystanders and, on the other, the negative feelings and behaviour of bullied pupils and bullies. Active bystanders who intervene become fewer and further-between with increasing age, which means that older pupils get less help than younger ones from both teachers and other pupils. Perhaps we become more sensitive to public shame and have a greater fear of making a fool of ourselves as we get older. It then seems safer to avoid the situation altogether. Avoidance, unfortunately, sets the stage for primitive revenge mechanisms and traumas in the victims, who risk turning into new perpetrators.

As a positive alternative, research shows how the atmosphere and the relations between pupils in a school are influenced in a positive way when bystanders are active, when adults are on the alert for conflicts and do something about them (Böhm, 2006a). Teachers, classes, and the school as a whole, share the responsibility for creating and for maintaining a workplace where bullying is counteracted. In certain schools, researchers have, for example, set up role play, which was filmed and used as a basis for discussion. Through role play, the pupils could practice taking an active role in preventing and stopping bullying (Staub, 2003).

In the classroom, active bystanders can play an important role by talking to both perpetrators and victims. If a pupil says something derogatory to a fellow pupil, the other pupils can turn to the victim and say: "What he said was awful and it's wrong of him to say it. We're your friends" (Staub, 2003). It is not hard to imagine the effect this would have on the perpetrator, the victim, and the other bystanders. Such a supportive society could help its members develop positive values and moral courage—civil courage.

Counteracting violence against women

In Chapter Eight, we brought up the gender perspective on revenge by analysing violence against women and the revenge motives by which men are driven. We now want to return to this theme and show ways to stop this destructive violence in society. It is a myth that violence necessarily has to be repeated, or that nothing can be done about it. The suggestions we put forth to counteract violence against women are built on experiences from the Men's Center in Stockholm, a professionally run clinic for men with violence issues, and the Norwegian project Alternatives to Violence (ATV).

At the Men's Center in Stockholm, group and individual psychological treatment is given to men who have abused a female partner. The interventions are based on a non-pathologizing psychotherapy with a pro-feminist ideology in order to encompass both personal and cultural aspects of the men's violence. The best results, according to the Men's Center, are found in the self-help groups with a group leader, where there is particular emphasis on learning how to identify and deal with risky situations.

In group treatment, the men's ability to reflect on and contain strong feelings as well as to refrain from violence is strengthened:

- Deficiencies in the ability to mentalize and to work through feelings internally are replaced by a shared working-through process in the group, where each member together with the other members can see, hear about, and think about the problems common to them all.
- The frame of the group offers a symbolic area for mental work, which can be incorporated in the members.
- Verbalizing is favoured, as is venting about uncertainties. Integration and tolerance of conflicting feelings such as the urge for revenge are encouraged.
- Being able to rely on the Men's Center, the group, and the group leaders relieves the men of their childish dependence on their women and their need to control them, whereby the women can be allowed more freedom of movement.

Alternatives to Violence was started in Norway in 1987, inspired by Emerge in Boston, the first institute in the USA to work with violence in close relationships. Their treatment can be characterized as empathetically confrontational and psychodynamic. Violent men often seek help when they have been subjected to outside pressures, often after an ultimatum from the woman.

There is to date no evaluation of the treatments at the Men's Center or at Alternatives to Violence that fulfils all the necessary scientific criteria. However, there is clinical experience showing that most men can cease being violent if they get help in working through their issues. There is also agreement among staff on how to work with these men. The men themselves, people close to them, and the treatment staffs at the Men's Center in Stockholm and ATV have provided information from which we can discern several desired measures to reduce violence against women in our society:

Each jurisdiction should be able to offer treatment according to the models of the Men's Center in Stockholm and ATV, where individual treatment and group treatment are made readily available to men in need. Many jurisdictions still lack such resources.

Society through social services and other municipal departments should develop a course of action so that rapid intervention can take place whenever there is violence against women. The blindfolds that cover this taboo-laden area should be removed, as should any distance-creating "we and them" thinking. Otherwise, there is always the risk that people who know the couple in question become passive bystanders to violence against the woman.

Society needs to make sure that teachers, childcare givers, and other adults are attentive to children who grow up with violence and substance abuse in their families.

Schools need to be on the alert towards these children's behavioural tendencies, take up questions of gender equality in their presence, and offer empathetic adult contacts as a counterbalance to the children's destructive home environments.

Schools and other authorities dealing with children should encourage them—both boys and girls—to develop strategies for zero tolerance towards psychic and physical violence. Active groups against bullying need to be especially on the alert and stop verbally disparaging treatment and destructive attitudes towards girls—and boys.

Schools should create space for thinking about and discussing the stress that some individual pupils can have been forced to endure because of the conflicts that have occurred during the school day.

The way that glorification of violence and a value system promoting domination by some people and submission by others are presented in the media needs to be vigorously pinpointed and challenged in school contexts. Consumption of violent films most likely has a destructive influence on insecure boys and needs to be brought to light and questioned.

Programmes should be developed that emphasize men's positive assets and resources, where men's ability to protect is accentuated along with their power of resistance against violence. This can be done, for example, by showing parts of ATV's development programmes, such as video films, at schools and other public venues. One idea would be to create a kind of Bamse role model for men. (Bamse is a Swedish comic-book character. He is the world's strongest bear but always uses his strength for the sake of the good.)

Even stronger societal stances are needed, where ideological and legislative power bases show that they reject all forms of violence, control, and domination over women.

Preventing genocide through radio programmes

In previous chapters of this book, we have described the dreadful consequences of genocide in the former Yugoslavia, Nazi-Germany, and Rwanda. We would now like to showcase a couple of projects where people are working to prevent new genocide and societal conflict. In the radio project Radio Benevolencija (Staub, 2004), the potential of the media combined with grassroots activities is utilized. The project started as a private initiative by radio producer George Weiss in Sarajevo in the former Yugoslavia. Two types of radio programmes within this project are now being broadcast in Rwanda (adapted by Weiss and Staub): an ongoing educational drama, a type of "soap opera", two times a week, and a monthly fact-presentation programme (Staub, 2011). The target audience for the shows is the entire population, most of whom live in rural areas. The goal is to encourage local discussion groups and facilitate generational linking (Kaplan, 2008). Particular attention is directed towards vulnerable groups, such as women and households led by orphaned children.

In the drama series *Musekewaya*, listeners follow the inhabitants of two villages as they fight over a piece of land. The tension between the villages escalates with time; the groups spread rumors about each other and subject each other to violent attacks. The fact-presentation programme *Kuki* then addresses the themes that the drama series has brought to the fore.

In the programmes, people learn how to prevent violence, how to start a reconciliation process and how to help trauma victims. They are given a chance to see how genocide develops gradually in a continuum of destruction. The programmes also give information on genocides that have taken place in other areas of the world. Both ordinary people and decision-makers listen to the programmes, which are broadcast nationally via Radio Rwanda but also in neighbouring country Burundi through Radio Isanganario.

The grassroots activities entail workshops and discussion groups out in the villages and take up the same topics as the radio broadcasts. These activities thus strengthen the radio information. Listener groups spread throughout the entire country give feedback on these programmes. The discussion groups also give the radio show producers the opportunity of finding out whether their message has come across adequately to its recipients.

CHAPTER THIRTEEN

Restoration and reconciliation

*R*estoration—*from the perspective of the individual—is to set boundaries for one's own integrity and to protect one's own interests. Revenge can feel sweet in the short term but its thrust is to hurt the other and invariably even oneself, since the vengeful individual becomes ensnared in bitterness. Restoration, in contrast, is a way to regain one's own dignity. In a broader sense, restoration can also be part of a political struggle, which can perhaps counteract earlier feelings of loss or failure. The individual, by regaining his dignity, does something good for himself and for his own group. In this concluding chapter, we intend to show the possibilities and difficulties involved in seeking and obtaining restoration.*

Justice, reconciliation, and forgiveness

A striving for restoration can imply an ambition to obtain justice. Many who have experienced cruel assaults towards their own person or towards people close to them say that justice is important. But what does that mean and what exactly is the difference between justice and revenge?

In his autobiography *Justice—But Not Revenge!* (1989), Nazi pursuer and concentration camp survivor Simon Wiesenthal (1990) describes how he is seen as a crusader for justice by the world at large while his fellow Austrians have seen him as the merciless avenger. After the Second World War, Wiesenthal tried to track down the whereabouts of as many Nazis in hiding as possible in order to put them on trial for their participation in the genocide of the Jews. He had a sense early in life of the need for balance between guilt and atonement, probably as a result of his Jewish upbringing. According to the Jewish reconciliation concept, a guilty act cannot be forgiven but must instead be atoned for. The extent of the guilty act determines the atonement needed.

Wiesenthal seems to mean that a human being can only receive forgiveness from God (psychologically by means of his own inner working-through of his guilt feelings, we would say), while what he can possibly do in relation to other humans is atonement and reconciliation. Psychologically speaking, it would appear that Wiesenthal is describing his own survival guilt—why was he allowed to live when so many were murdered?—as a background for his crusade for justice. He is paying a price for the fact that he himself was allowed to survive. The extreme cruelties that Wiesenthal was forced to endure unavoidably give rise to revenge fantasies, but he has taken command over his revenge impulses. A time of lawlessness demands the establishment of laws, he argues, and writes that the need for revenge must be subjected to well-defined rules while the truth must be ascertained by the courts.

Wiesenthal's view shows that revenge and justice concern different levels of awareness, maturity, and judgement. The revenge impulse is one of many risky reactions to cruelty and injustices while the quest for justice is either a societal or personal response that keeps the seeker of justice from becoming like the perpetrator. The quest for justice is something more than sublimated revenge. It is a striving to reach moral and psychic maturity, restoration, and development; in other words, a force directed against the act of revenge. Revenge is thus something other than justice, the latter accomplished through a legal process, and in a broad sense based on a more neutral and dispassionate position. The basis for justice is the need to set boundaries and to restore balance.

In this context, it is interesting to consider that different countries have different legislation concerning "self-defence", or, what a person has the right to do if attacked. In certain countries, it is permissible to defend oneself with violence, even more violence than the attack involved, with the aim of stopping the attack. According to our view, the person defending themselves in such cases risks coming close to an act of revenge.

Acknowledgement

In the film *Min morfars mördare* (*My Grandfather's Murderer*), the Danish documentary film-maker Søren Fauli (2004) seeks out the Danish Nazi who murdered his grandfather in 1943, during the war. Fauli's mother was 13 years old when her father was shot, which has marked her for life, and consequently had an indelible effect on the grandchild as well. Fauli succeeds in tracking down the murderer in Germany. Sixty years after the murder, he finds a man who is old and ill and who says that he is sorry for the pain he has caused the family.

When the murderer asks for forgiveness, it brings about an untying of the "psychic knots" that Fauli has felt, completely apart from the legal process, which remains unresolved. Fauli explains that he gets his "own existence confirmed" through meeting the perpetrator. The perpetrator is "no longer a ghost but has become a human being". However, when his mother hears him speak about his meeting with the murderer and sees a video recording of it, she says that she still cannot forgive him, even though her anger, her need to get revenge, and even her hatred have subsided.

Ethics researcher Ann Heberlein, who published a doctoral thesis in 1995 about forgiveness, commented on the film when it was shown on Swedish television. She argues that forgiveness re-establishes the value of life for the person who has been violated. What the murderer said when he met Fauli also serves as the acknowledgement that is essential for Fauli's reconciliation with what has happened. The murder of his grandfather was a violation for Fauli, who has felt that he did not count as a fully worthy human being. When the murderer acknowledges his guilt in the presence of Fauli, his existence receives justification again. A dialogue has come into being, which makes it possible for reconciliation to take place.

Revenge disguised as other motives

Max Rodenbeck (2005) writes about the West's reaction to the terrorist attacks of recent years—how there has been a desire to strike back. These strategic over-reactions, Rodenbeck argues, miss their mark.

In addition, the establishment in the USA—the Bush administration at the time—blended in other motives, such as an opportunistic grab for glory, an exploitation of people's fear, the common urge to be men of action—and also revenge. As we now know, such unbridled political drives are often translated into despicable excesses by officers in charge as well as by ordinary soldiers.

We thus sometimes see people mixing together revenge with legal aspects or the concept of justice, as if it were possible to motivate a prison sentence or a court verdict on the grounds of revenge. Court verdicts have instead—as we see it—an individually related deterrent effect and function as reprimands adjusted to the nature of the crime or as a way of protecting society in the case of more serious crimes. Justice is a neutral way of maintaining order in a society and setting up a suitable means of atonement for the perpetrator, who is forced to keep his revenge impulses in check. Justice also gives psychic space for necessary reflection to everyone involved. However, when the law is transformed by certain regressive forces and emotional motives take over, the revenge impulse can come to the surface again and set the tone.

In 1953, Americans Julius Rosenberg and his wife Ethel were executed in the electric chair for their alleged spying and revealing of information to the Soviet Union on the US atom bomb. In the USA and other countries that have capital punishment, revenge mechanisms are unusually open and unadorned. While there were those who demonstrated for the Rosenbergs to be released, there were also those who demonstrated under the slogan that they should "fry and die". FBI chief J. Edgar Hoover, as well as the then Vice President Richard M. Nixon, said baldly that the Rosenbergs were rats that should be exterminated (Swedish Television, 2005).

Annika Östberg is a Swedish citizen who spent over 27 years in an American prison. In 2011, she was released from a Swedish prison to which she had been transferred. In 2005, when she received a rejection of her plea to have her sentence commuted, the daughters of the policeman who had been murdered 25 years earlier by Östberg's boyfriend were there in the criminal commission room. The daughters, now middle-aged, participated in the commission's proceedings by snuffling and screaming: "I hate you!" and "I want my dad back!" There was thus no space for reconciliation. Instead, grief was used as a vengeful weapon. There seemed to be a widespread notion among people who followed the case that revenge would have a healing effect, which reminds us of the expression "positive revenge". Sweden's Minister of

Justice at the time, Thomas Bodström, commented, "Their feelings are completely natural. But their desire for revenge should not be allowed to determine the punishment ... the punishments [here] are influenced by emotional factors such as how the family members carry out their grief process" (Persson, 2005).

Forgiveness—sufficient or insufficient?

It can be worth reminding ourselves that forgiveness is usually a one-way process, whereas reconciliation is reciprocal, meaning that both the perpetrator and the victim are involved.

In a discussion at the Stockholm International Forum (2002), Ludvig Igra argued that forgiveness as a concept is closer to magical thinking than is reconciliation. Forgiveness is a more childish process, he asserted, a magical gesture that is carried out so that the one who forgives does not need to lose the respect of the one who is forgiven, upon whom he is dependent. This calls for an altogether too insufficient degree of psychic work on the part of the perpetrator. There is no demand upon him to work through the painful truth of what he has done and therewith to accept the burden of guilt in full. Forgiveness requires no transformation in the victim and the perpetrator. It is, according to Igra, more ceremonial than transformational. It demands nothing of the perpetrator but rather, it is more accurate to say, offers him relief. Certain actions are unforgivable and they require acknowledgement in order to make reconciliation possible.

If reconciliation is not reached, the risk for revenge and violence increases. If the perpetrator shows remorse for what he has done—as in the case of the Danish murderer who asks for forgiveness—we can see this as an open acknowledgement, important for both the perpetrator and the victim. The opposite is true of the shameful negotiation offers that the perpetrators in Rwanda have come up with and that amount to an avoidance of psychic pain: I will confess on the condition that I will be pardoned.

Reconciliation in society

We will now raise our perspective and discuss reconciliation on the societal level. Studies show that war creates war. Countries in prolonged conflict fall into what some call a conflict trap—a vicious cycle with recurring war. What is needed, then, for such a society to be able to break a vicious cycle of conflicts and revenge-related violence? We will give examples of some important factors that have been suggested by different researchers.

During the first decade of the twenty-first century, the concept *reconciliation* has been given more and more attention by societal researchers as a method of preventing continued conflicts in war-stricken societies. The implication of the concept is the subject of ongoing discussion.

Reconciliation is commonly considered to embrace a transformation of a relationship that goes beyond merely making it possible for the parties to co-exist. Reconciliation is preferably seen as a healing of traumas. Individual reconciliation is in this respect a precondition for national reconciliation. It is acknowledged that this process takes time, most likely several generations. The process entails building up broken relationships again and being able to exist together to form a lasting peace. The principles for the work are—justice, truth, acknowledgement, dialogue, acceptance of feelings, forgiveness, satisfaction of basic human needs, and social equality.

Peace and conflict researcher Karen Brounéus (2008) has arrived at the following definition after an extensive survey of the literature:

> Reconciliation is a societal process that means mutual acknowledgement of earlier suffering and a change of destructive attitudes and behavior into constructive relationships toward a lasting peace.

That reconciliation calls for an attitude change has to do with what Israeli social psychologist David Bar-Tai describes as the *conflict ethos*, which means that the people involved regard ongoing social conflicts as a normal state of affairs. The nature of the conflict ethos makes it reminiscent of the unquestioned vertical relationships that we have previously taken up. It also has points of correspondence with the elements that according to Volkan (see Chapter Five) characterize big group repression: the conviction on the part of each group member that he is right, a sense of security in this conviction, a positive self-image, a victim identity, a de-legitimizing of the opponent, patriotism, and unity (Bar-Tal, 1998). The conflict ethos is solidified in the population during long-term conflicts, in contrast to the *peace ethos* that is needed in order to reach a lasting peace (Bar-Tal, 2000).

Various studies show that the attitudes of the population seem to be changed as soon as a peace treaty is signed. Thereafter, they continue to be changed by other factors (Brounéus, 2008). Bar-Tal (2000) has made a compilation of the societal phenomena that facilitate reconciliation, create a peace ethos, and help to prevent acts of revenge:

- formal apologies from leaders
- truth and reconciliation commissions
- public trials (for example, the war tribunal in The Hague)
- economic compensation to victims
- a shared historical narrative
- education
- engagement on the part of the mass media
- reports from meetings between people from both sides
- work of individual organizations
- cooperative projects between former parties in the conflict
- tourism
- cultural exchanges

Social healing and reconstruction

Other researchers have also studied what is required in order for a society to reach reconciliation after having been devastated by brutal violence. In their book with the singularly telling title *My Neighbor, My Enemy* and the subtitle *Justice and Community in the Aftermath of Mass Atrocity*, Stover and Weinstein (2004) discuss the reconstruction of countries after ethnic cleansing and genocide. Their points of departure are Rwanda and the former Yugoslavia. How can survivors of wars with strong elements of ethnic hatred build up their lives again? How long does it take to re-establish trust among neighbours who have been torn apart by violence in their very neighbourhoods? How can people put an end to the revenge spiral and return to a "normal life"?

Stover and Weinstein argue that international and local trials have almost no relevance for the part of the reconciliation process that concerns the re-establishment of trust between ethnic groups: social healing. They point out that trials, to be sure, lead to the punishment of the guilty, but that this is not sufficient for the people. Those living in the society involved have a broader idea about justice than that held by international organizations. Nor is the relationship between trauma and trial outcomes, when it comes to healing, entirely clear.

Similar conclusions are apparent in a series of studies of daily life in the former Yugoslavia with a focus on preconditions for reconciliation (Corkalo et al., in ibid.). *The sense of having been betrayed*, and therewith violated, was found to be the greatest obstacle in the social healing process. People now expressed harsh criticism towards their former friends for not warning them about what would happen.

Reconstruction—of both the physical environment and social life—is essential for societal reconstruction. The faster the crumbled houses can be built up again, the faster the people who fled can move back.

It is also important to be quick about restoring buildings and other structures that have strong symbolic value. An example is the several-hundred-year-old bridge in Mostar, Stari Most, which was destroyed in 1993. The bridge has been described as a masterpiece and a unique symbol for an undivided city. To destroy the bridge was thus regarded as a brutal attack on a multicultural, richly historical heritage and on an important link between the inhabitants. For example, there was a long tradition of arranging diving contests from the bridge.

After the war, a great desire was expressed to get the bridge into good enough condition to resume the contests. The general idea was that everyone would be eligible: the criterion for participation on the bridge would not be nationality. One man commented, "What matters is that you're brave enough to dive. Everything else is irrelevant."

International aid organizations have been criticized many times for the fact that it took so long to get the bridge ready. We can, of course, see this prolonged time period as a symbol for the long and drawn-out course of the reconciliation process. Whatever the case, it is not possible to rush societal reconstruction. That life is to become "normal" again does not mean that it will be as before. After an ethnic cleansing, it is utterly impossible for the society involved to return to the way it was before. The inhabitants must find forms for co-existence at their own pace. It is necessary for the majority to accept the changes and thus they must be gradual. All changes can be reflected in small gestures, as for example in the way greetings are expressed. On the whole, the physical renovation has gone faster than the societal.

New patterns in a new generation

An important factor for future development, as observed by several researchers, is how members of the young, new generation, who have not experienced the time before the atrocities, take in new normative patterns that differ from the values of the earlier generations. In countries that have experienced ethnic cleansing, it is therefore within the school system that structural changes should be possible to carry out to great advantage.

The inhabitants of Mostar and Vukovar face a tough challenge in this respect. Nowhere in these cities is the ethnic division more obvious than in the schools. Both schools and classrooms are divided "along ethnical lines". Since this division has been carried out so thoroughly, children do not have any natural social interaction outside of school time, either. It is easy to think that pupil segregation has especially dire consequences since it instils a "we/they way of thinking" into the members of the new generation, who in their turn have not experienced and thus have not integrated a previous co-existence that they can pass on to the next generation.

It is all too easy for the education system to get stuck between, on the one hand, a programme that underscores the children's ethnic identities and, on the other, hand integrative models that do indeed facilitate societal recovery and reconciliation but that at the same time question the rights of the identity groups. If the denial of different identities is too strong, a backlash can occur whereby groups once again feel the urge to strengthen their own identities to the detriment of others'; such a state of affairs sparks the flames of new conflicts.

During the genocide in Rwanda in 1994, school buildings and infrastructure were totally destroyed. At least 75 per cent of the teachers were murdered or are now in prison. The difficulty and gravity of making a decision about which historical narrative to convey cannot be overemphasized (Freedman, Kambanda, in ibid.). The way in which memory, history, myths, and symbols are used can lead people to develop an identity that either aggravates the conflicts between groups or, to the contrary, helps to bring these groups closer to each other.

Fairly soon after the RPF took power in Rwanda in July of 1994, Rwanda's Ministry of Education declared a moratorium on history teaching in the schools. The goal was to have time to achieve unity concerning which history should be taught. Distorted, collective memories had been used earlier to construct identities built on division and differentiation. It was now clear that social identities could also be constructed for the opposite purpose, by emphasizing what people have in common and what encourages them to cooperate and join together over ethnic boundaries.

Several projects aiming to look over the teaching of history in Rwandan schools have been started in collaboration with non-profit organizations. These projects have included the development of a syllabus on human rights, symposia on possible ways to teach the subject of history and instruction for teachers on local societal issues. Despite these good initiatives, neither new textbooks nor new material for teachers had been published in Rwanda as late as 2004. Granted, most schools had been rebuilt but serious infrastructure problems remained. The discussion of ethnicity in Rwanda is extremely complex since the government officially denies the existence of ethnic groups. Denials and attempts to sweep possibly remaining conflicts under the rug increase the risk that repressed feelings will come to the surface again, as pointed out above.

Good treatment for trauma

In trouble spots all over the world, there are millions of victims of brutal violence. To prevent the escalation of revenge spirals in the world, we therefore also need high-level knowledge on the effects of psychic trauma and on ways of taking care of the victims of violence.

During the most recent decades, the continent of Africa has been torn apart by inner conflicts and revolts. In 2003, 18 of Africa's 53 countries were either involved in or on the way out of armed conflicts. The psychological traumas that African children and youths have suffered have different backgrounds and characteristics. A group that has been afflicted in an exceptionally violent way is composed of child soldiers, who in many cases have been brutally snatched from their homes and forced to participate in acts of war (Kaplan, 2005). In addition, children in war-torn countries are often direct or indirect victims of violence and/or witness to different forms of cruelty connected with war. The revenge potential—the urge to retaliate for injustices—is obvious.

A problem for afflicted children in many African countries is that the parents do not appear to talk to them about their emotional reactions to traumas. The children for the most part are excluded from the grieving process. The younger children might be taken to their relatives' homes and in an indirect way take part in the grieving process. Teenagers, who spend most of their time with each other, receive no such indirect opportunity. They are expected to act as adults—a huge demand to make on them after extreme traumatization—and no one discusses feelings with them (The Traumatic Stress Newsletter, 2004). Other studies from war-torn countries also show that teenagers suffer more than many others. A study in Cape Town shows that preschool boys and teenaged girls suffered most after an attack of political violence in their neighbourhood (Dawes, Tredoux & Feinstein, 1989). The children in-between, the ones between the ages of ten and twelve, are considered too young to understand feelings of sorrow and loss.

During the first decade of the twenty-first century, UNICEF, USAID, and many private voluntary organizations such as Save the Children have developed different types of psychosocial programmes to help children who have been afflicted by war situations. During the most recent years, different models have been tested for re-integrating vulnerable children, where consideration has also been given to the children's special psychological situation. Many of the reports on these efforts show the importance of integrating the local traditional healing processes with methods in Western psychotherapy (Kaplan, 2005).

In several African countries, such as Mozambique, traditional healing methods are used to relieve the afflicted of their trauma. Clothes worn by child soldiers are burned or the young people are bathed in the sea in order to help them break with their past (ibid.). Traditional healing rituals, such as cleansing, bring together several symbolic implications that aim to cut off the individual's links with the past (the war). This means, in turn, that the past is transformed to oblivion. At the same time, a space is created where the afflicted can talk about the traumatic events and speak about their nightmares. In this manner, the rituals can concur with Western methods that emphasize giving the torment a name. The most fundamental requirements for recovery in the long term are a linking of the individual to social and economic networks as well as cultural institutions and an atmosphere of respect for human rights (Bracken, Giller & Summerfield, 1995).

There are other concepts that are used to define the path to well-functioning, peaceful societies. One such concept is to *sensitivize* people, which is done in Rwanda to reach reconciliation, reunion, integration, or re-socialization. When experts from outside Africa advise local trauma experts without having knowledge of the cultural context, they can run into problems. In contrast, informative lectures on the origin of genocide, the psychological implications of trauma, paths towards healing and prevention of future violence can be highly successful, as has been documented in Rwanda (Pearlman, 2004).

Even so, the therapeutic methods in Africa are in a very early stage of development. A great deal of research is needed to determine which Western methods—developed originally to treat Europeans and Americans—would be appropriate and effective for work with children in Africa. For example, the therapeutic techniques commonly used in the West centre upon the individual, rather than upon the extended family or the village community, which could be a more meaningful approach in many African countries.

It is vital to gain a deeper understanding within this research field, to find out which knowledge gaps exist and which further research is necessary. Children who have been afflicted by war must not be stigmatized as chronically damaged. Models to prevent violence in schools also have high priority in the psychosocial programmes that the aid organizations carry out. In this context, violence against girls demands special attention.

The truth shall make us free?—Back to Rwanda

In the introduction, we explained that Rwanda was the starting point for our study on revenge. Now, as part of our concluding section, we would like to return to a discussion of the reconciliation process in Rwanda. First, some words about truth commissions are in order.

During the second half of the twentieth century, many countries were transformed from repressive, totalitarian regimes into democracies (Pagnier, 2004). Every new regime must deal with its violent history and create a peaceful future that makes some sort of reconciliation possible. There is no magic formula that works in all situations. The possibilities are limited by political, economic and military realities.

However, there is a broad agreement among researchers about the connections between justice, truth, and reconciliation; agreement that justice requires fair and impartial courts; that the truth about committed crimes helps society to go forward; that reconciliation requires openness about all crimes that have been committed by both parties in a conflict (Brounéus, 2008).

In Europe, the Nuremberg trials were created to condemn the perpetrators of the Holocaust. Ever since the first internationally known truth commission began its work in Argentina in 1984, the number of similar commissions has grown throughout the world. In Latin America, commissions have been created to investigate crimes against human rights. In South Africa, there is the Truth and Reconciliation

Commission, which has received a great deal of attention. In Rwanda, Gacaca has been established (ibid.).

Gacaca

Pancrace, a pardoned Hutu, says: "I have been accused, I have been condemned, I have been pardoned. I have not asked to be forgiven. It is futile to ask for a forgiveness that no one can give" (in Hatzfeld, 2009).

In 1998, the new government in Rwanda brought the old village courts, Gacaca, back into function (Pagnier, 2004). A decision was made to try cases related to genocide in a system that was based on the old tradition. In 2000, a Gacaca law was passed.

All crimes of genocide 1990–1994 were to be tried within Gacaca and the legal process was to involve the entire Rwandan society. With thousands of newly established village courts in smaller geographical units, it would be possible to try the more than 120,000 persons suspected of genocide. Thousands of judges and other personnel received accelerated training to prepare them for these courts. In eight different phases, the officials go through who has died in a certain province, who still lives there, who has disappeared, what people have seen and heard about those killed and what they have seen and heard about who killed them.

These commissions have been regarded as instruments of reconciliation and even if they have met under tense circumstances and have resulted in conflicting statements, they nevertheless do not seem to have had a detrimental effect on people's security and human rights (Brounéus, 2008).

In Rwanda, the handling of history is especially important because of the large numbers of victims and perpetrators. The difficulties are also considerable. The government in Rwanda also insists that there cannot be any reconciliation without justice. When anthropologist Jet Pagnier asked people in Rwanda what was needed in order to make reconciliation possible, she almost always got the same answer, "The guilty ones must tell the truth and ask for forgiveness and the victims must forgive them"; "Truth will heal the wounds"; "Justice will heal the wounds". They speak of the importance of reconciliation; that Hutus and Tutsis must be able to live as neighbours again in the same country. Gacaca is meant to function as a support for the regular judicial system and bring an end to a culture where people have been able to go unpunished.

However, when all of these mass murderers get out of prison and stand face to face with their victims, the process risks falling out of the boiling pot and into the fire (Berg, 2001). Documentation and research concerning the development and consequences of Gacaca are ongoing (de Jonge, 2002). One finding is that inhabitants have been enthusiastic about the procedures at the outset but that their interest has faded with the passing of time. The forced nature of participation in Gacaca is another problem, as is the need for the laymen judges, whose training was so accelerated, to receive further education. The fear on the part of the survivors of having their traumas reawakened is also an obstacle.

The need for trauma treatment for both survivors and perpetrators coincides with the need for careful documentation, since the events have a great historical value for memory and for reconciliation. Gacaca has been created because people want to have closure in relation to the past, but at the same time Gacaca has meant that the past has been brought to life again. In the best case, the people's courts result in a working through that lessens the risk for re-traumatization in individuals taken as individuals. When these courts are considered, both their possibilities and their limitations must be taken into account. The authoritarian nature of the system must be reckoned with when the value of Gacaca is assessed. Pagnier describes how shocked she was when she heard the prosecutor, a moderate and sensible man, exhort the participants in Gacaca to respect authorities and obey them at all times. When we ourselves were given an opportunity to listen to some Gacaca proceedings, the participants were urged to conduct themselves in an especially exemplary way this time: "You must remember to conduct yourselves properly, because today we are being visited by white people."

Pagnier studied the Gacaca process within a limited geographical area. Every area is characterized by its own special circumstances. Nonetheless, murderers and victims everywhere, in every hill and valley of Rwanda, are going to need to live side by side. They pass each other on the roads, they stop for a beer at the same bars and their children go to the same schools. Pagnier highlights the importance of looking at how people's daily lives are organized in order to understand the preconditions for the reconciliation process. The individual experiences of the Rwandan genocide differ from the official picture. What people remember and come back to when the official picture is peeled away is the collective insanity that transforms people into ruthless murderers. The private individual does not recognize the descriptions in academic treatises that are rooted in "cause–effect"—as though the acts of atrocity were comprehensible.

The fragmented narratives in Rwanda are reminiscent of the accounts given by the survivors of the Holocaust and by those caught in the break-up of the former Yugoslavia (Kaplan, 2008; Kirmayer, in Pagnier, 2004). The accounts, at times minutely precise, often concern external matters, such as the weather, and omit details about the actual killing (van der Port, in Pagnier, 2004). The most atrocious acts and experiences are not mentioned. Pagnier wonders whether this has to do with the degree of education of the afflicted or the cautious interview technique: "Do I have the right to ask?" Most likely, it has to do with the shock and the nature of the memory function. When there is no psychic space for dealing with experiences, the sensory impressions they have made are stored in their place.

René Lemarchand (2004), a genocide researcher in Belgium, writes about the problematical nature of throwing out the definitions of Tutsis and Hutus and instead calling everyone Rwandans. For example, the crime "divisionism" has been added to the penal code. Lemarchand questions whether the forbidding of ethnic memories can actually contribute to mutual trust and peaceful co-existence. To deny ethnic identities is one matter—to dissolve ethnic memories another matter entirely.

Once again, concepts have been coined that the authorities expect all citizens to take into themselves, make their own, and live by. The motto is reconciliation and national unity. The authorities object to the use of the words "Hutu" and "Tutsi". People are instructed to use language that underscores that all citizens are Rwandans. Tutsis who have survived are called survivors (rescapés in French). The Hutus, who have been called génocidaires, are now called "non-survivors", "non-rescapés". At the same time, Pagnier, who while doing her research lived with the inhabitants in a part of Rwanda where acts of revenge were especially prevalent, argues that it is impossible to talk about the genocide or questions related to the genocide without talking about the two categories Tutsi and Hutu. We cannot help but wonder whether the ban on mentioning the categories is a constructive policy or a way to deny what has happened—or at any rate, a way to gloss over feelings that remain and that would need to come out in the open and be worked through.

Pagnier focuses on the relationship between an authoritarian state and an obedient society. Large, formalized studies of Rwanda's genocide give one picture, she asserts, while individual's stories taken in themselves give another. Those who have been face to face with the murderers still feel a great distrust and the population as a whole is far from ready to establish a collective narrative about what happened. In addition, people mechanically repeat the "prepared" phrases of the authorities. Genocide, Gacaca, and reconciliation are sensitive subjects and there is much that is never said. Furthermore, the Rwandan cultural code is against a show of feelings, which means that faces are difficult to read. True experiences are sometimes given expression only after the tape recorder has been turned off.

The past is viewed through different ethnic lenses, and Hutus and Tutsis also remember different things. Surviving Tutsis, perpetrators and rescuers, have different memories. There are also, according to Lemarchand, a great number of Hutus who witnessed cold-blooded murders committed by RPF troops in Rwanda and East Congo. Moreover, proponents of different ideologies sometimes manipulate history for political reasons. Such people are found on both sides of the ethnic line and even beyond it.

Memories deviate from reality in many ways. Lemarchand refers to *stopped* memories, *manipulated* memories, and *forced* memories. These forms of distorted memories can prevent people who have witnessed genocide from working with their true memories. He argues that the process of seeking out the truth is going too fast. The necessary amount of time is not being taken, in contrast to the case of South Africa, to find out the truth. There is a tendency to sweep inopportune contexts under the carpet. There are therefore blind spots in Rwanda's official memories. Owing to the banning of all mention of ethnic identities, memories of the ethnic conflicts that have made their mark on perpetrators and victims alike are stopped. Furthermore, memories are stopped concerning the Hutus who had the backbone to refuse to turn over their Tutsi friends and neighbours to the militias and who offered protection at great risk to themselves and their families. An example is Damas Mutezintare, a Hutu who rescued and sheltered nearly 400 Tutsis, 300 children and 80 adults, in his orphanage in Nyamirambo.

Lemarchand asserts that parts of both Hutu and Tutsi groups are responsible for the catastrophe, but this is denied by Rwanda's official ideology. There is thus an official denial of a theme we have described in this book, namely that perpetrator and victim exist within one and the same individual. Perpetrators must be made to take responsibility for the crimes of which they are guilty, regardless of other considerations.

It is true that France played a criminal role throughout the entire crisis, that international organizations turned their backs and that the Belgian colonial policy had catastrophic consequences. However, Kagame, the leader of RPF, was also responsible through inciting the civil war that led to genocide. Lemarchand argues that there would not have been any genocide if Kagame had not let his exile warriors come into Rwanda in 1990, which was against international law. To be sure, he did stop the genocide in 1994 but he was also among those who incited it into being. The later murders of tens of thousands of Hutu refugees in East Congo—by roughly defining them as *génocidaires*—have been literally wiped out of history. The forced memory turns into a kind of saga, where the Tutsis are the victims and the Hutus are the perpetrators and nothing else is allowed to exist.

Co-existence instead of reconciliation

Experiences from the Holocaust show that survivors suffer from their memories. There is a constant risk that memories will return and emotional, traumatic memories can invade the individual time and time again. The feeling of being haunted by one's memories can also include elements of identification with the persecutor. The difficulty in forgetting can sometimes be more troubling that forgetfulness in itself (Schacter, 1996). The survivors want to be able either to work through their tormenting memories or to forget them.

What is the relationship, then, between governmental policies guiding people on how to remember past events on the one hand and reconciliation on the other? Lemarchand argues that co-existence is more realistic than reconciliation, since it carries with it no obligation to forgive. Acknowledgement of crime is more important than forgiveness. If Hutu victims are excluded from Rwanda's official memories, people get the feeling that the regime is using memories for its own sake. The obvious alternative—to give free space to ethnic memories—is no less problematical. Ethnic memories can be just as politicized and blind to the truth as specially constructed versions of history.

Another approach has been suggested by Eva Hoffman (2004). According to her, it is best for everyone to acknowledge and accept what has happened, from the standpoint that what has been done cannot be made undone. Acknowledgement in this sense means somewhat more than memories. It means to reconcile oneself with the indescribable cruelties that have been committed against Hutus and Tutsis by both Hutus and Tutsis. This is what Lemarchand means by working with the memory and something that Staub tests in his radio and teaching project, which we mentioned in the previous chapter. The memory by itself does not help—the question is which moral purpose the memory is meant to serve.

How can people go on living after they have spent so much time in hell? Everything in Rwanda was destroyed—one million people died. Streets, houses, schools, and infrastructure disappeared. Hundreds of thousands of children now live in households run by children who in many instances are just slightly older than they themselves are. We visited Josephine, fourteen years old, who was taking care of three younger siblings after her mother, her only remaining parent, died of AIDS. In a mature, caring way, she managed the household and supported her siblings so that they could go to school. We can ask ourselves how this forced premature adulthood, this "age distortion" (Kaplan, 2008), is going to affect young people in their development towards their true adulthood and their future parenthood.

We end on a somewhat pessimistic tone with a quotation from Philip Gourewitch, pessimistic but at the same time a starting point for constructive reflections. However, before quoting Gourewitch, we would like to give another quotation, which mirrors a way of thinking that can give us hope, a way that does not leave people in situations where they are tempted to carry out acts of revenge.

> In my heart there will always be sorrow and anger. I will not be able to reconcile myself with what happened but I accept it.
>
> (Alain, a Rwanda youth)

> *History tells us that in these times of crisis, the test is put to people … will you behave honourably … or will you be on the side of killers and torturers …?*
>
> … It's not a heartening lesson, but the vast majority of people in such situations show moral weakness … So what does that teach us?
>
> … When we look at how we want to construct society maybe the most valuable thing we could possibly do is hope never to be tested.
>
> (Philip Gourewitch, in an interview on *Kobra*, Swedish Television, 10 August 2009, about his books on Abu Ghraib and on the genocide in Rwanda)

REFERENCES

Åkesson, P. (2005). Vi krigar mot svenskarna. Unga rånare om hur och varför de begår brott. (We make war with the Swedes. Young muggers about how and why they commit crimes.) *Research report, 3,* Lund University, Sweden.

Alberoni, F. (1991). *Avund* (*Envy,* Gli invidiosi). Göteborg: Bokförlaget Korpen.

Alderdice, J. (2010). Off the couch and round the conference table. In: A. Lemma & M. Patrick (Eds.), *Contemporary Psychoanalytic Applications* (pp. 15–32). New York and London: Routledge.

Arendt, H. (2006). *Eichmann in Jerusalem: A Report on the Banality of Evil.* London: Penguin Classics.

Arriaga, X. & Oskamp, S. (Eds.) (1999). *Violence in Intimate Relationships.* London: Sage.

Asch, S. (1956). Opinions and social pressure. *Scientific American, 193*: 31–35.

Bacon, F. (1625). *On Revenge.* Wikipedia.

Bar-Tal, D. (1998). Societal beliefs in times of intractable conflict: the Israeli case. *The International Journal of Conflict Management, 9*: 22–50.

Bar-Tal, D. (2000). From intractable conflict through conflict resolution to reconciliation: psychological analysis. *Political Psychology, 21(2)*: 351–365.

Bauman, Z. (1989). *Modernity and the Holocaust.* Ithaka: Cornell University Press.

Beattie, H. J. (2005). *Revenge*: Panel. *J. Amer. Psychoanal. Assn.*, *53*: 513–524.

Beck-Friis, J. (2010). *Den nakna skammen: grund för depression eller väg till ömsesidighet?* (The naked shame: ground for depression or road to mutuality). Stockholm: Natur och Kultur.

Berg, L. (2001). *Rwanda i stort »rättsexperiment«*. (Rwanda in a large "judicial experiment"). Stockholm: *Dagens Nyheter (Daily News)*, 7 December.

Bloom, S. (Ed.) (2001). *Violence, a Public Health Menace and a Public Health Approach*. London: Karnac Books.

Blum, H. P. (1985). Superego formation, adolescent transformation and the adult neurosis. *Journal of the American Psychoanalytic Association*, 4: 887–909.

Böhm, T. (1993). *Inte som vi! Psykologiska aspekter på främlingsfientlighet och rasism*. (Not like us! Psychological aspects of xenophobia and racism). Stockholm: Natur och Kultur.

Böhm, T. (1998). *Att ha rätt*. (To be right). Stockholm: Natur och Kultur.

Böhm, T. (2000). *The Vienna Jazz Trio*. Stockholm: Natur och Kultur [*The Vienna Jazz Trio*, Virginia: Pitchstone, 2010].

Böhm, T. (2001). *Kärleksrelationen*. (The Love Relationship). Stockholm: Natur och Kultur.

Böhm, T. (2003). Mäns våld mot kvinnor. (Men's violence against women). *Insikten, 5 (12)*: 20–27.

Böhm, T. (2004a). One man can make a difference. Paper to the Raoul Wallenberg exhibition, Jewish Museum of Stockholm.

Böhm, T. (2004b). *Bortresta*. (Gone Away). Göteborg: Lindelöws förlag.

Böhm, T. (2006a). *Passiva åskådare—en vetenskaplig introduktion. »Spelar roll«* (Passive bystanders—a scientific introduction to "*Does it matter*"). Stockholm, Forum för Levande Historia (Forum for Living History).

Böhm, T. (2006b). Psychoanalytic aspects on perpetrators of genocide: experiences in Rwanda. *Scandinavian Psychoanalytic Review, 29 (1)*: 1–11.

Böhm, T. & Kaplan, S. (2009). Rache—Zur Psychodynamik einer unheimlichen Lust und ihrer Zähmung. (Revenge—on the psychodynamics of a frightening lust and its taming). Giessen: Psychosozial-Verlag and (2009) Hämnd eller Upprättelse—om hämndspiralens psykologi (Revenge or Restoration—on the psychology of the spiral of revenge), Stockholm: Natur och Kultur.

Bond, M. (2004). Culture and aggression. *Personality and Social Psychology Review, 8*: 62–68.

Bracken, P., Giller, J. & Summerfield, D. (1995). Psychological responses to war and atrocity: the limitations of current concepts. *Social Science Medicine, 40*: 1073–1082.

Brenman, E. (2006). *Recovery of the Lost Good Object*. East Sussex: Routledge.

Brounéus, K. (2008). Rethinking reconciliation: concepts, methods, and an empirical study of truth telling and psychological health in Rwanda. Report Number 81, doctoral thesis, Uppsala University, Peace and Conflict Research, S. 3–74.

Browning, C. R. (1992). *Ordinary Men: Reserve Police Battalion 101 and the Final Solution in Poland*. New York: Harper Perennial.

Burstein, M., Narrowe, M. & Rubinstein, H. (2006). *Denna afton*. (This evening). Stockholm: Hillelförlaget.

Carnahan, T. & McFarland, S. (2007). Revisiting the Stanford prison experiment: could participant self-selection have led to the cruelty? *Personality and Social Psychology Bulletin, 33 (5)*: 603–614.

Columbia Guide to Standard American English (1993). Columbia University Press.

Damasio, A. R. (1999). *The Feeling of What Happens: Body and Emotion in the Making of Consciousness*. London: Harcourt.

Darley, J. & Bateson, C. (1973). From Jerusalem to Jericho: a study of situational and dispositional variables in helping behaviour. *Journal of Personality and Social Psychology, 27*: 100–108.

Dawes, A., Tredoux, C. & Feinstein, A. (1989). Political violence in South Africa: some effects on children of the violent destruction of their community. *International Journal of Mental Health, 18*: 16–43.

Dencik, L. (2004). Personal communication.

Dumas, A. (2003). *The Count of Monte Cristo*. London: Penguin Classics.

Durham, M. (2000). *The Therapist's Encounters with Revenge and Forgiveness*. London: Jessica Kingsley.

Dyberg, N. (2008). Konsten att säga förlåt. (The art of saying "Forgive me"). *Dagens Industri* (Daily Industry), 11 May.

Eliasson, P. E. (2000). *Män, kvinnor och våld*. (Men, women and violence). Stockholm: Carlssons Bokförlag.

Elliott, M., Bishop, K. & Stokes, P. (2004). Societal PTSD? Historic shock in Northern Ireland. *Psychotherapy and Politics International, 2*: 1–16.

Engstrand, M. (2005). Personal communication.

Eriksson, B. (2009). *Antonias Revansch*. Sweden: T. Fischer.

Erlich, H. S. (2010). A beam of darkness—understanding the terrorist mind. In: H. Brunning & M. Perini (Eds.), *Psychoanalytic Perspectives on a World* (pp. 3–15). London: Karnac Books.

Ferro, A. (2005). Bion: theoretical and clinical observations. *International Journal of Psychoanalysis, 86*: 1541.

Fiske, S. T., Harris, L. T. & Cuddy, A. J. C. (2004). *Why ordinary people torture enemy prisoners. Science, 306(5701)*: 1482–1483.

Fonagy, P. (1998). Attachment, the Holocaust and the outcome of child psychoanalysis: the third generation. Paper presented at the 3rd Congress of the European Federation for Psychoanalytic Psychotherapy in the Public Sector. Köln, Germany, 28 March.

Fonagy, P. (1999). Male perpetrators of violence against women: an attachment theory perspective. *Journal of Applied Psychoanalytic Studies*, 1: 7–27.

Fonagy, P. (2005). Keynote lecture, presented at IPA 44th Congress of Trauma. *Attachment Trauma and Psychoanalysis Meets Neuroscience: New Developments in Psychoanalysis*. Rio de Janeiro, 28 July.

Fonagy, P., Gergely, G., Jurist, E. L. & Target, M. (2002). *Affect Regulation, Mentalization and the Development of the Self*. New York: Other Press.

Fornari, F. (1966). *The Psychoanalysis of War*. [Trans. A. Pfeifer. Bloomington: Indiana University Press, 1975].

Forum för Levande Historia (2004). (Forum for Living History). *Intolerans. Antisemitiska, homofobiska, islamofobiska och invandringsfientliga tendenser bland unga*. (Intolerance, anti-Semitic, homophobic, islamophobic and immigration hostile tendencies among young people). *Brottsförebyggande Rådet*. Stockholm: BRÅ, Council for the Prevention of Crime.

Freud, A. (1993). *The Ego and the Mechanisms of Defense*. London: Karnac Books.

Freud, S. (1905). *Fragment of an Analysis of a Case of Hysteria*. Standard Edition, Volume 7: 3–122. [London: Hogarth Press, 2003].

Freud, S. (1917). *Mourning and Melancholia*. Standard Edition, Volume 14: 237–258. [London: Hogarth Press, 2003].

Freud, S. (1920). *Beyond the Pleasure Principle*. Standard Edition, Volume 18: 1–64. [London: Hogarth Press, 2003].

Freud, S. (1921). *Group Psychology and the Analysis of the Ego*. Standard Edition, Volume 18: 65–144. [London: Hogarth Press, 2003].

Freud, S. (1932). *Why War?* Standard Edition, Volume 22: 197–215. [London: Hogarth Press, 2003]

Garland, C. (1998). *Understanding Trauma: A Psychoanalytical Approach*. London: Duckworth.

Gentry, J. E., Baggerly, J. & Baranowsky, A. (2004). Training as treatment. *International Journal of Emergency and Mental Health*, 6: 147–155.

Gilbert, G. M. (1977). *Nürnberger Tagebuch*. Frankfurt am Main (Fischer-Taschenbuch-Verlag).   http://en.wikiquote.org/wiki/Hermann_Göring

Glover, E. (1947). *War, Sadism, and Pacifism: Further Essays on Group Psychology and War*. London: Allen and Unwin.

Goldschmidt, L. (Hg.) (1897–1935). *Der babylonische Talmud*. (The Babylonian Talmud). Berlin: Calvary; Leipzig: Harrasowitz; Haag: Nijhoff.

Gourevitch, P. (1998). *We Wish to Inform You that Tomorrow We Will Be Killed with Our Families*. New York: Farrar, Strauss & Giroux.

Gourevitch, P. (2009). Interview on *Kobra*, Swedish Television, about his books on Abu Ghraib and on the genocide in Rwanda, 19 August.

Grubrich-Simitis, I. (1984). From concretism to metaphor: thoughts on some theoretical and technical aspects of the psychoanalytic work with children of Holocaust survivors. *Psychoanalytic Study of the Child, 39*: 301–319.

Haffner, S. (2000). *Geschichte Eines Deutschen: Die Erinnerungen 1914–1933. (A German Man's Story: Memories 1914–1933). Stuttgart—München: Deutsche Verlags-Anstalt (DVA)*.

Hatzfeld, J. (2005). *Machete Season—The Killers in Rwanda Speak*. New York: Farrar, Straus & Giroux.

Hatzfeld, J. (2009). *A Strategy of Antelopes: Rwanda after the Genocide*. London: Profile Books.

Heberlein, A. (2008). *Det var inte mitt fel. Om konsten att ta ansvar.* (It was not my fault. About the art of taking responsibility). Stockholm: ICA bokförlag.

Herman, J. (1992). *Trauma and Recovery: The Aftermath of Violence—from Domestic Abuse to Political Terror*. New York: Basic Books.

Hjärpe, J. (2005). *Den som behandlas som terrorist blir det.* (He who is treated as a terrorist becomes one). *Svenska Dagbladet* (Swedish Daily Paper), 15 July.

Hoffman, E. (2004). *After Such Knowledge: Memory, History and the Legacy of the Holocaust*. New York: Public Affairs.

Holmes, J. (1996). *Attachment, Intimacy, Autonomy*. London: Jason Aronson.

Hollander, N. (1997). *Love in a Time of Hate: Liberation Psychology in Latin America*. New York: Other Press.

Hollander, N. (2010). *Uprooted Minds: Surviving the Political Terror in the Americas*. New York: Taylor & Francis.

Hydén, M. (1995). *Kvinnomisshandel inom äktenskapet: Mellan det omöjliga och det möjliga.* (Women battering in marriage: between the impossible and the possible). Stockholm: Liber.

Igra, L. (1983). *Objektrelationer och psykoterapi.* (Object relations and psychotherapy). Stockholm: Natur och Kultur.

Igra, L. (2001). *Den tunna hinnan. Mellan omsorg och grymhet.* (The thin membrane. Between care and cruelty). Stockholm: Natur och Kultur.

Igra, L. (2002). Truth, Justice and Reconciliation. Stockholm International Forum, 23, 24 April.

Jonge, K., de (2002). Interim Report on Research on Gacaca Jurisdictions and its Preparations, Penal Reform International Research Team, Kigali.

Jorjani, S. (2006). Personal communication.

Jukes, A. (1999). *Men Who Batter Women*. London: Taylor & Francis.

Kakar, S. (1996). *The Colors of Violence: Cultural Identities, Religion, and Conflict*. Chicago: University of Chicago Press.

Kaplan, S. (2002). Children in the Holocaust: affects and memory images in trauma and generational linking. Doctoral thesis, University of Stockholm, Department of Education.

Kaplan, S. (2005). Children in Africa with experiences of massive trauma: a research review. Stockholm. SIDA Department for Research Cooperation, S.: 3–56.

Kaplan, S. (2006). Children in genocide: extreme traumatization and the "affect propeller". *International Journal of Psychoanalysis, 87*: 725–746.

Kaplan, S. (2008). *Children in Genocide: Extreme Traumatization and Affect Regulation*. London: International Psychoanalysis Library.

Kaplan, S. & Eckstein, H. (2004). *Kinderchirurg Dr Alfred Jahn und die Waisenkinder von Kigali*. (Child surgeon Dr Alfred Jahn and the orphans from Kigali). Nierstein am Rhein: Iatros-Verlag.

Kaplan, S. & Laub, D. (2009). Affect regulation in extreme traumatization— fragmented narratives of survivors hospitalized in psychiatric institutions, *Scandinavian Psychoanalytic Review* 33 (2): 95–106.

Keilson, H. (1992). *Sequential Traumatization in Children*. Jerusalem: Magnes Press.

Kernberg, O. (1992). *Aggression in Personality Disorders and Perversions*. New Haven: Yale University Press.

Kihlbom, M. (2004). *Livshotande tillstånd hos barn i asylsökande familjer (Life-threatening conditions in children from asylum-seeking families)*. Panel at the Annual Medical Congress of Sweden, 26 November.

Klefbeck, E.-L. (2004). *Extremtraumatisering och skam*. (Extreme traumatization and shame). *Psykoterapieexamensuppsats*. Stockholm: Karolinska Institutet.

Klein, M. (1961). *Narrative of a Child Analysis: The Conduct of the Psychoanalysis of Children as Seen in the Treatment of a Ten-Year-Old Boy*. [Reprinted London: Hogarth Press, 1975].

Klein, M. (1975). *Envy and Gratitude, and Other Works, 1946–1963. The Writings of Melanie Klein*, Volume III. London: Hogarth Press.

Kleist, H. (2005). *Michael Kohlhaas*. Hoboken, NJ: Melville House.

Klintberg, B. (1996). Why are there so many modern legends about revenge? In: G. Bennett & P. Smith, *Contemporary Legend: A Reader* (pp. 261–265). New York and London: Garland.

Kohut, H. (2009a). *The Analysis of the Self*. Chicago: University of Chicago Press.

Kohut, H. (2009b). *The Restoration of the Self*. Chicago: University of Chicago Press.

Königsberg, R. (2004). The logic of the Holocaust: why the Nazis killed the Jews. *libraryofscience@earthlink.net*

Lansky, M. (2007). Clinical topics: unbearable shame, splitting and forgiveness in the resolution of vengefulness. *J. Amer. Psychoanal. Assn., 55 (2)*: 571–594.

Laub, D. & Auerhahn, N. (1993). Knowing and not knowing massive psychic trauma: forms of traumatic memory. *International Journal of Psychoanalysis, 74*: 287–302.

Laufer, M. & Laufer, E. (1989). *Developmental Breakdown and Psychoanalytic Treatment in Adolescence*. New Haven and London: Yale University Press.

Lemarchand, R. (2004). The politics of memory and the prospects for reconciliation. Lecture: The Rwandan Genocide of 1994, Lessons Learned Still to Learn of, 6 May Danish Institute for International Studies.

Leuzinger-Bohleber, M. (2010). *Transgeneratives Trauma—eine unerwartete klinische Beobachtung in extraklinischen Studien*. (Transgenerative Trauma—an unexpected clinical observation in extra-clinical studies). Lecture at the 11th Joseph Sandler Research Conference, Frankfurt.

Lifton, R. J. (1999). *The Protean Self-Human Resilience in an Age of Fragmentation*. Chicago: University of Chicago Press.

Lindner, E. G. (2001). Humiliation and human rights: mapping a minefield. *Human Rights Review, 2*: 46–63.

Loewenberg, P. (1991). Uses of anxiety. *Partisan Review, 3*: 514–525.

Mamdani, M. (2001). *When Victims Become Killers*. Princeton, NJ: Princeton University Press.

McDermott, R. (2004). *Political Psychology in International Relations*. Ann Arbor: University of Michigan Press.

Meltzer, D. & Williams Harris, M. (1988). *The Apprehension of Beauty*. London: The Clunie Press.

Melvern, L. (2000). *A People Betrayed—The Role of the West in Rwanda's Genocide*. London and New York: Zed Books.

Milgram, S. (1974). *Obedience to Authority*. New York : Harper & Row.

Mironko, C. (2004). Igitero: means and motive in the Rwandan genocide. *Journal of Genocide Research, 6 (1)*: 47–60.

Mitscherlich, A. (1971). Psychoanalysis and aggression of large groups. *International Journal of Psychoanalysis, 52*: 161–167

Mitscherlich, A. & Mitscherlich, M. (1975). *Die Unfähigkeit zu trauern. Grundlagen kollektiven Verhaltens*; 1967; 2004–18. A. ISBN 3-492-20168-7. *The Inability to Mourn: Principals of Collective Behavior*. Trans. B. R. Placzek. New York: Grove Press.

Moses, R. (1982). The group-self and the Arab-Israeli conflict. *International Review of Psychoanalysis, 9*: 55–65.

Narrowe, M. (2005). *En tretvinnad tråd*. (A thread made of three). Stockholm: Bonniers.

Nathanson, D. L. (1994). *Shame and Pride: Affect, Sex and the Birth of the Self*. New York and London: Norton.

Pagnier, J. (2004). Gacaca tribunals: justice and reconciliation in Rwanda? Master thesis, University of Amsterdam, Department of Cultural Anthropology.

Pearlman, L. (2004). A community-based approach to trauma healing. Lecture, *International Society of Political Psychology, Annual Conference*, Lund, Sweden, 16 July.

Pearlman, L. & Saakvitne, K. W. (1995). *Trauma and the Therapist: Countertransference and Vicarious Traumatization in Psychotherapy with Incest Survivors*. New York and London: Norton.

Persson, A. (2005). *Bodström besviken över beslutet om Östberg*. (Bodström disappointed about the decision concerning Östberg). *Dagens Nyheter* (Daily News), 6 January.

Pollack, M. (2008). *Dead Man in the Bunker*. London: Faber & Faber.

Raakil, M. (2000). Treatment for men battering their partners: beyond psycho-educational programs. Unpublished thesis.

Rakita, S. (2003). Rwanda lasting wounds: consequences of genocide and war for Rwanda's children. *Human Rights Watch, 15 (5)*: 1–74. http://hrw.org/reports/2003/rwanda0403/

Rangell, L. (2003). Affects: in an individual and a nation. First Annual Volkan Lecture, University of Virginia, Charlottesville, VA, 15 November.

Reich, W. (1943). *Was ist Klassenbewusstsein? Ein Beitrag zur Diskussion über die Neuformierung der Arbeiterbewegung*. (What Is Class Consciousness?). Copenhagen, Paris, Zürich: Verlag für Sexualpolitik.

Reich, W. (1997). *Mass Psychology of Fascism*. London: Souvenir Press.

Ring, J. & Morgentau, S. (2004). Intolerance Report, Brå (Council for the Prevention of Crime).

Rodenbeck, M. (2005). The truth about jihad. *New York Review of Books*, 11 August.

Rosen, I. C. (2007). Clinical topics. Essay: Revenge, the hate that dare not speak its name: a psychoanalytic perspective. *J. Amer. Psychoanal. Assn., 55 (2)*: 585–620.

Rössel, R. (2005). *Skammen som fräter själen* (Shame that corrodes the soul). Lecture, Swedish Psychoanalytic Society, Stockholm.

Roth, E. (2005a). *Emerich är mitt namn. Hatet, förnedringen, kärleken*. (Emerich is my name. The hatred, denigration, love). Stockholm: Carlsson.

Roth, E. (2005b). Personal communication.

Schacter, D. L. (1996). *Searching for Memory: The Brain, the Mind and the Past*. New York: Basic Books.

Schore, A. N. (2003). *Affect Dysregulation and Disorders of the Self*. New York and London: Norton.

Schüllerqvist, L. (2006). *Värdigheten tar ton* (Dignity speaks out). *Dagens Nyheter* (Daily News), 24 April.

Šebek, M. (1994). Psychopathology of everyday life in the post-totalitarian society. *Mind and Human Interaction, 5*: 104–109.

Shakespeare,W. *Hamlet.* [London: Palgrave MacMillan, 2008].

Shakespeare, W. *Romeo and Juliet.* [London:Wordsworth Editions, 2000].

Socarides, C. (1966). On vengeance: the desire to get even. *J. Amer. Psychoanal. Assn., 14*: 356–375.

Staub, E. (1989). *The Roots of Evil.* Cambridge: Cambridge University Press.

Staub, E. (2000). Genocide and mass killing: origins, prevention, healing and reconciliation. *Political Psychology, 21 (2)*: 367–382.

Staub, E. (2003). *The Psychology of Good and Evil.* Cambridge: Cambridge University Press.

Staub, E. (2011). *Overcoming Evil—Genocide, Violent Conflict, and Terrorism. New York: Oxford University Press.*

Staub, E. & Weiss, G. (2004). Radio Benevolencija; *http://www.labenevolencija.org*

Steiner, J. (1996). Revenge and resentment in the Oedipus situation. *International Journal of Psychoanalysis, 77*: 433–443.

Stover, E. & Weinstein, H. M. (Eds.) (2004). *My Neighbor, My Enemy: Justice and Community in the Aftermath of Mass Atrocity.* Cambridge: Cambridge University Press.

Sundh, O. (2003). *Seminarium om dissociation.* (Seminar about dissociation). Stockholm: Ericastiftelsen.

Svenska Dagbladet/Debate (2005). *Främlingen kan bli din vän.* (The stranger can become your friend). *Svenska Dagbladet* (Swedish Daily Paper), 12 September.

Swartz, R. (2004). *Sonen till en förövare söker svar.* (The son of a perpetrator seeks an answer). *Svenska Dagbladet* (Swedish Daily Paper), 26 November.

Teurnell, L. (2002). *Traumasymposium.* Unpublished lecture, Swedish Psychoanalytic Association, Stockholm.

Tomkins, S. (1995). *Exploring Affects.* Cambridge: Cambridge University Press.

Valentino, B. (2000). Final solutions: the causes of mass killing and genocide. *Security Studies, 9 (3)*: 1–62.

Varvin, S. (2003). *Mental Survival Strategies after Extreme Traumatisation.* Köpenhamn: Multivers Academic.

Varvin, S. (2004). *Dissociation, Unowned Experience, Trauma and the Mind.* Lecture at the EPF Congress in Helsingfors, Finland.

Varvin, S. & Volkan, V. D. (Eds.) (2003). *Violence and Dialogue.* London: International Psychoanalytic Library.

Volkan, V. (2004). *Blind Trust*. Charlottesville, VA: Pitchstone.

Volkan, V. D. (1979). *Cyprus: War and Adaptation, A Psychoanalytic History of Two Ethnic Groups in Conflict*. Charlottesville, VA: University of Virginia Press.

Volkan, V. D. (1988). *The Need to Have Enemies and Allies: From Clinical Practice to International Relationships*. Northvale, NJ: Jason Aronson.

Volkan, V. D. (1997). *Bloodlines: From Ethnic Pride to Ethnic Terrorism*. New York: Farrar, Straus & Giroux.

Volkan, V. D. (2004). *Blind Trust: Large Groups and Their Leaders in Times of Crisis and Terror*. Charlottesville, VA: Pitchstone.

Volkan, V. D. (2006a). Psikodinâmica da violência de grandes grupas e da violência de massas. *Ciência & Saúde Coletiva, 11*: 303–314.

Volkan, V. D. (2006b). *Killing in the Name of Identity: A Study of Bloody Conflicts*. Charlottesville, VA: Pitchstone.

Volkan, V. D., Ast, G. & Greer, W. F. (2002). *The Third Reich in the Unconscious: Transgenerational Transmission and its Consequences*. New York: Brunner-Routledge.

Volkan, V. D. & Itzkowitz, N. (1994). *Turks and Greeks: Neighbours in Conflict*. Cambridgeshire, England: Eothen Press.

Volkan, V. D. & Kayatekin, S. (2006). Extreme religious fundamentalism and violence: some psychoanalytic and psychopolitical thoughts. *Psyche & Geloof, 17*: 71–91.

Waelder, R. (1971). Psychoanalysis and history. In: B. B. Wolman (Ed.), *The Psychoanalytic Interpretation of History* (pp. 3–22). New York: Basic Books.

Waller, J. (2002). *Becoming Evil: How Ordinary People Commit Genocide and Mass Killing*. New York: Oxford University Press.

Weingarten, K. (2003). *Common Shock: Witnessing Violence Every Day, How We Are Harmed, How We Can Heal*. New York: Dutton Penguin Group.

Wiesenthal, S. (1990). *Justice Not Vengeance: Recollections*. New York: Grove Press.

Winnicott, D. W. (1971). *Playing and Reality*. London: Tavistock.

Wretling, O. (2005). Interview: *Stiftelsen Röda Korsets Center för torterade flyktingar*. (Red Cross Center for Tortured Refugees). Stockholm.

Wurmser, L. (1981). *The Mask of Shame*. Baltimore and London: John Hopkins university Press.

Zimbardo, P. (1996). *Psychology and Life*. New York: Harper Collins College Publications.

Websites

http://www.sociologi.lu.se/krim/vi_krigar.pdf
http://de.wikiquote.org/wiki/Hermann_Göring
http://www.bibleserver.com (Smedjeback, 2004)
http://www.bra.se
http://www.krf.se

Films

Abu-Assad, Hany: *Paradise Now*, Palestine/France/Germany/Netherlands/ Israel 2005, Augustus Film, Haarlem.

Dones, Elvira: *Inchiodato*, Switzerland 2004, Schweizer Fernsehen, Zurich.

Fauli, Søren: *Min morfars mörder*, Denmark 2004, Tju Bang, Copenhagen.

Kershner, Irvin: *Star Wars*: Episode V: *The Empire Strikes Back*, USA 1980, Lucasfilm, Presidio of San Francisco/California.

Kurosawa, Akira: *Shichinin no samurai*, Japan 1954, Toho Company, Tokio.

Reynolds, Kevin: *The Count of Monte Cristo*, UK/USA/Ireland 2002, Touchstone Pictures, Burbank/California.

Spielberg, Steven: *Schindler's List*, USA 1993, Universal Pictures, Los Angeles/California.

Verhoeven, Paul: *Basic Instinct*, USA/Frankrike 1992, Canal+, Issy-les-Moulineaux.

INDEX